Prentice Hall LITERATURE

PENGUIN EDITION

Unit Six
Resources

Grade Six

PEARSON

Upper Saddle River, New Jersey
Boston, Massachusetts
Chandler, Arizona
Glenview, Illinois

BQ Tunes Credits
Keith London, Defined Mind, Inc., Executive Producer
Mike Pandolfo, Wonderful, Producer
All songs mixed and mastered by Mike Pandolfo, Wonderful
Vlad Gutkovich, Wonderful, Assistant Engineer
Recorded November 2007 – February 2008 in SoHo, New York City, at
Wonderful, 594 Broadway

ISBN–13: 978-0-13-366434-8
ISBN–10:   0-13-366434-1

3 4 5 6 7 8 9 10   12 11 10 09

CONTENTS

For information about the Unit Resources, assessing fluency, and teaching with BQ Tunes, see the opening pages of your Unit One Resources.

"The Tiger Who Would Be King"; "The Ant and the Dove"

"The Lion and the Bulls" "A Crippled Boy"

"The Lion and the Bulls"; "A Crippled Boy"

"Arachne" by Olivia E. Coolidge

Prologue *from* The Whale Rider by Witi Ihimaera

"Arachne" and Prologue *from* The Whale Rider

 **BQ Tunes**

Roots, performed by The Dave Pittinger Band

One **generation** passes to its children
The **values** and the things that they believe in
To **influence** and help them make decisions
In the hope that they'll have a better life

So please don't **isolate** yourself — let them in

One **belief** I've got
Is the confidence that we **support** and hold each other up
Our **community**, the people who surround us and
Make us who we are

Just like a bird is affected by the wind
Our **culture** and surroundings help to shape us
If there's a bond, a **connection** with those around us,
We have a better chance to grow

Together as a **group** we strengthen each other
By working toward the **common** goals we share
Our loved ones and our **families** all benefit from knowing that
We'll all make a better world

One **belief** I've got
Is the confidence that we **support** and hold each other up
Our **community**, are the people who surround us and
Make us who we are

When we pitch in and get **involved**
When we join in and **participate**
History has shown that in the past
We've had a better chance, a better chance

One **belief** I've got
Is the confidence that we **support** and hold each other up
Our **community**, are the people who surround us and
Make us whvo we are

Roots, *continued*

Song Title: **Roots**
Artist / Performed by The Dave Pittenger Band
Vocals & Guitar: Dave Pittenger
Bass Guitar: Jon Price
Drums: Josh Dion
Lyrics by Dave Pittenger
Music composed by Dave Pittenger
Produced by Mike Pandolfo, Wonderful
Executive Producer: Keith London, Defined Mind

x

Name _____ Date _____

Unit 6: Themes in Folk Literature
Big Question Vocabulary—1

The Big Question: How much do our communities shape us?

For many people, family is their most important community. This may include extended family—grandparents, cousins, aunts, and uncles; just immediate family—parents and siblings; or any group of people that a person lives with and has close ties to.

common: shared by all

family: a group of people who are all related and usually live together

generation: a group of people who were all born around the same time

influence: to have an effect on the way someone or something develops, behaves, or thinks without using force

support: to agree with someone else and offer your help

DIRECTIONS: *Answer the following questions using the vocabulary words in parentheses.*

1. What are the names of the people you live with? **(family)**

   _____

   _____

   _____

2. What are the ages of people in your family? How many people in your extended family are in similar age groups? **(generation)**

   _____

   _____

   _____

3. What do you share with your family? **(common)**

   _____

   _____

   _____

4. How have you helped other members of your family and/or how have they helped you? **(support)**

   _____

   _____

   _____

5. What effect do other members of your family have on you? **(influence)**

   _____

   _____

   _____

Name _____ Date _____

Unit 6: Themes in Folk Literature
Big Question Vocabulary—2

The Big Question: How much do our communities shape us?

Larger groups of people that we are associated with form our communities. They can be the people in our neighborhood, our school, a club that we belong to, or at the place where we work.

belief: the feeling that something is definitely true or definitely exists

community: a group of people who live in the same area or a group of people who share a common interest

connection: a situation where two or more people understand each other

participation: taking part in an activity or event

values: a person's principles about what is right and wrong and what is important in life.

Elana belongs to a youth group. She is making a brochure for new members, but she is having trouble finishing her sentences. Finish Elana's sentences for her. Include all of the above vocabulary words at least once.

Webbville Youth Group (WYG)

WYG is more than just a youth group. We are a (1) _____.
This is demonstrated by (2) _____ _____
_____.

The members of WYG share the (3) _____ that helping
one another and being there for one another is (4) _____
_____.

If you decide to join WYG, you won't regret it. Your (5) _____
_____
_____.

WYG'S (6) _____

Be kind.
Be supportive of your friends.
Be polite.
Help others.

2

Name _____ Date _____

Unit 6: Themes in Folk Literature
Unit 6 Big Question Vocabulary—3
The Big Question: How much do our communities shape us?

People who share a similar background often understand each other more easily than people with diverse backgrounds. But through communication, people can learn about and feel comfortable with those from other backgrounds.

culture: ideas, beliefs, and customs that are shared by people in a society

group: several people or things that are related in some way.

history: everything that has happened in the past

involve: to include something as a necessary part

isolate: to stop something or someone from having contact with particular people or ideas

Brian just moved from a small town to a big city. He was feeling lonely. In his town he knew everybody. He also shared the same ideas, beliefs and customs as his small town friends. Here, he didn't understand the ideas, beliefs and customs.

Brian told his old friend Steve,

> **1. (isolate, culture)**

Steve advised Brian to find others with similar interests as himself so that he will meet people. He said

> **2. (involve, group)**

Brian was grateful for Steve's advice. Brian understood him because they shared a similar past. He said

> **3. (history)**

Name _____ Date _____

Unit 6: Themes in Folk Literature
Applying the Big Question

 How much do our communities shape us?

DIRECTIONS: *Complete the chart below to apply what you have learned about ways that communities shape the lives of their members. One row has been completed for you.*

Example	Community	Description of this community	Problem or issue	Outcome of the problem or issue	What I learned
From Literature	animals in "He Lion, Bruh Bear, and Bruh Rabbit"	various large and small animals in a wilderness area	A loud, threatening lion scares the other animals.	community gets two wise members to teach the lion that he is not all-powerful	A community can use its resources to change the behavior of a member who is causing a problem.
From Literature					
From Science					
From Social Studies					
From Real Life					

Name _____

Unit 6: Themes in Folk Literature Skills Concept Map—1
How much do our communities shape us?

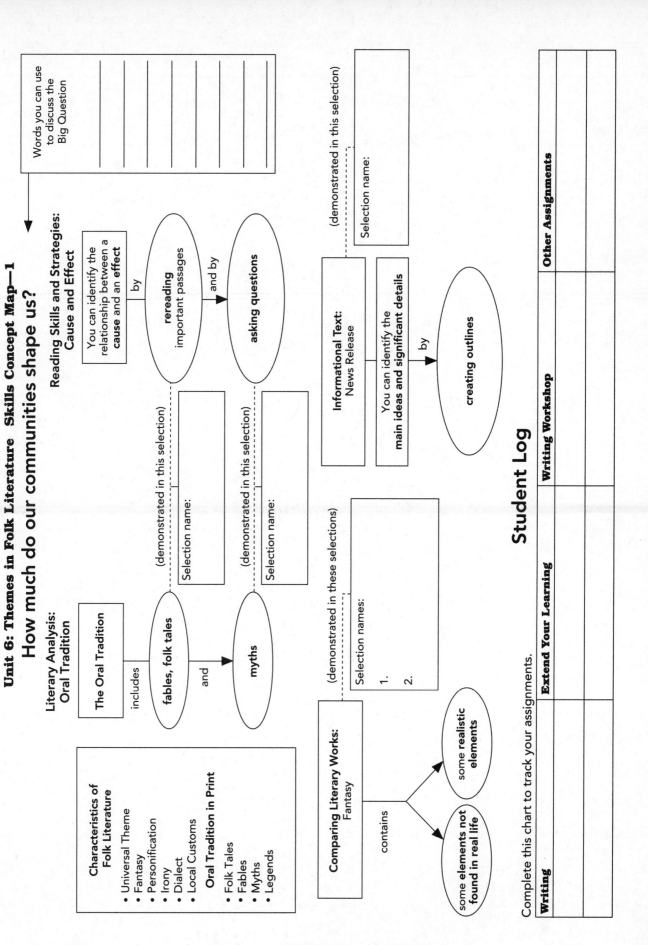

Literary Analysis:
Oral Tradition

The Oral Tradition — includes → fables, folk tales — and → myths

(demonstrated in this selection)
Selection name: _____

(demonstrated in this selection)
Selection name: _____

Characteristics of Folk Literature
- Universal Theme
- Fantasy
- Personification
- Irony
- Dialect
- Local Customs

Oral Tradition in Print
- Folk Tales
- Fables
- Myths
- Legends

Reading Skills and Strategies:
Cause and Effect

You can identify the relationship between a **cause** and an **effect** — by → **rereading** important passages — and by → **asking questions**

Informational Text:
News Release

You can identify the **main ideas and significant details** — by → **creating outlines**

(demonstrated in this selection)
Selection name: _____

Comparing Literary Works:
Fantasy — contains → some realistic elements / some elements not found in real life

(demonstrated in these selections)
Selection names:
1. _____
2. _____

Words you can use to discuss the Big Question
_____
_____
_____
_____
_____

Student Log

Complete this chart to track your assignments.

Writing	Extend Your Learning	Writing Workshop	Other Assignments

Vocabulary Warm-up Word Lists

Study these words from "Black Cowboy, Wild Horses." Then, complete the activities that follow.

Word List A

corral [kuh RAL] *n.* fenced-in area for holding animals
  The boy led his horse through the gate and into the <u>corral</u>.

distinct [dis TINGKT] *adj.* clear and definite
  The stronger athlete had a <u>distinct</u> advantage.

grazed [GRAYZD] *v.* fed on growing grass
  As the shepherds watched, the sheep <u>grazed</u> in the field.

herd [HURD] *n.* group of cattle or other large animals feeding or moving together
  The cowboys drove the <u>herd</u> of cattle hundreds of miles.

maintaining [mayn TAYN ing] *v.* keeping
  <u>Maintaining</u> her self-control, she did not panic in the crisis.

plains [PLAYNZ] *n.* large areas of flat, open country
  Buffalo used to roam the <u>plains</u> of North America.

presence [PREZ uhns] *n.* being in a place
  Everyone was surprised at his <u>presence</u> at the meeting.

scarcely [SKAIRS lee] *adv.* not quite; only just
  We had <u>scarcely</u> arrived when the show started.

Word List B

dusk [DUSK] *n.* the beginning of darkness in the evening
  When the sun went down, <u>dusk</u> settled on the town.

faint [FAYNT] *adj.* weak; hard to see or hear
  We barely saw the <u>faint</u> touches of blue in the painting.

flickered [FLIK erd] *v.* shined or burned unsteadily
  The birthday candles <u>flickered</u>, but did not go out.

milled [MILLD] *v.* moved around slowly
  People <u>milled</u> around, waiting for the doors to open.

peering [PEER ing] *v.* looking closely and searchingly
  They kept <u>peering</u> through the window, but they could not see.

steep [STEEP] *adj.* having a sharp rise or slope
  Those hills were too <u>steep</u> for the children to climb easily.

suspended [sus PEN ded] *v.* hung from above
  The acrobat was <u>suspended</u> by one thin rope.

vastness [VAST nes] *n.* greatness of size
  The <u>vastness</u> of the ocean must have terrified the sailors.

"Black Cowboy, Wild Horses" by Julius Lester
Vocabulary Warm-up Exercises

Exercise A *Fill in each blank in the paragraph below with an appropriate word from Word List A. Use each word only once.*

The bus full of tourists pulled into the front entrance of the dude ranch. A dude ranch is a place where city people get a taste of the life of the Old West. There is a [1] _____ difference between life in the city and life on a ranch. The tourists had [2] _____ arrived when they saw things they had never seen before. A [3] _____ of cattle was being carefully guided into a huge wooden [4] _____. These animals had just been brought in from the open country around the ranch, the [5] _____ that stretched on for miles. The cattle [6] _____ there every day, feeding on the grass. The cattle looked at the curious tourists, but the [7] _____ of these strangers did not disturb them at all. In fact, the ranch workers are very skilled at showing how the ranch works while [8] _____ the daily routine that the animals need.

Exercise B *Answer each question in a complete sentence. Use a word from Word List B to replace each underlined word or group of words without changing the meaning.*

1. Did the air become cooler at <u>the time just before evening</u>?

   _____

2. The lights <u>shined unsteadily</u> during the night, didn't they?

   _____

3. Have you ever climbed a mountain <u>with a sharp slope</u>?

   _____

4. In the fog, were the warning lights <u>weak and difficult to see</u>?

   _____

5. Why do you think the students just <u>moved around slowly</u> instead of taking their seats?

   _____

6. Were you <u>looking</u> through the telescope, searching for the ship?

   _____

7. Is that a spider <u>hanging</u> over your plate?

   _____

8. Are you amazed by the <u>tremendous size</u> of the universe?

   _____

Name _____   Date _____

"Black Cowboy, Wild Horses" by Julius Lester
Reading Warm-up A

Read the following passage. Pay special attention to the underlined words. Then, read it again, and complete the activities. Use a separate sheet of paper for your written answers.

The wild horses of America are called mustangs. Most mustangs are reddish brown in color. Some are gray, tan, black, or white. For hundreds of years, mustangs have grazed the fields of the American West and Midwest. They eat grass and plants. They drink water from rivers and lakes.

Mustangs are distinct from trained horses because they run wild. They have some features that tame horses do not have. For example, they have stronger legs. They have heavier bones than horses that are not wild. They also have very hard feet. This helps them to travel over many kinds of difficult ground. After all, they do not have any human beings to protect them in a corral or to make iron horseshoes for them!

Herds of mustangs once ran wild over the American plains, the open spaces. These large groups of horses traveled together in order to protect themselves. They knew that there is safety in numbers. The leader of the group is a male horse called the stallion. A big part of his job is to keep the herd safe. Sometimes mountain lions and bears would attack the herd. Now the stallion has to help protect the group from people too.

In the modern world, there are more people than before. There are more cities and less open space than before. This has changed the world of the mustangs. Scientists think that long ago there were over two million mustangs. Compared to that large number, there are now scarcely any left.

People have different opinions about mustangs. Some people think they should be left alone. Some people think that mustangs need more protection. These people have started groups. These groups aim at maintaining the herds that still run on the plains, keeping them safe and healthy. To these people, the presence of wild horses is part of the beauty of America.

1. Circle the words that explain what grazed means. Name another animal that *grazed*.

2. Underline the words that explain the meaning of distinct. Use *distinct* in a sentence of your own.

3. Circle the word that tells one of the purposes of a corral. Where would you be most likely to see a *corral*?

4. Circle the words that explain the meaning of herds. What other animals live in *herds*?

5. Circle the words that describe the plains. What landforms would you usually not find on *plains*?

6. Underline the words that suggest the meaning of scarcely. Define *scarcely* in your own words.

7. Circle the word that means the same as maintaining. Name something else that needs *maintaining*.

8. Circle the words that tell where the presence of mustangs is important. If someone asks for your *presence*, what are they asking?

Name _____ Date _____

"**Black Cowboy, Wild Horses**" by Julius Lester
Reading Warm-up B

Read the following passage. Pay special attention to the underlined words. Then, read it again, and complete the activities. Use a separate sheet of paper for your written answers.

I will never forget the time I saw my first sunset at the Grand Canyon, one of the natural wonders of the world. We had driven all day, and we were hot and tired. By the time we arrived at the national park, it was <u>dusk</u>. There were only a few minutes of daylight left, but we had to see the canyon before night fell. After all that driving, we did not want to wait until morning.

We parked our car and began to walk from the parking lot to the edge of the Grand Canyon. The sun was going down. Growing less and less bright, it was <u>faint</u> on the horizon. The sky was red, orange, and yellow, but mixed with gray and blue-black. It was like a spectacular painting. However, nothing could have prepared us for the Grand Canyon itself.

There it was, an open space larger than anything I had ever seen. Its <u>vastness</u> was greater than anything I had imagined. Its sharply sloping cliffs and <u>steep</u> sides gave the canyon boundaries, but it was almost impossible to see them. To me, the space seemed to have no boundaries at all.

The last light in the sky faded, finally <u>flickered</u>, and went out. My eyes straining, I stood <u>peering</u> out into absolute blackness. I felt like I was standing on the edge of the planet. I felt <u>suspended</u> in space, hanging there in midair. People <u>milled</u> about, silently moving around, not willing to leave the spot. No one spoke. After a while, we all turned back to the comfort and the lights of the buildings behind us. But our sense of our place in the universe had been changed.

1. Underline the words that give clues to the meaning of <u>dusk</u>. Based on the definition of *dusk*, what do you think *dusky* means?

2. Circle the words that suggest the meaning of <u>faint</u>. Name a word that means the opposite of *faint*.

3. Underline the words that help explain the meaning of <u>vastness</u>. Name something else that has the quality of *vastness*.

4. Circle the words that tell the meaning of <u>steep</u>. Use *steep* in a sentence of your own.

5. Circle the words that suggest the meaning of <u>flickered</u>. If a light bulb *flickered*, what would you do with it?

6. Underline the words that help explain the meaning of <u>peering</u>. Which physical sense do you use when you are *peering*?

7. Underline the words that explain the meaning of <u>suspended</u>. If a mountain climber is *suspended* from a rope, what is he doing?

8. Circle the words that tell the meaning of <u>milled</u>. If a group of students *milled* about after class, what might they be waiting to do?

Name _____ Date _____

Julius Lester
Listening and Viewing

Segment 1: Meet Julius Lester
- What types of stories does Julius Lester write? Why do you think it is important to retell these stories?

_____

_____

_____

_____

Segment 2: Themes in Folk Literature
- Who was Bob Lemmons, and why did Julius Lester write a story about him? Why do you think details and vivid language are important when writing a story like the story of Bob Lemmons?

_____

_____

_____

_____

Segment 3: The Writing Process
- How is the process of writing an act of discovery for Julius Lester? What do you think he means by "writing is also an act of self-discovery"?

_____

_____

_____

_____

Segment 4: The Rewards of Writing
- How do Julius Lester's stories act as a bridge between the past and the present? How do you think reading can help you "make sense" of your own life?

_____

_____

_____

_____

Unit 6 Resources: Themes in Folk Literature
© Pearson Education, Inc. All rights reserved.
11

Learning About the Oral Tradition

Passing along stories from one generation to the next is called the **oral tradition.**
Here are some common characteristics:

Characteristics of Stories in the Oral Tradition	Definitions and Examples
Universal theme	A **universal theme** is a message about life that can be understood by people of many cultures (the value of hard work).
Fantasy	**Fantasy** is writing that is highly imaginative and contains elements that are not found in real life (a man who can fly).
Figurative language	**Hyperbole** is exaggeration or overstatement. It is often used to create humor (a man as tall as a tree). **Personification** is the giving of human characteristics to a nonhuman subject (an animal that can talk).
Story types	**Folk tales** often deal with heroes, adventure, magic, or romance ("Jack and the Beanstalk"). Some folk tales are **tall tales**—stories that contain hyperbole (stories about Paul Bunyan or Pecos Bill). **Myths** are tales that explain the actions of gods and heroes (the Greek god Apollo) or explain things in nature (how the leopard got its spots). **Legends** are stories about the past. They are often based on facts, but storytellers have added imaginative details (George Washington cutting down the cherry tree). **Fables** are brief stories, usually with animal characters, that teach a moral or lesson (Aesop's fable "The Tortoise and the Hare," which has the moral *Slow and steady wins the race*).

DIRECTIONS: *Underline the term in each pair that best describes each numbered item.*

1. Friendship is the most valuable gift   universal theme   personification
   of all.

2. The god Zeus hurls a bolt of thunder   myth   folk tale
   across the sky.

3. A fox learns that it is important to be   tall tale   fable
   loyal and honest.

4. Raindrops feel sorry for a hot traveler.   hyperbole   personification

5. An elf grants a hardworking farmer   tall tale   folk tale
   three magic wishes.

Name _____ Date _____

"Black Cowboy, Wild Horses" by Julius Lester
Model Selection: The Oral Tradition

"Black Cowboy, Wild Horses" is an example of literature in the **oral tradition**. A story in the oral tradition was passed down from generation to generation by word of mouth long before it was written down. Stories in the oral tradition often contain a **universal theme,** a message about life. They also contain **fantastic details** that could not happen in real life and **personification,** figurative language that gives human characteristics to nonhuman subjects. **Hyperbole,** an exaggeration or an overstatement, is often found in these stories as well.

Stories written in the oral tradition may be **folk tales** told to entertain and to communicate the shared values of a culture. Folk tales often deal with heroes, adventure, magic, or romance. **Myths** explain the actions of gods and heroes or explain natural phenomena. **Legends** are stories that are widely told about the past. These stories are often based on fact and are a culture's familiar and traditional stories.

A. DIRECTIONS: *Answer the following items.*

1. In the opening paragraph, the author states that the land stretched out "as wide as love." What term is used to describe this type of exaggeration? _____

2. Find another example of this type of exaggeration. _____

3. The author also states that at the edge of the world, "land and sky kissed." What term describes this type of figurative language? _____

4. Find another example of this type of figurative language. _____

5. In what ways is Bob similar to other cowboys? In what ways is he different?

    _____

    _____

    _____

B. DIRECTIONS: *Tell what type of story you think "Black Cowboy, Wild Horses" is. Explain what features of the story led to your answer.*

_____

_____

_____

_____

_____

Name _____   Date _____

"**Black Cowboy, Wild Horses**" by Julius Lester
Open-Book Test

Short Answer *Write your responses to the questions in this section on the lines provided.*

1. In folk literature, a flower that speaks to children is an example of what characteristic? Define the characteristic.

   _____

   _____

2. A grandmother tells her grandchildren a folk tale about a boy whose nose gets longer each time he tells a lie. What two characteristics of folk literature does this story have? Define the characteristics.

   _____

   _____

   _____

3. You read a story about a mouse and a lion that ends with the following: "One good turn deserves another." What kind of folk literature is the story? Explain.

   _____

   _____

4. Eventually, folk tales were collected and written down. How might this have affected the stories? Think about what happened to them as they were told orally.

   _____

   _____

5. In the first paragraph of "Black Cowboy, Wild Horses," how does the author use personification? Give an example from the text.

   _____

   _____

   _____

6. In "Black Cowboy, Wild Horses," the author writes, "Bob could make the horses think he was one of them—because he was." What characteristic of folk literature is Lester using? Explain.

   _____

   _____

7. In "Black Cowboy, Wild Horses," Bob realizes he must "smell of sun, moon, stars, and wind" before he gets to the mustangs. Explain why.

   _____

   _____

8. In "Black Cowboy, Wild Horses," Lester describes the rain as "hard and stinging as remorse." Explain how a heavy rain can be like remorse. Base your answer on the definition of *remorse*.

_____

_____

_____

9. In order to take over the herd, Bob and Warrior must defeat the stallion who is the leader. Why does Bob choose the moment he does to attack? Use details from the story to explain.

_____

_____

_____

10. At the end of "Black Cowboy, Wild Horses," what are Bob and Warrior longing for?

_____

_____

_____

Essay

Write an extended response to the question of your choice or to the question or questions your teacher assigns you.

11. Describe Bob Lemmons's character In "Black Cowboy, Wild Horses." Base your answer on the things he does and on his abilities. Use specific details from the story to support your answer. Use the chart to help organize your points

Things Bob Lemmons Does	Bob Lemmons's Abilities

12. Julius Lester combined fact and fiction to write the legend "Black Cowboy, Wild Horses." In an essay, explain how Lester's story brings history to life. Consider the way in which Lester describes the setting and characters in the story. Use detailed examples to support your ideas.

13. A universal theme is a message about life that can be understood by people of most cultures. What universal theme does "Black Cowboy, Wild Horses" suggest to you? Use details from the story to respond in a brief essay.

14. **Thinking About the Big Question: How much do our communities shape us?** Reread the last paragraph of "Black Cowboy, Wild Horses." Do you think Bob's community shapes his decision not to ride away onto the plains? In a brief essay, explain your opinion and tell whether you think Bob made the right choice. Use details about Bob from the selection.

Oral Response

15. Go back to question 5, 7, or 10 or to the question your teacher assigns to you. Take a few minutes to expand your answer and prepare an oral response. Find additional details in "Black Cowboy, Wild Horses" that support your points. If necessary, make notes to guide your response.

Unit 6 Resources: Themes in Folk Literature
16

"Black Cowboy, Wild Horses" by Julius Lester
Selection Test A

Learning About the Oral Tradition *Identify the letter of the choice that best answers the question.*

_____ 1. Why are some stories said to be part of the oral tradition?
A. They have been told by many generations.
B. They teach lessons about life and nature.
C. They contain heroes, magic, and adventure.
D. They tell about the traditions of a people.

_____ 2. What is a universal theme?
A. a story that comes from another country or another time
B. a message about life that can be understood in many cultures
C. a message about what qualities a hero should have
D. a description of natural events such as storms

_____ 3. A cat who tells jokes is an example of
A. myth.
B. hyperbole.
C. moral.
D. personification.

_____ 4. What is a legend?
A. a folk tale that contains many characters
B. a story that explains the actions of gods
C. a true story about a real person doing real things
D. a story based on facts that also contains imaginative details

_____ 5. Which word has the same meaning as hyperbole?
A. fantasy
B. lesson
C. exaggeration
D. hero

Critical Reading

_____ 6. In "Black Cowboy, Wild Horses," the author writes, "the earth lay napping like a curled cat." What kind of figurative language is this?
A. hyperbole
B. personification
C. fable
D. moral

____ **7.** Which statement is the BEST description of Bob Lemmons?

    A. He is a doctor who treats horses.

    B. He is a rancher who owns many horses.

    C. He is a cowboy who tames wild horses.

    D. He is a cowboy who tracks and rounds up wild horses.

____ **8.** What adjective BEST describes the mustangs?

    A. tame

    B. pretty

    C. mean

    D. wild

____ **9.** Who is Warrior?

    A. Bob's horse

    B. Bob's guide

    C. Bob's cowboy friend

    D. Bob's dog

____ **10.** Why can't Bob light a fire at night?

    A. The horses will see it.

    B. The horses will try to put it out.

    C. The horses will smell the smoke on him.

    D. The horses will run from the light.

____ **11.** What helps Bob find the horses?

    A. their hoofprints

    B. their scent

    C. the river

    D. the storm

____ **12.** Why is the stallion the most important horse in the herd?

    A. He is the fastest of the herd.

    B. He is the oldest of the herd.

    C. He is the youngest of the herd.

    D. He is the leader of the herd.

____ **13.** Why do the horses think that Bob is a horse?

    A. He makes sounds like a horse.

    B. He runs and rears up like a horse.

    C. He thinks and acts like a horse.

    D. He is as wild as a horse.

_____ **14.** How does Bob take control of the herd?

    A. He puts ropes on the horses and drives them into a fenced corral.

    B. He defeats the stallion and takes his place as the leader.

    C. He kills the rattlesnake and wins the trust of the herd.

    D. He leads the horses into a ravine during a storm.

_____ **15.** Why do the cowboys open the corral gate when they hear Bob coming?

    A. They want to welcome him home.

    B. They want to put the mustangs in a fenced-in area.

    C. They want to keep the mustangs from entering the barn.

    D. They want to ride the mustangs.

Essay

16. At the end of *Black Cowboy, Wild Horses*, Bob and Warrior stand on a bluff, looking out over the plains. Warrior rears and whinnies loudly, and Bob says, "I know. Maybe someday." What does he mean? What might he be hoping to do "someday"?

17. Which part of *Black Cowboy, Wild Horses* did you enjoy most? Summarize the main events of your favorite part and tell why you liked it.

18. Thinking About the Big Question: How much do our communities shape us?
Reread the last paragraph of "Black Cowboy, Wild Horses." Do you think Bob's community of cowboys shapes his decision not to ride away onto the plains? In a brief essay, explain your opinion and tell whether you think Bob made the right choice. Use details about Bob from the selection.

"**Black Cowboy, Wild Horses**" by Julius Lester
Selection Test B

Learning About the Oral Tradition *Identify the letter of the choice that best completes the statement or answers the question.*

____ 1. In the oral tradition, a story that deals with heroes, adventure, magic, or romance is
    A. a fable.
    B. a folk tale.
    C. a drama.
    D. realism.

____ 2. Which statement is always true about a universal theme?
    A. It is an exaggeration that is used to add humor to a story.
    B. It teaches a lesson about life such as "Hard work pays off."
    C. It is a message about life that can be understood in many different cultures.
    D. It is an imaginative way to explain a natural occurrence.

____ 3. An angry storm that seems to punish an evil man is an example of
    A. theme.
    B. hyperbole.
    C. moral.
    D. personification.

____ 4. Which of the following is the BEST definition of fantasy?
    A. writing that is highly imaginative and contains elements not found in real life
    B. writing that conveys a central message about life
    C. writing that attempts to explain something that occurs in nature
    D. writing that attempts to teach readers an important lesson

____ 5. Tall tales are folk tales that always contain
    A. hyperbole.
    B. morals.
    C. animal characters.
    D. personification.

____ 6. Which is the BEST definition of a legend?
    A. a tale that explains the actions of gods and heroes
    B. an animal story that contains a lesson
    C. a story about the past that mixes facts and imaginative details
    D. a folk tale that contains personification

Critical Reading

____ 7. Julius Lester writes, "The sky was curved as if it were a lap on which the earth lay napping like a curled cat." This is an example of
    A. hyperbole.
    B. personification.
    C. universal theme.
    D. moral.

____ 8. At the beginning of the story, what job sends Bob Lemmons out onto the plains?
   A. He has been sent to find a runaway horse.
   B. He has been sent to find an injured colt.
   C. He has been sent to round up a herd of wild horses.
   D. He has been sent to find new pasture land for a herd of horses.

____ 9. Which word means "wild horses"?
   A. grazers
   B. stallions
   C. mares
   D. mustangs

____ 10. Which statement is true about Bob Lemmons?
   A. He couldn't read words, but he could read animal tracks.
   B. He couldn't ride a horse, but he could find herds of wild horses.
   C. He could read animal tracks, but he couldn't round up wild horses alone.
   D. He couldn't read words, but he could write messages using pictures.

____ 11. When he stops for the night, Bob Lemmons does not make a campfire because
   A. the grass is very dry, and he is afraid that the fire might spread.
   B. he is afraid that Warrior might be frightened by the flames.
   C. he doesn't want the wild horses to smell the smoke on his clothes.
   D. he doesn't want the wild horses to see the glow of the fire.

____ 12. What dangerous event occurs while Bob is tracking the herd of wild horses?
   A. A thunderstorm frightens Warrior and causes Bob to take shelter in a ravine.
   B. A poisonous snake attacks Warrior.
   C. A smoldering campfire spreads across the prairie as a wildfire.
   D. A fierce dust storm makes it impossible for Bob to find his way across the plains.

____ 13. At one point, Bob doesn't blink his eyes because he is afraid that the stallion will hear the sound. This is an example of
   A. personification.
   B. myth.
   C. hyperbole.
   D. universal theme.

____ 14. As he approaches the herd, Bob is careful not to alarm the stallion because
   A. as the leader of the herd, the stallion will make them run away if he senses a threat.
   B. as the leader of the herd, the stallion will fight to the death to protect them.
   C. the stallion is very large and strong, capable of attacking and killing Warrior.
   D. the stallion has been attacked by a rattlesnake, and Bob wants to help him.

_____ 15. Bob and Warrior attack the stallion because
   A. Bob doesn't think the stallion is strong enough to lead the herd back to the corral.
   B. Bob is angry at the way the stallion treated the mare after the death of her colt.
   C. Bob must defeat the stallion and take over the leadership of the herd.
   D. Bob wants to tame the stallion and make him a trustworthy workhorse.

_____ 16. Bob rides with the horses out on the plains for a few days because
   A. he wants to tame them.
   B. he enjoys being part of the herd.
   C. a storm causes him to lose his way back to the corral.
   D. the cowboys need more time to finish building the corral.

_____ 17. The cowboys put the wild horses into a fenced enclosure because
   A. they intend to keep the wild horses and eventually tame them.
   B. they want to prevent the stallion from coming back to the herd.
   C. they want to protect the wild horses from rattlesnakes and other dangers.
   D. they have to separate the wild horses from their tame horses.

_____ 18. What is the most probable reason that Warrior rears and whinnies as they look out onto the plains at the end of the story?
   A. He feels pride for leading the wild horses home to the fenced corral.
   B. He is concerned about what might have happened to the stallion.
   C. He longs for the freedom of running with wild horses.
   D. He senses that another terrible thunderstorm is coming across the plains.

Essay

19. What universal theme does "Black Cowboy, Wild Horses" suggest to you? Use details in the story to support your ideas.

20. Based on his actions and abilities, describe what kind of character Bob Lemmons is. Be sure to use specific details from the story to support your ideas.

21. Pick one of the following images from "Black Cowboy, Wild Horses." In your own words, describe the picture the image creates in your mind. How does the image contribute to your understanding of the story?

   • "Near dusk, clouds appeared, piled atop each other like mountains made of fear."
   • "By mid-afternoon he could see the ribbon of river shining in the distance."
   • "Bob saw the rattler, as beautiful as a necklace, sliding silently through the tall grasses."

22. **Thinking About the Big Question: How much do our communities shape us?**
   Reread the last paragraph of "Black Cowboy, Wild Horses." Do you think Bob's community shapes his decision not to ride away onto the plains? In a brief essay, explain your opinion and tell whether you think Bob made the right choice. Use details about Bob from the selection.

"The Tiger Who Would Be King" by James Thurber
"The Ant and the Dove" by Leo Tolstoy
Vocabulary Warm-up Word Lists

Study these words. Then, complete the activities that follow.

Word List A

creature [KREE chuhr] *n.* a living being, human or animal
Raul thought that the monkey in the zoo was a strange <u>creature</u>.

cubs [KUHBZ] *n.* young lions, wolves, tigers, or bears
The mother lion watched over her young <u>cubs</u>.

den [DEN] *n.* the home of a wild animal, such as a lion or tiger
The bear slept in his <u>den</u> throughout the entire winter.

greet [GREET] *v.* to welcome somebody in a friendly or familiar way
Haley rushed to <u>greet</u> her friend with a hug.

jungle [JUHNG guhl] *n.* land in tropical areas covered with trees, bushes, and vines
Chimpanzees are one type of animal that lives in the trees of the <u>jungle</u>.

prowled [PROWLD] *v.* moved around quietly or secretly, like an animal hunting
The hungry wolf <u>prowled</u> the forest looking for food.

sake [SAYK] *n.* the good or benefit of someone or something
Angela raised money for the <u>sake</u> of getting new uniforms for her soccer team.

stripes [STRYPS] *n.* narrow bands of color
The flag of the United States has red and white <u>stripes</u>.

Word List B

defend [di FEND] *v.* to protect something or someone from harm
Nadia wanted to <u>defend</u> the environment from polluters.

horror [HAWR uhr] *n.* great fear or terror
Peter jumped back in <u>horror</u> when he saw a spider in front of him.

imaginary [i MAJ uh ner ee] *adj.* existing only in the mind, not in reality
A unicorn is an <u>imaginary</u> animal.

inquired [in KWYRD] *v.* asked about someone or something
George <u>inquired</u> at the box office about the time of the next movie.

monarch [MAHN ark] *n.* a single, unelected ruler, such as a king or a queen
The <u>monarch</u> ruled over his land with justice.

numbered [NUHM buhrd] *adj.* limited; close to the end of a total or amount
It was June, and the days of school left before summer vacation were <u>numbered</u>.

struggle [STRUG uhl] *n.* a big fight to overcome difficulties
Martin Luther King, Jr., fought hard in the <u>struggle</u> for civil rights.

surveyed [ser VAYD] *v.* looked at the whole scene or situation
The teacher <u>surveyed</u> the classroom to make sure all the students were seated at their desks.

Name _____ Date _____

"The Tiger Who Would Be King" by James Thurber
"The Ant and the Dove" by Leo Tolstoy
Vocabulary Warm-up Exercises

Exercise A *Fill in each blank in the paragraph below with an appropriate word from Word List A. Use each word only once.*

A [1] _____ is a tropical forest that is home to many plants, birds, insects, and animals. One [2] _____ that lives there is the tiger. The tiger has narrow markings or [3] _____ on its fur. Young tigers are called [4] _____. They live with their mothers in a home called a [5] _____. Some nights, the mother tiger leaves her young, returning in the morning with meat. To get this meat, the mother tiger will have [6] _____ her territory, hunting. She will return to [7] _____ her young by bringing them the meat. A mother tiger will act for the [8] _____ of her young, protecting them from danger.

Exercise B *Answer the questions with complete explanations.*

1. If you <u>inquired</u> about a topic, would you want to know more about it? Explain.
   _____

2. Would you choose to witness something that made you feel <u>horror</u>? Why or why not?
   _____

3. Is a <u>monarch</u> a type of ruler that is elected? Explain.
   _____

4. Would you want to <u>defend</u> those you love? Why or why not?
   _____

5. If your vacation days are <u>numbered</u>, are there many of them left? Explain.
   _____

6. Would you expect a <u>struggle</u> to be easy? Explain.
   _____

7. When a person has <u>surveyed</u> a situation, has he or she gained a greater knowledge of it? Why or why not?
   _____

8. If you were told that something is <u>imaginary</u>, would you believe it is real? Why or why not?
   _____

24

"The Tiger Who Would Be King" by James Thurber
"The Ant and the Dove" by Leo Tolstoy
Reading Warm-up A

Read the following passage. Pay special attention to the underlined words. Then, read it again, and complete the activities. Use a separate sheet of paper for your written answers.

Few living animals are as impressive as the tiger. This <u>creature</u> is known for its strength and cunning. Tigers are the largest members of the cat family. An adult tiger can weigh over five hundred pounds. A large tiger can measure up to nine feet in length. Tigers have narrow bands of color on their fur. These <u>stripes</u> help a tiger blend in with its surroundings.

Tigers live mostly in Asia. They live as far north as the arctic regions of Siberia. Tigers also live in the warm forests of India and Indonesia. Most tigers in the wild today live in the <u>jungle</u>. There, they are protected by the thick plant growth of these tropical areas.

Tigers are solitary animals. One tiger needs a large amount of land on which to live and hunt. When two tigers meet, they usually do not <u>greet</u> each other in a friendly manner. Instead, they are likely to fight. Each tiger will fight for the rights to its territory.

Young tigers, or <u>cubs</u>, are cared for by their mothers. They live with their mothers in their <u>den</u> until they are about two years old. Then the young tigers will leave this home and go in search of their own territory.

Once, tigers <u>prowled</u> the forests all over Asia hunting for prey. Now, humans have moved into much of the tigers' territory. Tigers no longer have enough room to roam and hunt, so the number of them in the wild is getting smaller. Scientists believe that there are only about six thousand tigers living in the wild today. Laws have been passed for the <u>sake</u> of these remaining tigers. These laws act to benefit tigers by protecting their territory from human development and hunting.

1. Underline the words that describe the word <u>creature</u>. Then, define **creature** in your own words.

2. Circle the words that tell what <u>stripes</u> are. What is something that you know that has **stripes?**

3. Circle the sentence that describes how the <u>jungle</u> helps tigers. Then, write a sentence using the word **jungle**.

4. Underline the words that explain the word <u>greet</u>. Then tell how you usually **greet** someone.

5. Underline the words that tell what <u>cubs</u> are. Then use the word **cubs** in a sentence.

6. Circle the words that tell you what a <u>den</u> is. Then, explain **den** in your own words.

7. Underline the phrase that tells the meaning of the word <u>prowled</u>. Then use the word **prowled** in a sentence.

8. Circle the words that tell you about what has been done for the tigers' <u>sake</u>. What is something you would work hard for the **sake** of?

Name _____ Date _____

Read the following passage. Pay special attention to the underlined words. Then, read it again, and complete the activities. Use a separate sheet of paper for your written answers.

A coup is a sudden change in the government of a country. Coups have happened in many countries around the world. They occur when a group seeks to replace the existing government with a new one. Often, a monarch is replaced with another ruler. The king or queen, for example, might be replaced with a military dictator.

While coups happen quickly, they usually spring from a long political struggle. They are the end result of a great effort to change the government. Those who plan a coup have usually surveyed the government carefully. They have looked at the government and found its weaknesses. Once a coup has been planned, the government's days are usually numbered. There is only a small amount of time left before the coup occurs.

Most coups are not done in a democratic manner. Few military dictators, for example, have inquired to see what the people in their country truly desire from their government. Instead, the new ruler might address imaginary problems, ignoring the country's real concerns. This failure to ask the proper questions often leads to another failed government.

A coup can happen in a few days, perhaps even overnight. Often the leaders of a coup believe it is the best way to defend their country and protect it from the injustices of the first government.

The goal of many coups is to remain bloodless. However, the change in government is rarely good for the citizens. Many "bloodless" coups are followed by the horror of war. Political parties representing either side begin to fight and the country must face the terror of battle.

The dangers of coups can be overcome through democracy. When citizens have a say in their government, the chance of a coup occurring is reduced.

1. Underline the nearby words that are similar to monarch. Then, tell what a *monarch* is.

2. Circle the words that explain what a struggle is. Then, write a sentence about a political *struggle* you are familiar with.

3. Underline the words that tell you how the planners of a coup have surveyed the government. Then, write a sentence using the word *surveyed*.

4. Underline the sentence that tells what numbered means. Then, use the word *numbered* in a sentence.

5. Underline the words that tell what inquired means. What have you *inquired* about lately?

6. Circle the nearby word that means the opposite of imaginary. Then, explain *imaginary* in your own words.

7. Underline the words that tell you what the leaders of a coup seek to defend their country from. Then, use the word *defend* in a sentence.

8. Circle the word that tells you what horror is. Then, write a sentence using the word *horror*.

"**The Tiger Who Would Be King**" by James Thurber
"**The Ant and the Dove**" by Leo Tolstoy
Writing About the Big Question

How much do our communities shape us?

Big Question Vocabulary

common	community	connection	culture	family
generation	group	history	influence	involve
isolate	participation	support	values	belief

A. *Use one or more words from the list above to complete each sentence.*

1. Juan enjoyed going to the town picnic because it made him feel he was part of a _____.

2. Every time Elizabeth played a tennis match, she had a strong _____ that she would win.

3. David and Shauna discovered that being in the photography club had begun to _____ the kinds of photos they took, since they were learning from the other members.

4. Before Raj decided to work on the senator's re-election campaign, he checked into her _____, including her voting record and speeches.

B. *Follow the directions in responding to each of the items below.*

1. List two different times when being part of a group made you act in a certain way.

   _____

   _____

2. Write two sentences explaining one of the preceding experiences, and describe how it made you feel. Use at least two of the Big Question vocabulary words.

   _____

   _____

   _____

C. *Complete the sentence below. Then, write a short paragraph in which you connect this experience to the Big Question.*

Members of my community helped one another when _____

_____

_____

_____

_____

"The Tiger Who Would Be King" by James Thurber
"The Ant and the Dove" by Leo Tolstoy
Reading: Reread to Analyze Cause-and-Effect Relationships

A **cause** is an event, an action, or a feeling that produces a result. The result that is produced is called an **effect.** Sometimes an effect is the result of a number of different causes. To help you identify the relationships between an event and its causes, **reread** important passages in the work, looking for connections. In some stories, all the causes (the events) lead in one way or another to the effect (how the story turns out).

You can use a chart like the one below to record events and actions that work together to produce an effect. You may need to rearrange the lines and arrows for different works. This chart shows you how causes lead to two effects in "The Tiger Who Would Be King."

DIRECTIONS: *Fill in the missing causes and effect.*

1. **CAUSE:** The tiger wants to be king of beasts.

EFFECT A: The tiger challenges the lion.

2. **CAUSE:** _____

3. **CAUSE:** The lion defends his crown.

4. **CAUSE:** _____ **EFFECT B:** _____

5. **CAUSE:** _____

Name _____ Date _____

"The Tiger Who Would Be King" by James Thurber
"The Ant and the Dove" by Leo Tolstoy
Literary Analysis: Fables and Folk Tales

Fables and **folk tales** are part of the oral tradition of passing songs, stories, and poems from generation to generation by word of mouth.

- **Fables** are brief stories that teach a lesson or moral. They often feature animal characters.
- **Folk tales** feature heroes, adventure, magic, and romance. These stories often entertain while teaching a lesson.

DIRECTIONS: *Read "The Tiger Who Would Be King" and "The Ant and the Dove." Answer the following items as you read.*

"The Tiger Who Would Be King"

1. Who are the main characters in this fable? _____

_____

2. Which character, if any, is someone you can admire as a hero? _____

3. Give one reason for your answer to question 2. _____

_____

4. In your own words, what is the moral or lesson of the fable? _____

_____

_____

"The Ant and the Dove"

5. Who are the main characters in this folk tale? _____

_____

6. Which character, if any, is someone you can admire as a hero? _____

7. Give one reason for your answer to question 6. _____

_____

8. What lesson about life docs this folk tale teach? _____

_____

_____

"The Tiger Who Would Be King" by James Thurber
"The Ant and the Dove" by Leo Tolstoy
Vocabulary Builder

Word List

inquired   monarch   prowled   repaid   repulse   startled

A. DIRECTIONS: *Write a* **synonym** *for each vocabulary word. Use a thesaurus if you need one. Write a sentence that includes the synonym. Be sure that your sentence makes the meaning of the word clear.*

Vocabulary word: defend

Synonym: protect

Sentence: The tigress fought to <u>protect</u> her cubs during the battle.

1. Vocabulary word: **startled**   Synonym: _____

   Sentence: _____

2. Vocabulary word: **prowled**   Synonym: _____

   Sentence: _____

3. Vocabulary word: **repulse**   Synonym: _____

   Sentence: _____

4. Vocabulary word: **inquired**   Synonym: _____

   Sentence: _____

5. Vocabulary word: **repaid**   Synonym: _____

   Sentence: _____

6. Vocabulary word: **monarch**   Synonym: _____

   Sentence: _____

B. WORD STUDY: The suffix *-ment* means "the act, art, or process of." Complete each of the following sentences about a word containing *-ment-*.

1. As *repayment* to a friend for a favor, you might

   _____

2. The *argument* between the two teams involved

   _____

3. The candidate gave a *statement* in which

   _____

"The Tiger Who Would Be King" by James Thurber
"The Ant and the Dove" by Leo Tolstoy
Enrichment: Cooperation

In "The Ant and the Dove," the dove performs an act of kindness for the ant. Soon afterward, the ant repays the favor. By following the example of the ant and the dove, people can make their lives and the lives of others more pleasant. Think about acts of kindness that you can perform at school and in your community. Remember, if you want others to help you, *you* have to be a helper.

A. DIRECTIONS: *Read the imaginary situations below. On the lines, write how you could be a helper to the other person.*

1. Your friend has a job delivering newspapers on her bicycle every morning before school. One day she tells you that her bicycle needs to be fixed, and she is worried about not being able to make her deliveries the following morning. How can you help?

   _____

   _____

2. Your younger brother is having a lot of trouble doing his math homework. He says he just doesn't understand how to do long division, and he is worried that he will receive a low grade on his report card. How can you help?

   _____

   _____

3. Your parents work hard all week, and by Friday they are very tired. This Friday, friends are coming for dinner. How can you help?

   _____

   _____

B. DIRECTIONS: *In a few sentences, write about a time when someone helped you do a job or solve a problem. If you prefer, make up a story in which one person helps another, write about a friend or relative who was helped by someone, or write about how someone helped another person in a book, movie, or television show.*

   _____

   _____

   _____

   _____

   _____

   _____

"The Tiger Who Would Be King" by James Thurber
"The Ant and the Dove" by Leo Tolstoy
Open-Book Test

Short Answer *Write your responses to the questions in this section on the lines provided.*

1. In "The Tiger Who Would Be King," what causes the death of so many animals?

   _____

   _____

   _____

2. What kind of story is "The Tiger Who Would Be King"? How do you know?

   _____

   _____

   _____

3. How would you describe the character of the tigress in "The Tiger Who Would Be King"? Explain using examples from the selection.

   _____

   _____

   _____

   _____

4. In "The Tiger Who Would Be King," the tiger causes two things to happen. Fill in the cause/effect chart. Then, on the lines below, tell whether tiger really got what he wanted.

Cause tiger attacks lion

Effect	**Effect**

   _____

   _____

5. In "The Tiger Who Would Be King," the tiger prowled through the jungle. Why did he move this way? Base your answer on the definition of *prowled.*

_____

_____

6. Like most fables, "The Tiger Who Would be King" has a moral at the end. Explain what you think the lesson of the fable is.

_____

_____

_____

7. Folk tales often reveal the shared ideas of a culture. "The Ant and the Dove" reveals that the people of Russia admired what character trait? Use details from the tale to explain.

_____

_____

_____

_____

8. What two feelings is the dove experiencing at the end of "The Ant and the Dove"? Explain.

_____

_____

_____

9. In "The Ant and the Dove," what causes the hunter to drop his net? Explain.

_____

_____

_____

10. Explain how "The Ant and the Dove" is a folk tale.

_____

_____

_____

_____

Essay

Write an extended response to the question of your choice or to the question or questions your teacher assigns you.

11. "The Ant and the Dove" and "The Tiger Who Would be King" both teach a lesson. In a brief essay, explain the lesson of each story and tell which one you think is more important. Use details from the selections in your answer.

12. Think about the lesson taught by "The Ant and the Dove." Do you think the lesson is simply "Be kind," or is it "Be kind because it might get you something in return"? In a brief essay, explain what you think. Include in your answer what you think the better lesson is. Use details from the fable to support your opinion.

13. Both "The Tiger Who Would Be King" and "The Ant and the Dove" use animal characters. How would the stories be different if they were about human characters instead? In a brief essay, explain which story would change more and whether it would be more or less effective. Use details from the stories.

14. **Thinking About the Big Question: How much do our communities shape us?** Consider the community of jungle animals in "The Tiger Who Would Be King." In what ways did they allow themselves to be shaped by their community? Explain your answer in a brief essay. Include in your answer an opinion on whether the animals acted wisely.

Oral Response

15. Go back to question 1, 3 or 6 or to the question your teacher assigns you. Take a few minutes to expand your answer and prepare an oral response. Find additional details in "The Tiger Who Would Be King" or "The Ant and the Dove" that support your points. If necessary, make notes to guide your oral response.

"The Tiger Who Would Be King" by James Thurber
"The Ant and the Dove" by Leo Tolstoy
Selection Test A

Critical Reading *Identify the letter of the choice that best answers the question.*

____ 1. In "The Tiger Who Would Be King," the tiger and the tigress share several characteristics. However, they are different in one main way. Which adjective best describes the tigress but not the tiger?
   A. practical
   B. ferocious
   C. boastful
   D. ambitious

____ 2. In "The Tiger Who Would Be King," what is the main cause for the death of so many animals?
   A. They are on the losing side.
   B. They do not want change.
   C. They join in the fight.
   D. They attack the tiger.

____ 3. How do you know that "The Tiger Who Would Be King" is a fable?
   A. It contains human characters who act like animals.
   B. It teaches a lesson that is stated as a moral at the end.
   C. It has parts that are funny and parts that are sad.
   D. It has animal characters that talk and act like humans.

____ 4. In "The Ant and the Dove," what causes the hunter to drop the net?
   A. The dove flies away.
   B. The dove drops a twig to rescue the ant.
   C. The hunter changes his mind.
   D. The ant bites his foot.

____ 5. How does the dove feel toward the ant at the end of "The Ant and the Dove"?
   A. jealous
   B. grateful
   C. embarrassed
   D. indifferent

____ 6. What is the storyteller's main purpose in "The Ant and the Dove"?

    A. to make readers laugh   C. to teach a lesson

    B. to explain something natural   D. to surprise and amaze

Vocabulary and Grammar

____ 7. Which sentence uses the underlined vocabulary word *incorrectly*?

    A. A goose honked loudly as it <u>prowled</u> across the lake.

    B. Bears <u>prowled</u> through the campsite looking for food.

    C. The bird, <u>startled</u> by the cat, flew away.

    D. The <u>startled</u> audience gasped when the magician disappeared.

____ 8. Which of the following statements about the words *cause* and *reason* is true?

    A. Either word can be used in place of the word *effect*.

    B. They are synonyms; they have the same basic meaning.

    C. They both mean "the consequence of."

    D. They are antonyms; they have opposite meanings.

____ 9. In which of the following sentences is the underlined Academic Vocabulary word used *incorrectly*?

    A. No one could remember the <u>cause</u> of the war.

    B. There is a clear <u>relationship</u> between the fable and its moral.

    C. The <u>effect</u> of the storm was seen in the broken tree limbs.

    D. Give me one good <u>result</u> to explain why you are late.

____ 10. Which of the following is an independent clause in the sentence shown below?

    Folk tales sometimes entertain while they teach a lesson.

    A. Folk tales sometimes entertain

    B. while they

    C. teach a lesson

    D. while they teach a lesson

Essay

11. What lesson does "The Tiger Who Would Be King" teach? What lesson does "The Ant and the Dove" teach? Choose one story. In an essay, tell the lesson that the story teaches. Then, explain how the lesson might apply to human society.

12. **Thinking About the Big Question: How much do our communities shape us?** Consider the community of jungle animals in "The Tiger Who Would Be King." In what ways did they let themselves be shaped by their community? Explain your answer in a brief essay. Include your opinion about whether the animals acted wisely.

"The Tiger Who Would Be King" by James Thurber
"The Ant and the Dove" by Leo Tolstoy
Selection Test B

Critical Reading *Identify the letter of the choice that best completes the statement or answers the question.*

____ 1. In "The Tiger Who Would Be King," the tiger feels he should be king because
    A. the lion is doing a poor job.
    B. he is smarter than the lion.
    C. he is stronger than the lion.
    D. he wants to be.

____ 2. In "The Tiger Who Would Be King," the adjective that best describes the tigress is
    A. practical.
    B. ferocious.
    C. boastful.
    D. ambitious.

____ 3. In "The Tiger Who Would Be King," the main cause for the death of almost all the animals is that
    A. they take the side of the tiger.
    B. they take the side of the lion.
    C. they join in the fight.
    D. they do not want change.

____ 4. You know that "The Tiger Who Would Be King" is a fable because
    A. it contains both human and animal characters.
    B. it teaches a lesson or moral that is stated at the end.
    C. it is humorous but has a serious message.
    D. it is a fictional story with animal characters that can talk.

____ 5. "The Ant and the Dove" reveals that the people—the folk—of Russia admired which character trait?
    A. strength
    B. fairness
    C. cleverness
    D. kindness

____ 6. As a folk tale, "The Ant and the Dove" does all of the following except
    A. entertain.
    B. explain something in nature.
    C. teach a lesson.
    D. contain human and animal characters.

____ 7. Which statement below best expresses the lesson in "The Ant and the Dove"?
    A. Good deeds inspire other good deeds.
    B. Virtue is its own reward.
    C. It takes courage to stand up to power.
    D. Kindness is not always repaid.

____ 8. In "The Ant and the Dove," what is the effect of the ant's biting the hunter's foot?
   A. The hunter steps on the ant and kills it.
   B. The dove drops a twig for the ant to grab.
   C. The hunter changes his mind about killing the dove.
   D. The hunter drops the net, and the dove flies away.

Vocabulary and Grammar

____ 9. Which sentence uses the underlined vocabulary word *incorrectly*?
   A. Geese <u>prowled</u> across the lake, honking loudly as they reached the opposite shore.
   B. Raccoons <u>prowled</u> through the campsite at night, hunting for something to eat.
   C. <u>Startled</u> by the cat, the bird flew off the deck and up into the tree.
   D. The jets swooped low, and the <u>startled</u> audience at the air show gasped.

____ 10. Which of the following statements is true about the words *cause* and *reason*?
   A. *Cause* is used more often than *reason.*
   B. Finding the cause leads to the reason.
   C. They are opposites.
   D. They have the same basic meaning.

____ 11. Which sentence uses the underlined Academic Vocabulary word *incorrectly*?
   A. None of the animals could remember the <u>cause</u> of the war.
   B. There is a clear <u>relationship</u> between the story and its moral.
   C. The <u>result</u> of the argument was a simple misunderstanding.
   D. The <u>reason</u> for their friendship was mutual respect and kindness.

____ 12. In which of the following sentences is the independent clause underlined?
   A. <u>When the ant saw what was happening</u>, it walked right up to the man.
   B. When the ant saw what was happening, <u>it walked right up to the man.</u>
   C. When the ant saw <u>what was happening</u>, it walked right up to the man.
   D. When the ant saw what was happening, it walked <u>right up to the man</u>.

Essay

13. The characters in both "The Tiger Who Would Be King" and "The Ant and the Dove" are animals, but they are portrayed quite differently in the two stories. In an essay, tell two ways in which the animals in one story are different from the animals in the other story. Explain how these differences cause the stories to have different effects on the reader. Use specific details from the stories to support your ideas.

14. Cultural values are often expressed in folk literature and may give you clues about what was (or still is) important to a certain culture. In an essay, explain the values expressed in "The Ant and the Dove" and tell how the characters and the events in the story contribute to the lesson that is taught.

15. **Thinking About the Big Question: How much should our communities shape us?** Consider the community of jungle animals in "The Tiger Who Would Be King." In what ways did they allow themselves to be shaped by their community? Explain your answer in a brief essay. Include in your answer an opinion on whether the animals acted wisely.

Vocabulary Warm-up Word Lists

Study these words. Then, complete the activities that follow.

Word List A

attempted [uh TEMPT id] *v.* tried to do something
George <u>attempted</u> to make a home run but only hit a triple.

attention [uh TEN shuhn] *n.* close and careful thought
Rita gave her homework assignment a great deal of <u>attention</u>.

extremely [ek STREEM lee] *adv.* to a very high degree
Above the Arctic Circle, the weather is <u>extremely</u> cold.

interrupted [in tuh RUHPT id] *v.* stopped something briefly
John <u>interrupted</u> me before I had finished making my point.

miserable [MIZ uhr uh buhl] *adj.* very unhappy or dejected
They stray cat looked cold, hungry, and <u>miserable</u>.

reports [ri PAWRTS] *n.* written or spoken accounts of events
The journalist sent <u>reports</u> back to the newspaper about what she saw at the trial.

success [suhk SES] *n.* a good or desired result
Richard knew his party was a <u>success</u> because everyone enjoyed it.

unusual [un YOO zhoo uhl] *adj.* rare, uncommon
A ferret is an <u>unusual</u> type of pet.

Word List B

demonstrate [DEM uhn strayt] *v.* to show something clearly
Carla wanted to <u>demonstrate</u> her ability to sing at the recital.

lure [LOOR] *v.* to attract strongly
Manuel put cheese in the mousetrap to <u>lure</u> mice.

official [uh FISH uhl] *n.* an important person in an organization
The king's top advisor was a very important <u>official</u>.

palace [PAL is] *n.* a large, grand house for a king, queen, or ruler
The queen's <u>palace</u> had one hundred rooms.

provided [pruh VY did] *v.* supplied things that are needed
The local farm <u>provided</u> the restaurant with fresh vegetables.

remained [ri MAYND] *v.* stayed in the same place
Angela <u>remained</u> after class to ask her teacher a question.

treasured [TREZH uhrd] *v.* valued something highly
Paul <u>treasured</u> the antique watch that he was given by his grandfather.

withdrew [with DROO] *v.* dropped out or went away
Stephanie wanted to be alone, so she <u>withdrew</u> to her bedroom.

39

"The Lion and the Bulls" by Aesop
"A Crippled Boy" by My-Van Tran
Vocabulary Warm-up Exercises

Exercise A *Fill in each blank in the paragraph below with an appropriate word from Word List A. Use each word only once.*

Alexis had always wanted to travel, so she was [1] _____ glad to have the chance to go to Mexico. She had read [2] _____ that said Mexico was a very beautiful country. She looked forward to seeing [3] _____ things that she had never seen before. To prepare for her trip, Alexis focused all of her [4] _____ on learning Spanish. Once she got to Mexico, she [5] _____ to speak Spanish with as many people as possible. Once, a man [6] _____ her before she could finish her sentence and spoke to her in English. She responded in Spanish, to show that she knew the language. Alexis loved Mexico and felt [7] _____ when she had to leave. The trip had been a [8] _____. Alexis had had the time of her life.

Exercise B *Revise each sentence so that the underlined vocabulary word is used in a logical way. Be sure to keep the vocabulary word in your revision.*

Example: Gina <u>treasured</u> her books so much that she left them sitting out in the rain.
Gina <u>treasured</u> her books so much that she kept them in order on a shelf.

1. Joey <u>provided</u> his family with company by never seeing them.
   _____

2. The <u>official</u> had one of the least important jobs in the organization.
   _____

3. Lauren <u>withdrew</u> from the race by participating in it.
   _____

4. Anthony tried to <u>lure</u> the bird into his hand by scaring it away.
   _____

5. A <u>palace</u> is a place where a very poor person lives.
   _____

6. Kerry chose to <u>demonstrate</u> her skill as a writer by using poor grammar.
   _____

7. Marco <u>remained</u> at his friend's house and walked out the door.
   _____

Name _____ Date _____

"The Lion and the Bulls" by Aesop
"A Crippled Boy" by My-Van Tran
Reading Warm-up A

Read the following passage. Pay special attention to the underlined words. Then, read it again, and complete the activities. Use a separate sheet of paper for your written answers.

Lions rule the African plains. These regal animals have long captured our <u>attention</u>. People have been interested in lions for hundreds of years. Most of the information we have about lions comes from <u>reports</u> by naturalists working in Africa. These accounts tell us how lions live in the wild.

Lions are <u>unusual</u> among cats because they live in groups. This behavior is rare among members of the cat family. Lions are <u>extremely</u> social. They enjoy the company of other lions very much. A group of lions is called a pride. Most prides are made up of fifteen to twenty lions. If a lion is separated from its pride, it becomes <u>miserable</u>. The lion will remain very unhappy until it has found a new pride to join.

Lions may look fierce, but they are actually lazy animals. Most lions sleep all day. They hunt only rarely at night. A male lion will not hunt at all. Female lions do all the hunting. They hunt for animals such as giraffes and zebras. A lioness on the hunt only has a one in five chance of catching her prey. If a lioness has <u>attempted</u> to capture an animal and failed, she must try again. Once the hunt ends in <u>success</u>, however, the male lion will get to eat first.

It is the male lion's job to protect the pride's territory. Sadly, this task has become harder in recent decades. Humans have <u>interrupted</u> the lions' natural way of life. As people have taken over the African plains, they have stopped the lions from roaming freely. As a result, the number of lions in the wild has been cut in half in the last fifty years. Today, there are only about 21,000 lions living in the wild.

1. Underline the words that describe <u>attention</u>. Then, explain what it means to give *attention* to something.

2. Circle a nearby word with a meaning similar to <u>reports</u>. Then, use *reports* in a sentence.

3. Circle the word that means the same thing as <u>unusual</u>. What is something you find *unusual*?

4. Underline the words that explain the meaning of <u>extremely</u>. Describe something you do *extremely* well.

5. Underline the phrase that describes the word <u>miserable</u>. Then, define *miserable* in your own words.

6. Circle the words that tell you what a lioness must do if she has <u>attempted</u> to hunt and failed. Describe something you *attempted* to do recently.

7. Underline the words that describe what happens when the hunt is a <u>success</u>. Then, use *success* in a sentence.

8. Circle the words that tell what humans have <u>interrupted</u>. Have you *interrupted* anything or anyone lately? Explain, using the word.

Name _____   Date _____

Read the following passage. Pay special attention to the underlined words. Then, read it again, and complete the activities. Use a separate sheet of paper for your written answers.

When Aya found out that she could work in the king's palace, she was thrilled. She had never been inside such a large and grand building in her life. Aya was also excited to be able to work as a chef in the kitchen. There, she would have a chance to demonstrate her cooking ability. Aya wanted to show how well she could cook delicious food. Aya also knew that it was an honor to cook for the king and his guests.

One day, Aya was working in the kitchen making a large pot of soup. The delicious smell of the soup was so strong, it began to lure people in from the hallway. A maid and a butler were drawn in to the kitchen by the smell. Once they had tasted the soup, they liked it so much that they remained in the kitchen. The two servants stayed there for a while, eating happily.

Soon, a man dressed in fancy clothes entered the kitchen. Aya gasped when she recognized the official, knowing that this man held one of the most important positions in the king's government. Filled with shyness, Aya withdrew into a corner and hoped that the official would not notice that she was there.

"Where is that smell coming from?" the official asked. "I must taste some of whatever is cooking."

Nervously, Aya came out from the corner. She greeted the official and ladled him a bowl of her soup.

"Remarkable," said the official. "You have provided me with the best soup I have ever eaten. Thank you for giving me this delicious treat. I will let the king know what a fine cook he has in his kitchen."

Aya treasured the official's words. They meant a lot to her. After that day, Aya cooked the soup often, and always made sure that the official got a steaming hot bowl.

1. Underline the words that describe what a palace is. Would you like to live in a *palace*?

2. Circle the words that explain what it means to demonstrate something. Then define *demonstrate*.

3. Underline the words that describe the meaning of lure. Then, use *lure* in a sentence.

4. Underline the words that show what the servants did when they remained in the kitchen. Explain *remained* in your own words.

5. Circle the words that explain why the official was important. Then, write a sentence using the word *official*.

6. Underline the words that tell what reason Aya had when she withdrew into the corner. Then, use *withdrew* in a sentence.

7. Underline the words that tell what Aya did when she provided the official with soup. Then, tell what *provided* means.

8. Circle the sentence that describes the word treasured. Describe something that you have *treasured*.

Name _____ Date _____

"The Lion and the Bulls" by Aesop
"A Crippled Boy" by My-Van Tran
Writing About the Big Question

How much do our communities shape us?

Big Question Vocabulary

common	community	connection	culture	family
generation	group	history	influence	involve
isolate	participation	support	values	belief

A. *Use one or more words from the list above to complete each sentence.*

1. When Dariah broke her leg and had to quit the soccer team, she felt _____ and alone, since she didn't see her teammates as often.

2. Gene feels stronger and happier about himself on days when he spends a little time with his parents because his _____ encourages him to do well.

3. Teaching a youth church group was important to Will because it allowed him to share some of his _____ with others.

4. Working on the block's garage sale was fun, and contributing to the _____ good of her neighbors made Susannah feel productive.

B. *Follow the directions in responding to each of the items below.*

1. List two different times when you felt alone, like an outsider.

   _____.

   _____.

2. Write two sentences explaining one of the preceding experiences, and describe how it made you feel. Use at least two of the Big Question vocabulary words.

   _____

   _____

   _____

C. *Complete the sentence below. Then, write a short paragraph in which you connect this experience to the Big Question.*

One time, someone asked me for help with _____ because

_____

_____

_____

_____

Unit 6 Resources: Themes in Folk Literature

Name _____ Date _____

Reading: Reread to Analyze Cause-and-Effect Relationships

A **cause** is an event, an action, or a feeling that produces a result. The result that is produced is called an **effect.** Sometimes an effect is the result of a number of different causes. To help you identify the relationships between an event and its causes, **reread** important passages in the work, looking for connections. In some stories, all the causes (the events) lead in one way or another to the effect (how the story turns out).

You can use a chart like the one below to record events and actions that work together to produce an effect. You may need to rearrange the lines and arrows for different works. This chart shows you how causes lead to two effects in "The Lion and the Bulls."

DIRECTIONS: *Fill in the missing causes and effect.*

1. CAUSE: The lion tries to lure away a bull.

 EFFECT A: The bulls are safe.

2. CAUSE: _____

3. CAUSE: The lion thinks of a plan.

4. CAUSE: _____ **EFFECT B:** _____

5. CAUSE: _____

"The Lion and the Bulls" by Aesop
"A Crippled Boy" by My-Van Tran
Literary Analysis: Fables and Folk Tales

Fables and **folk tales** are part of the oral tradition of passing songs, stories, and poems from generation to generation by word of mouth.

- **Fables** are brief stories that teach a lesson or moral. They often feature animal characters.
- **Folk tales** feature heroes, adventure, magic, and romance. These stories often entertain while teaching a lesson.

DIRECTIONS: *Reread "The Lion and the Bulls" and "A Crippled Boy." Answer the following items as you read.*

"The Lion and the Bulls"

1. Who are the main characters in this fable? _____

   _____

2. Which character, if any, is someone you can admire as a hero? _____

3. Give one reason for your answer in question 2. _____

   _____

4. In your own words, what is the moral or lesson of this fable? _____

   _____

   _____

"A Crippled Boy"

5. Who are the main characters in this folk tale? _____

   _____

6. Which character, if any, is someone you can admire as a hero? _____

7. Give one reason for your answer in question 6. _____

   _____

8. What lesson about life does this folk tale teach? _____

   _____

   _____

Name _____ Date _____

"The Lion and the Bulls" by Aesop
"A Crippled Boy" by My-Van Tran
Vocabulary Builder

Word List

crippled   demonstrate   lure   official   provided   slanderous

A. DIRECTIONS: *Revise each sentence so that the underlined vocabulary word is used logically. Be sure to keep the vocabulary word in your revision.*

1. People enjoy hearing <u>slanderous</u> remarks about their friends.

   _____

2. In schools of the future, a cat may be <u>provided</u> to help students with homework.

   _____

3. To <u>demonstrate</u> the law of gravity, Tom read a book about falling rocks.

   _____

4. The rabbit with the <u>crippled</u> foot hopped away quickly.

   _____

5. The <u>official</u> Web site for the store says, "Our prices are too high!"

   _____

6. I tried to <u>lure</u> my cat to sit on my lap by growling like an angry dog.

   _____

B. WORD STUDY: The suffix *-ous* means "having, full of, or characterized by." Answer the following questions about these words containing *-ous: slanderous, humorous, laborious.*

1. How would a *slanderous* magazine article about someone you admire make you feel, and why? _____

2. What would you do if you heard a *humorous* story, and why? _____

   _____

3. If someone told you something is a *laborious* job, how would you feel about doing it, and why? _____

"The Lion and the Bulls" by Aesop
"A Crippled Boy" by My-Van Tran

Enrichment: Devising a Strategy

In Aesop's fable "The Lion and the Bulls," the lion fails at first because he does not have a strategy, or plan. He just roams around the field, accomplishing nothing. When he devises a strategy—turning the bulls against one another—he finally succeeds. The moral of this story, from the bulls' point of view, is "United we stand, divided we fall." The fable could have another moral from the lion's point of view: "If you want to succeed, devise a strategy."

This moral applies to succeeding in school and in other areas of your life. Sometimes you may have a hard time studying or getting your work done because you cannot decide what to do first. Perhaps you waste time on something that's not important, or you spend all your study time on one subject and don't leave enough time for the others. To avoid these and similar problems, you need to devise a strategy.

An important strategy for success is to **make a list** of things you need to do. When you make a to-do list, you should write down everything you have to do for the day—or week or month—and then number the items on your list in order of importance. Then, rewrite the items in numerical order, in the order of their importance, with the most important item first.

DIRECTIONS: *Fill in the chart below with six items that you (or any student) might need to do in a typical day. In the first column, write the items as you think of them. In the second column, number the items in order of importance. In the third column, rewrite the list in numerical order.*

List of Things to Do	Order of Importance	Re-ordered List

"The Tiger Who Would Be King" by James Thurber
"The Ant and the Dove" by Leo Tolstoy
"The Lion and the Bulls" by Aesop
"A Crippled Boy" by My-Van Tran

Integrated Language Skills: Grammar

Clauses: Independent and Subordinate

A **clause** is a group of words with its own subject and verb. An **independent clause** has a subject and a verb and can stand on its own as a complete sentence. A **subordinate clause** has a subject and a verb but cannot stand on its own as a complete sentence.

Independent clause: All winter we went to school.

Subordinate clause: All winter after we went to school

A subordinate clause depends on an independent clause to complete its meaning.

Subordinate clause   **Independent clause**

All winter after we went to school, we played in the snow.

A. Practice: *Identify each of the following items as an independent or a subordinate clause.*

Example: Before the tiger left his den   <u>subordinate</u>

1. Most people fear tigers and lions _____

2. When you read a fable _____

3. He learned his lesson well _____

4. Before he got into trouble again _____

B. Writing Application: *Add to each subordinate clause to make a complete sentence. Write the complete sentence on the line following each subordinate clause.*

As we came to the end of the path,
As we came to the end of the path, we saw a cabin.

1. After we finished eating,

_____

2. By the time we saw the bear,

_____

3. Although we got away that time,

_____

"The Tiger Who Would Be King" by James Thurber
"The Ant and the Dove" by Leo Tolstoy
"The Lion and the Bulls" by Aesop
"A Crippled Boy" by My-Van Tran

Support for Writing a Fable

Before you write your fable, figure out the causes and effects that lead up to the lesson of your story. Begin by writing down your story ideas on the chart below.

Lesson	
Animal characters	
Their situation or conflict	

Next, decide on the action in your fable. Write one story event on each line. Use only as many lines as you need. Draw arrows between events to show causes and effects that are connected. Finally, write how your fable will end.

Story events:

_____
_____
_____
_____

How my fable will end:

Now, use your notes to draft a fable that teaches a lesson.

Name _____ Date _____

"The Tiger Who Would Be King" by James Thurber
"The Ant and the Dove" by Leo Tolstoy
"The Lion and the Bulls" by Aesop
"A Crippled Boy" by My-Van Tran
Support for Extend Your Learning

Listening and Speaking: "The Tiger Who Would Be King" and "The Ant and the Dove"

Use the following lines to take notes for your oral report on James Thurber or Leo Tolstoy.

Early life: _____

_____

How and why he became a writer: _____

_____

What I'm going to read and why I chose it: _____

_____

Listening and Speaking: "The Lion and the Bulls" and "A Crippled Boy"

Use the following lines to take notes for your oral report on Aesop or My-Van Tran.

Early life: _____

_____

How and why he/she became a writer: _____

_____

What I'm going to read and why I chose it: _____

_____

"The Lion and the Bulls" by Aesop
"A Crippled Boy" by My-Van Tran
Open-Book Test

Short Answer *Write your responses to the questions in this section on the lines provided.*

1. Use the graphic organizer to show what effects the lion's lies cause in "The Lion and the Bulls." On the lines below, explain how the bulls are also a cause of their own downfall.

Cause

Effect	Effect

_____

_____

2. The lion said slanderous things about each bull. Explain how you would feel if someone made slanderous comments about you. Use the definition of *slanderous* in your answer.

_____

_____

3. In "The Lion and the Bulls," what character trait did the bulls show that got them into trouble? Explain.

_____

_____

4. What is the storyteller's main purpose for telling the fable of "The Lion and the Bulls"? How do you know?

_____

_____

_____

5. The King asks Theo to demonstrate his skill in "A Crippled Boy." What do the mandarins demonstrate at the beginning of the meeting? Use the definition of *demonstrate*.

_____

_____

Unit 6 Resources: Themes in Folk Literature
51

6. In "A Crippled Boy," what are the two effects of Theo's stone throwing in the King's palace? Consider short-term and long-term effects. Use details to explain.

_____

_____

_____

_____

7. In "A Crippled Boy," how does Theo's disability cause both positive and negative results for him? Explain.

_____

_____

_____

8. In "A Crippled Boy," the King has Theo sit behind a curtain. Explain the purpose of the curtain and why it is important to the King's plan.

_____

_____

_____

9. How is the King in "A Crippled Boy" similar to the lion in "The Lion and the Bulls"? Explain, using details from the stories.

_____

_____

10. Folk tales were often meant to entertain and to teach a lesson. What is the lesson in "A Crippled Boy"? Use details from the story to explain.

_____

_____

_____

_____

Essay

Write an extended response to the question of your choice or to the question or questions your teacher assigns you.

11. Choose either the King in "A Crippled Boy" or the lion in "The Lion and the Bulls." Write an essay comparing the two characters and telling which one you find more admirable. Use details from the stories to support your ideas.

12. Folk tales and fables are often intended to teach a lesson. Compare the lessons taught in "The Lion and the Bulls" and "A Crippled Boy." In an essay, explain which lesson you think is more important in our culture today. Use details from the selections to support your position.

13. In "The Lion and the Bulls," the bulls are not entirely without fault. In an essay, explain how the bulls help bring about their own end and how they could have prevented it. Use details from the fable to describe the flaw in the bulls' personalities.

14. **Thinking About the Big Question: How much do our communities shape us?** Think about Theo in "A Crippled Boy." Is his life shaped, or affected, more by his community or by other factors? Use details from the story to support your ideas in a brief essay.

Oral Response

15. Go back to question 3, 7, or 10 or to the question your teacher assigns you. Take a few minutes to expand your answer and prepare an oral response. Find additional details in "The Lion and the Bulls" or "A Crippled Boy" to support your points. If necessary, make notes to guide your oral response.

Unit 6 Resources: Themes in Folk Literature
53

Name _____ Date _____

Selection Test A

Critical Reading *Identify the letter of the choice that best answers the question.*

_____ 1. In "The Lion and the Bulls," the lion's evil reports about the bulls is a cause for what happens later. What effect follows the lion's evil reports?
   A. The bulls fight against the lion.
   B. The bulls spread reports about the lion.
   C. The lion loses all his friends.
   D. The bulls stay away from each other.

_____ 2. Which description below best fits the lion in "The Lion and the Bulls"?
   A. thinks and plans before he acts
   B. fears the other animals
   C. proud of being king of beasts
   D. eager to make friends

_____ 3. What is the moral of "The Lion and the Bulls"?
   A. Don't listen to lies.
   B. Stick together and be stronger.
   C. Never trust a stranger.
   D. It's always good to have a plan.

_____ 4. In "A Crippled Boy," where does the King have Theo sit?
   A. under a banyan tree
   B. next to the mandarins
   C. behind a curtain
   D. with him on the throne

_____ 5. In "A Crippled Boy," what causes the mandarins to stop interrupting the King?
   A. Theo tells the mandarins that they have been rude to the King.
   B. Every time a mandarin opens his mouth, Theo throws a pebble into it.
   C. Every time a mandarin speaks, Theo makes him bite his tongue.
   D. The King threatens to cut off their heads.

_____ 6. Which of the following statements is true about "A Crippled Boy"?
   A. It is a fable.
   B. The King is the hero.
   C. It is an entertaining story that teaches a lesson.
   D. All of the characters are talking animals.

Vocabulary and Grammar

___ 7. Which sentence uses the underlined vocabulary word in a way that *does not* make sense?
   A. Please <u>demonstrate</u> how I can safely feed the snake.
   B. Will you <u>demonstrate</u> how that robot toy works?
   C. A television <u>provided</u> all the entertainment they wanted.
   D. We <u>provided</u> to Mom that we had finished all our chores.

___ 8. Which of the following statements about the words *effect* and *result* is true?
   A. They both mean "why something happens."
   B. They only relate to fables.
   C. They are opposites.
   D. They are synonyms.

___ 9. Which sentence uses an underlined Academic Vocabulary word *incorrectly*?
   A. There's a good <u>reason</u> why birds fear cats.
   B. The <u>cause</u> of a cold is bacteria or a virus.
   C. The word <u>relationship</u> means "complete separation."
   D. The <u>effect</u> of gossiping about friends is sometimes losing friends.

___ 10. Which of the following is a subordinate clause in the sentence shown below?
   If anybody opened his mouth to speak, he would shut it again.

   A. opened his mouth
   B. If anybody opened his mouth to speak
   C. he would shut it again
   D. shut it again

Essay

11. Choose "The Lion and the Bulls" or "A Crippled Boy." Write an essay in which you explain the purpose of the tale. Does it entertain, teach, or both entertain *and* teach? Support your answer with details from the text.

12. **Thinking About the Big Question: How much do our communities shape us?**
   Think about Theo in "A Crippled Boy." His life is shaped, or affected, by his community. It is also affected by other things—his disability and his skill. In an essay, discuss whether Theo's life is shaped more by his community or by the other factors. Use details from the story to support your ideas in a brief essay.

"The Lion and the Bulls" by Aesop
"A Crippled Boy" by My-Van Tran
Selection Test B

Critical Reading *Identify the letter of the choice that best completes the statement or answers the question.*

_____ 1. In "The Lion and the Bulls," the effect of the lion's evil reports about the bulls is that
   A. the bulls unite against the lion.
   B. the bulls spread reports about the lion.
   C. the lion loses all the bulls' friendship.
   D. the bulls begin to avoid one another.

_____ 2. In "The Lion and the Bulls," the lion might best be described as an animal who
   A. thinks before he acts.
   B. is a coward.
   C. is king of beasts.
   D. is always successful.

_____ 3. In "The Lion and the Bulls," the bulls are safe as long as they
   A. are brave.
   B. stay alert.
   C. stay together.
   D. are friendly.

_____ 4. The storyteller's main purpose in "The Lion and the Bulls" is to
   A. entertain.
   B. teach a lesson.
   C. surprise and amaze.
   D. explain the nature of bulls.

_____ 5. In "A Crippled Boy," Theo learns to throw pebbles because
   A. he cannot play with the other children.
   B. he wants to get a job with the King.
   C. he needs to defend himself.
   D. he wants to hit fruit in the trees.

_____ 6. In "A Crippled Boy," why does the King have Theo sit behind a curtain?
   A. He knows Theo is shy.
   B. He doesn't want the mandarins to see Theo.
   C. He wants Theo to surprise the mandarins at the end.
   D. He doesn't want his bodyguards to interfere.

_____ 7. In "A Crippled Boy," Theo's job for the King is to make the mandarins
   A. speak up.
   B. talk quietly.
   C. leave.
   D. stop talking.

Unit 6 Resources: Themes in Folk Literature
56

_____ 8. Which statement below best expresses the lesson in "A Crippled Boy"?
　　　　A. Listening is more important than speaking.
　　　　B. Skill and practice will be rewarded.
　　　　C. Kings should be respected and listened to.
　　　　D. Kings can profit from their own charity.

Vocabulary and Grammar

_____ 9. Which sentence uses the underlined vocabulary word *incorrectly*?
　　　　A. Please demonstrate how to feed and handle snakes safely.
　　　　B. I may buy that robot toy if you can demonstrate that it works easily.
　　　　C. A slanderous attack in the newspaper pleased and flattered the actress.
　　　　D. His slanderous accusations angered us because we thought we were friends.

_____ 10. Which statement is true about the words *effect* and *result*?
　　　　A. They mean *cause* and *reason*.
　　　　B. They are synonyms.
　　　　C. They have opposite meanings.
　　　　D. They show a connection.

_____ 11. Which sentence uses the underlined Academic Vocabulary word *incorrectly*?
　　　　A. What might be a reason that some birds fear cats and others tease them?
　　　　B. The cause of their argument was a simple misunderstanding.
　　　　C. Every writer has a good effect for writing a story.
　　　　D. The relationship between fables and folk tales is a close one.

_____ 12. In which of the following sentences is the subordinate clause underlined?
　　　　A. If anybody opened his mouth to speak, he would be stopped.
　　　　B. If anybody opened his mouth to speak, he would be stopped.
　　　　C. If anybody opened his mouth to speak, he would be stopped.
　　　　D. If anybody opened his mouth to speak, he would be stopped.

Essay

13. In both "The Lion and the Bulls" and "The Crippled Boy," characters are rewarded or punished for their actions. In an essay, explain how one or more characters in each tale cause—and therefore deserve—the fate they receive. Give details from each tale to support your argument.

14. The moral for "The Lion and the Bulls" is given at the end of the fable: "United we stand, divided we fall." In an essay, tell at least one other lesson that you might gain from this fable. Then, tell what lesson you learn from "A Crippled Boy." Explain which lesson you think is more relevant to people today. Give reasons for your answer.

15. **Thinking About the Big Question: How much do our communities shape us?**
Think about Theo in "A Crippled Boy." Is his life shaped, or affected, more by his community or by other factors? Use details from the story to support your ideas in a brief essay.

Vocabulary Warm-up Word Lists

Study these words from "Arachne." Then, complete the activities that follow.

Word List A

challenged [CHAL uhnjd] *v.* dared someone to participate in a contest
   Rita <u>challenged</u> her friends to a race to prove how fast she was.

descend [dee SEND] *v.* to climb down or go lower
   Tomorrow, Jake plans to <u>descend</u> the mountain and hike the valley.

goddess [GAHD is] *n.* a female god or deity
   The ancient Egyptians worshipped Isis, the <u>goddess</u> of fertility.

judged [JUHJD] *v.* decided the winner of a competition
   Stephen <u>judged</u> the writing contest and gave Pablo's essay first prize.

marvelous [MAHR vuh luhs] *adj.* creating surprise or wonder
   The fireworks display was a <u>marvelous</u> sight and impressed everyone.

olive [AHL iv] *adj.* relating to the small green fruit that can be eaten or crushed for oil
   The <u>olive</u> trees were ready to be harvested.

presence [PREZ uhns] *n.* the position near a person or thing
   Marco felt smarter in the <u>presence</u> of his teacher.

products [PROD uhktz] *n.* things that are made or created
   <u>Products</u> like cheese and butter can be made from cow's milk.

Word List B

amid [uh MID] *prep.* in the middle of or surrounded by
   The bird flew <u>amid</u> the branches of a tree to reach its nest.

deceived [dee SEEVD] *v.* purposefully tricked
   The wolf in sheep's clothing <u>deceived</u> the sheep.

fate [FAYT] *n.* consequence, result, or destiny
   It was Evan's <u>fate</u> to always be the last person picked for the team.

gorgeous [GOR juhs] *adj.* very beautiful or attractive
   Linda thought the beautiful rose bushes in the park were <u>gorgeous</u>.

overtaken [oh ver TAY kuhn] *v.* caught up with and passed
   The runner was <u>overtaken</u> by his rival and finished in second place.

reckless [REK lis] *adj.* careless about safety
   Marla was a <u>reckless</u> bicycle rider, and she often had accidents.

skillful [SKIL fuhl] *adj.* able to do something well
   Diego was a <u>skillful</u> guitarist and could play many songs well.

strands [STRANDZ] *n.* long, thin threads
   Alice wove the <u>strands</u> of wool into a beautiful blanket.

Name _____ Date _____

"**Arachne**" by Olivia E. Coolidge
Vocabulary Warm-up Exercises

Exercise A *Fill in each blank in the paragraph below with an appropriate word from Word List A. Use each word only once.*

Irene looked out onto the beautiful valley. She thought the view was

[1] _____. From the mountaintop she began to [2] _____

the slope to where the farmhouse stood. The valley below was covered in

[3] _____ and plum trees. It was harvest season. Some families kept the

tradition of making offerings to the harvest [4] _____. Now they were

picking the fruit. Later they would make oil and jam. Irene soon found herself in the

[5] _____ of a group of farmers. While she was there, one farmer

[6] _____ another to a contest. Each farmer thought his plum jam was

the best. They asked Irene to try their [7] _____. Irene tasted the jams

and [8] _____ the first farmer's plum jam the best. The farmers smiled

and laughed. Irene loved this valley. She felt as if she could stay here forever.

Exercise B *Answer the questions with complete explanations.*

Example: Would you be happy if someone did <u>skillful</u> work for you? Why or why not?
   Yes, I would be happy, because <u>skillful</u> work is good work, since it is done with a lot of skill.

1. If a boy found out that he had been <u>deceived</u>, would he be angry? Explain.

   _____

2. If a cow is <u>amid</u> a herd of cattle, is that cow alone or with others? Explain.

   _____

3. Would you get in a car with a <u>reckless</u> driver? Why or why not?

   _____

4. Are <u>strands</u> of thread stronger than woven cloth? Explain.

   _____

5. If something were <u>gorgeous</u>, would you like to look at it? Why or why not?

   _____

6. Would a runner in a race like to be <u>overtaken</u>? Why or why not?

   _____

7. If it is your <u>fate</u> to grow old some day, will it happen? Explain.

   _____

"**Arachne**" by Olivia E. Coolidge
Reading Warm-up A

Read the following passage. Pay special attention to the underlined words. Then, read it again, and complete the activities. Use a separate sheet of paper for your written answers.

The ancient Greeks believed in many different gods. They thought their gods lived on a mountain called Mt. Olympus. Sometimes these gods would <u>descend</u> from Mt. Olympus. They would come down to Earth to watch the activities of the mortals.

The city of Athens in Greece is named after Athene, the ancient Greek <u>goddess</u> of wisdom. A goddess is a female god or deity. Sculptures of Athene show the goddess wearing a helmet and decorated armor.

In Athens, people tell a legend about how the city was named. Athene <u>challenged</u> the god of the sea, Poseidon, to a contest. The winner would rule over the city. The competition was to see who could give the best gift to the city of Athens.

Poseidon said that he would give the people of Athens water. In the <u>presence</u> of many onlookers, Poseidon threw his spear to the ground. A <u>marvelous</u> saltwater spring arose. The spring created a sense of wonder in all who were there and saw it. Unfortunately, people could not drink the salt water. It turned out not to be such a good gift.

Athene threw her spear to the ground and brought forth an <u>olive</u> tree. From this tree came many <u>products</u>. This tree created small fruits called olives that could be eaten. The olives could also be pressed for oil. This oil could be used for cooking and made into fuel for lamps.

The gods of Mt. Olympus <u>judged</u> the competition. They decided that the olive tree was the better gift. Athene was the winner. That is why the city of Athens was named for this goddess.

1. Underline the sentence that explains the word <u>descend</u>. Then, write a sentence using the word **descend**.

2. Underline the sentence that tells you what a <u>goddess</u> is. What **goddess** is this passage about?

3. Circle the words that give a clue to the meaning of <u>challenged</u>. Have you ever **challenged** someone to do something?

4. Circle the words that help you know what <u>presence</u> means. Define **presence** in your own words.

5. Underline the words that describe why people thought the spring was <u>marvelous</u>. Then, use the word **marvelous** in a sentence.

6. Circle the words that tell you what an <u>olive</u> tree is. Explain why the **olive** tree was an important gift.

7. Circle the <u>products</u> that came from the olive tree. Write a sentence using the word **products**.

8. Underline the sentence that tells what the word <u>judged</u> means. Have you ever **judged** a contest?

Name _____ Date _____

"**Arachne**" by Olivia E. Coolidge
Reading Warm-up B

Read the following passage. Pay special attention to the underlined words. Then, read it again, and complete the activities. Use a separate sheet of paper for your written answers.

Have you ever wondered why spiders weave webs? Spiders live in the webs they create. These webs can be as large as three feet across and can come in many different, <u>gorgeous</u> patterns. Very beautiful spider webs can be found all over the world.

Spiders weave webs from <u>strands</u> of silk. A spider makes these long, thin threads out of a special protein created by its body. A spider makes a web by carefully weaving these threads together in a pattern. Spiders are <u>skillful</u> in their ability to do this.

To make a web, a spider first anchors itself to its starting point. Then, the creature makes a <u>reckless</u> jump into the wind. It lands at a point where it can connect the second end of its strand. This seemingly careless maneuver is the most dangerous part of making a web. The spider will then crawl back along the first strand while creating a second strand. The spider will continue to move <u>amid</u> the strands to add more silk. As the spider crawls within these strands, the web grows larger and more complex.

Spiders not only live in their webs but also use them to catch their food. The barely visible webs trick other insects, which then fly right into them. An insect that gets <u>deceived</u> by the web becomes trapped. Then, the spider will move quickly to catch the bug. Once a spider has <u>overtaken</u> the insect, it will coat the bug with more strands of silk. At that point, the insect's <u>fate</u> is sealed. It will be eaten by the spider.

Next time you see a spider in its web, think about how this special animal creates and uses its unusual home.

1. Circle the words that explain what <u>gorgeous</u> means. Use the word *gorgeous* in a sentence.

2. Underline the phrase that tells you how spiders make <u>strands</u> of silk. What is something else that comes in *strands*?

3. Circle the words that tell you what the spiders are <u>skillful</u> at doing. Then write about something that you are *skillful* at doing.

4. Underline the words that explain the word <u>reckless</u>. Then, explain the word *reckless* in your own words.

5. Underline the phrase that describes the word <u>amid</u>. Then, write a sentence using the word *amid*.

6. Circle the words that tell you how insects get <u>deceived</u> by a web. Define *deceived* in your own words.

7. Underline the sentence that explains the word <u>overtaken</u>. Then, write a sentence with the word *overtaken*.

8. How is the insect's <u>fate</u> sealed? Explain.

"Arachne" by Olivia E. Coolidge
Writing About the Big Question

How much do our communities shape us?

Big Question Vocabulary

common	community	connection	culture	family
generation	group	history	influence	involve
isolate	participation	support	values	belief

A. *Use one or more words from the list above to complete each sentence.*

1. Diana's grandmother said that her parents had told her animal stories with lessons, as a way to pass wisdom on from one _____ to the next.

2. Sanjay enjoys reading myths from the Hindu tradition and is happy that his _____ has a strong tradition of old stories.

3. Stories like "Jack and the Beanstalk" and *To Kill a Mockingbird* _____ the idea that it is good to fight evil, no matter how small you are.

4. Len's dad told interesting stories about the odd jobs he did to pay for college as a way of passing onto his kids the _____ of education and hard work.

B. *Follow the directions in responding to each of the items below.*

1. List two different times when you learned a lesson from doing something wrong.

   _____.

   _____.

2. Write two sentences explaining one of the preceding experiences, and describe what you learned and how you felt about it. Use at least two of the Big Question vocabulary words.

   _____

   _____

C. *Complete the sentence below. Then, write a short paragraph in which you connect this experience to the Big Question.*

   The story of _____ taught me that _____

   _____

   _____

   _____

   _____

   _____

Name _____ Date _____

"**Arachne**" by Olivia E. Coolidge

Reading: Ask Questions to Analyze Cause-and-Effect Relationships

A **cause** is an event, an action, or a feeling that makes something happen. An **effect** is what happens. Sometimes, an effect can become the cause of another event. For example, seeing an empty soda can on the sidewalk can cause you to pick it up. The good example you set can then cause someone else to pick up litter when he or she sees it. As you read, look for clue words such as *because, as a result, therefore,* and *so* to signal a cause-and-effect relationship. Then, **ask questions** such as "What happened?" and "Why did this happen?" to help you follow the cause-and-effect relationships in a literary work.

DIRECTIONS: *Look at the organizer below. Some of the causes and effects and the questions you might ask about them in the first half of "Arachne" have been listed for you. Fill in the missing causes, questions, and effects. Notice as you work that events may follow each other without one causing the next. Also, notice that an effect can become the cause of another event.*

CAUSE		EFFECT
1. Arachne becomes famous as a weaver.	2. What happened?	3. People say Athene must have taught Arachne.
4. _____ _____	5. _____ _____	6. _____ _____
7. _____ _____	8. Why?	9. The old woman shows herself to be Athene.
10. _____ _____	11. _____	12. Arachne competes with Athene.

Name _____ Date _____

"**Arachne**" by Olivia E. Coolidge
Literary Analysis: Myths

Myths are fictional tales that describe the actions of gods or heroes. Every culture has its own collection of myths. A myth can do one or more of the following:

- tell how the universe or a culture began
- explain something in nature, such as the return of spring after winter
- teach a lesson
- express a value, such as courage or honor

DIRECTIONS: *As you read "Arachne," look for examples of each characteristic of a myth. Use the examples to fill in the chart below. If you do not find an example of a particular characteristic, write "None" in the second column.*

A Myth Can . . .	How "Arachne" Shows This
1. Describe the actions of gods or heroes	
2. Tell how the universe or a culture began	
3. Explain something in nature	
4. Teach a lesson	
5. Express values and traditions that are important to the culture	

"**Arachne**" by Olivia E. Coolidge
Vocabulary Builder

Word List

humble   indignantly   mortal   obscure   obstinacy   strive

A. DIRECTIONS: *Complete each sentence below. Use examples or details from the story to show that you understand the meaning of the underlined vocabulary word. You may write additional sentences if necessary.*

Example: Some of Arachne's visitors were *nymphs*, _____.

Some of Arachne's visitors were nymphs, minor nature goddesses.

1. Arachne lived in an <u>obscure</u> village, a place that was _____

   _____

2. Someone who is <u>mortal</u> must eventually _____

   _____

3. Arachne showed her <u>obstinacy</u> when she _____

   _____

4. Far from being <u>humble</u>, Arachne was actually _____

   _____

5. The goddess spoke <u>indignantly</u>, because _____

   _____

6. When we <u>strive</u> for a goal, we _____

   _____

B. WORD STUDY: The Latin root -*mort*- means death. Each of the following statements contains a word based on -*mort*-. Correct each statement to make it more logical.

1. His speed record seemed *immortal*, since it lasted about a week.

   _____

2. The young woman was a *mortal*, and so she was equal to the mythological gods.

   _____

"**Arachne**" by Olivia E. Coolidge
Enrichment: The Craft of Weaving

Weaving is an ancient craft that has been practiced in almost every culture. Weaving can be done for the creation of useful objects, such as clothing, or it can be for purely decorative or artistic purposes, as in "Arachne." Usually weavers and other craftspeople combine the two purposes, creating useful objects that are also beautiful. Other crafts that combine usefulness and beauty are pottery, glassblowing, wood carving, and basket weaving. Each craft uses special tools and equipment and requires special skills.

A. DIRECTIONS: *The following technical terms about the craft of weaving are mentioned in "Arachne." Use a dictionary to find the definition of each word as it relates to weaving. Using your own words, write the definition on the lines.*

1. spin: _____

_____

2. loom: _____

_____

3. embroidery: _____

_____

4. shuttle: _____

_____

5. distaff: _____

_____

6. skein: _____

_____

B. DIRECTIONS: *Use the Internet or other library resources to research tools used in one of the other crafts listed at the top of the page. In the box below, write the name of the craft you researched. Then, write the name of a tool used for the craft, describe the purpose of the tool, and draw a picture of it.*

Name _____ Date _____

"**Arachne**" by Olivia E. Coolidge
Open-Book Test

Short Answer *Write your responses to the questions in this section on the lines provided.*

1. Arachne lives in an obscure little village. Does her village remain obscure as the myth goes on? Use the definition of *obscure* to explain.

_____

_____

_____

_____

2. What causes Arachne to boast that her skill at weaving is greater than Athene's?

_____

_____

_____

_____

3. What causes the old woman to visit Arachne?

_____

_____

_____

4. What causes Athene to tear Arachne's work?

_____

_____

_____

_____

5. What skill did the ancient Greeks value according the myth "Arachne"?

_____

_____

_____

6. Fill in the chart to show characteristics of a myth in "Arachne." Then, on the lines below, explain what lesson the myth teaches.

Characters	Explains Nature	Value

_____

_____

7. The lesson taught to Arachne by the goddess Athene is stated at the end of the myth. What other lessons can we learn from the myth?

_____

_____

8. What part of the myth shows Arachne's foolishness? Use details from the myth to explain your answer.

_____

_____

_____

9. How are Athene and Arachne alike? Use details from the myth to explain.

_____

_____

10. At the end of the myth, Athene chooses to keep Arachne alive. Explain why.

_____

_____

_____

Essay

Write an extended response to the question of your choice or to the question or questions your teacher assigns you.

At the end of the myth, Arachne is punished by Athene. In a brief essay, explain how many times Arachne could have avoided her fate. Use details from the myth to support your response.

12. Both Arachne and Athene weave messages into their cloths as they compete against each other. Tell what each message was meant to convey and what they tell about the ancient Greeks' feelings toward the gods. Use details from the myth.

13. Choose one of the lessons taught by "Arachne." In a brief essay, explain whether this lesson is still important today. Use details from the myth and your own knowledge.

14. **Thinking About the Big Question: How much should our communities shape us?** How much was Arachne shaped by her community? Explain your answer in a brief essay. Use details from the myth. Consider whether Arachne was helped or hurt by her community.

Oral Response

15. Go back to question 6, 7, or 10 or to the question your teacher assigns you. Take a few minutes to expand your answer and prepare an oral response. Find additional details in "Arachne" that support your points. If necessary, make notes to guide your oral response.

Unit 6 Resources: Themes in Folk Literature
69

"Arachne" by Olivia E. Coolidge
Selection Test A

Critical Reading *Identify the letter of the choice that best answers the question.*

____ 1. Why is "Arachne" considered a myth?
   A. It tells a story about a goddess.
   B. It tells an entertaining story.
   C. It tells a very old story.
   D. It tells about a character who is punished.

____ 2. What is one of the purposes of "Arachne"?
   A. to explain how weaving developed
   B. to explain the creation of the gods
   C. to explain how spiders came into the world
   D. to explain how the first rules were established

____ 3. Arachne boasts that she can weave better than the goddess Athene. What is the immediate effect of that boast?
   A. The villagers believe her.
   B. The nymphs begin to worship her.
   C. Arachne sells her cloth at higher prices.
   D. Athene comes to visit her.

____ 4. Arachne refuses to take the old woman's advice and calls her stupid. How would the ancient Greeks describe Arachne's behavior?
   A. unimportant
   B. foolish
   C. cruel
   D. normal

____ 5. What happens right after Arachne insults the old woman?
   A. The old woman leaves immediately.
   B. The old woman starts to weave.
   C. The old woman changes into Athene.
   D. The old woman changes into a spider.

____ 6. During the weaving contest, Athene weaves a warning to Arachne. What does Athene's weaving show?
   A. the natural beauty of Greece
   B. what happens to mortals who compete against gods
   C. the miraculous powers of the gods
   D. humans being rewarded for respecting the gods

_____ 7. Why does Arachne try to hang herself?
   A. She thinks she will not die.
   B. Her weaving is not good.
   C. She is angry with her father.
   D. Athene has insulted her.

_____ 8. What is the effect of Athene's touching the rope and then touching Arachne?
   A. Arachne turns into a spider.
   B. Athene disappears.
   C. Arachne disappears.
   D. Arachne changes into an old woman.

_____ 9. Why does Arachne's punishment fit her crime?
   A. She will no longer be able to spin.
   B. In her new form, she will live on and spin.
   C. Everyone will fear her instead of admiring her.
   D. In her new form, she will be tiny.

_____ 10. Which character trait is the cause of Arachne's downfall?
   A. silliness
   B. curiosity
   C. pride
   D. selfishness

_____ 11. What does "Arachne" show you that the ancient Greeks valued?
   A. weaving skill
   B. disguises
   C. healthy competition
   D. games

Vocabulary and Grammar

_____ 12. Which sentence about "Arachne" uses the underlined vocabulary word *incorrectly*?
   A. The <u>obscure</u> village was far away from any main roads or cities.
   B. An <u>obscure</u> weaver at first, Arachne quickly became well known.
   C. Athene's <u>mortal</u> hands were better at weaving than Arachne's.
   D. Arachne's <u>obstinacy</u> caused problems when she refused to give in.

___ 13. *Cause* and *reason* have the same basic meaning. Which of the following words has the same basic meaning as *effect*?
   A. reason
   B. result
   C. cause
   D. relationship

___ 14. Which sentence about "Arachne" uses the underlined Academic Vocabulary word *incorrectly*?
   A. The cause of Athene's anger was the insulting design that Arachne wove.
   B. The effect of Athene's anger was that she tore Arachne's design.
   C. The relationship between gods and humans could be good or bad.
   D. The reason for Arachne's overconfidence was punishment.

___ 15. Which of the following sentences about Arachne is a compound sentence?
   A. Arachne was a girl who became famous.
   B. She lived in Greece, and her father was a dyer of wool.
   C. Arachne was even more skillful than her father.
   D. The Greeks never forgot the contest.

Essay

16. Think about the way Arachne looks and how she behaves. In an essay, describe Arachne's appearance and her personality. Explain how her appearance and personality cause the events of the story, including the ending. How does Athene use Arachne's character traits as part of her punishment?

17. What lesson does the story of Arachne teach? In an essay, tell what lesson you find in the tale. Explain why you think this is or is not an important lesson for people to learn even today.

18. **Thinking About the Big Question: How much should our communities shape us?** Think about the mortal community in which Arachne lived. In a brief essay, explain how the community shaped Arachne and whether their actions helped or hurt her. Use details from the myth to support your answer.

Name _____ Date _____

"**Arachne**" by Olivia E. Coolidge
Selection Test B

Critical Reading *Identify the letter of the choice that best completes the statement or answers the question.*

_____ 1. "Arachne" is a myth because it
   A. describes the actions of a god or goddess.
   B. entertains while teaching a lesson.
   C. is a very old story from ancient Greece.
   D. tells about a character who is punished.

_____ 2. "Arachne" is considered an origin myth because it explains how
   A. weaving developed.
   B. contests started.
   C. spiders came into the world.
   D. human justice was established.

_____ 3. Arachne's skill and fame cause
   A. jealousy in her family and village.
   B. people to say Athene must have taught her.
   C. Athene to become jealous of her.
   D. Arachne to challenge Athene to a contest.

_____ 4. The effect of Arachne's boasting that she can weave better than Athene is that
   A. more and more people watch her.
   B. the nymphs begin to worship her.
   C. her cloth becomes more expensive.
   D. Athene comes to visit her.

_____ 5. The old woman cautions Arachne not to claim equality to the gods. What does this cause Arachne to do?
   A. She tells the old woman to leave.
   B. She challenges the old woman to a contest.
   C. She calls the old woman "stupid."
   D. She embraces the old woman and apologizes.

_____ 6. In "Arachne," the old woman who cautions Arachne
   A. is really a nymph.
   B. is Arachne's mother.
   C. is Athene in disguise.
   D. turns into a spider.

_____ 7. In "Arachne," Athene weaves a warning to Arachne that shows
   A. a series of battles that have occurred between all the gods.
   B. what happens to mortals who compete against the gods.
   C. the cruel tricks and disguises used by the gods.
   D. humans respecting and worshiping the gods.

____ 8. During the contest, Arachne becomes angry because
    A. Athene is more popular.
    B. Athene is the better weaver.
    C. Athene weaves more quickly.
    D. she thinks Athene is cheating.

____ 9. Athene tears up Arachne's work because
    A. Arachne's design insults her.
    B. Arachne's design is better than hers.
    C. she does not want their work to be judged.
    D. she wants to teach Arachne a lesson.

____ 10. Arachne tries to hang herself because
    A. she fears that Athene will kill her.
    B. Athene has insulted her.
    C. she is angry with everyone.
    D. she has lost the contest.

____ 11. What is the effect of Athene's touching the rope and Arachne?
    A. The rope kills Arachne.
    B. Arachne changes into a spider.
    C. Arachne changes into an old woman.
    D. A spider bites Arachne.

____ 12. The character trait that is most important in bringing about Arachne's downfall is
    A. foolishness.
    B. anger.
    C. impulsiveness.
    D. pride.

____ 13. Athene's punishment for Arachne fits Arachne's crime because
    A. spiders cannot compete against the gods.
    B. spiders are tiny, spindly, and distorted.
    C. most humans fear spiders.
    D. spiders spin and weave.

____ 14. One lesson that "Arachne" teaches is that the gods will punish humans who
    A. are cruel to the weak and elderly.
    B. say they are equal to the gods.
    C. become too skillful at what they do.
    D. attempt to take their own lives.

____ 15. The story of "Arachne" shows that the ancient Greeks valued
    A. weaving skill.
    B. fine thread.
    C. competition.
    D. disguises.

Vocabulary and Grammar

____ 16. Which sentence about "Arachne" uses the underlined vocabulary word *incorrectly*?
  A. Arachne's village was <u>obscure</u> until her cloth made it famous.
  B. An <u>obscure</u> weaver will become well known if she is talented enough.
  C. Athene's <u>mortal</u> skills were more than equal to Arachne's weaving abilities.
  D. Arachne's <u>obstinacy</u> caused problems because she refused to give in.

____ 17. A cause and a reason are related to each other in the same way that an effect is related to a
  A. reason.
  B. result.
  C. cause.
  D. relationship.

____ 18. Which sentence about "Arachne" uses the underlined Academic Vocabulary word *incorrectly*?
  A. The <u>effect</u> of her father's skill in dyeing cloth could be seen in the colorful skeins.
  B. The <u>cause</u> of Athene's anger was Arachne's arrogance.
  C. One design showed how bad the <u>relationship</u> could be between gods and humans.
  D. The <u>result</u> of Arachne's punishment was overconfidence.

____ 19. Which of the following sentences about Arachne is a complex sentence?
  A. Arachne was a maiden who became famous throughout Greece.
  B. She lived in an obscure little village, and her father was a humble dyer of wool.
  C. Even more skillful than her father was Arachne.
  D. Her eyes were light, and her hair was a dusty brown.

Essay

20. Myths often blend realistic characters and actions with fantastic events. In an essay, explain how "Arachne" combines realism with fantasy.

21. One of the main ideas in "Arachne" is that people should respect others and be content with what they have. In an essay, show how Arachne's lack of respect and her discontent are the causes of her downfall.

22. **Thinking About the Big Question: How much do our communities shape us?** How much was Arachne shaped by her community? Explain your answer in a brief essay. Use details from the myth. Consider whether Arachne was helped or hurt by her community.

Unit 6 Resources: Themes in Folk Literature
75

Study these words from the Prologue from The Whale Rider. *Then, complete the activities that follow.*

Word List A

blessing [BLESS ing] *n.* prayer of thanks
My mother said a blessing before every meal.

brilliant [BRIL yuhnt] *adj.* shining very brightly
The brilliant moon lit up the clear night sky.

dazzled [DAZ uhld] *v.* amazed and impressed
The vocalist dazzled the audience with her performance.

downward [DOWN wuhrd] *adj.* moving toward a lower level
Carmen took the downward elevator to reach the first floor.

noble [NOH buhl] *adj.* showing greatness of character
Most people think of the horse as a noble animal.

perfumes [PER fyoomz] *n.* pleasing smells or odors
The perfumes of the flowers filled the air in the garden.

reflected [ri FLEKT id] *v.* showed an image on a shiny surface
Rajiv saw his face reflected in the mirror on his locker door.

swirling [SWERL ing] *v.* moving around in circles
Julie Ann loved to dance by swirling around the room.

Word List B

depths [DEPTHS] *n.* deep, remote parts
Strange creatures live in the depths of the ocean.

gigantic [jy GAN tik] *adj.* huge or enormous
The elephant looked gigantic next to the mouse.

hurling [HER ling] *v.* forcefully throwing
James loved hurling his basketball against the garage door to make a loud noise.

lush [LUHSH] *adj.* thick and healthy
The forest was lush with springtime growth.

similar [SIM uh luhr] *adj.* alike or close to the same
The two chairs were similar in style and color.

sufficient [suh FISH uhnt] *adj.* as much as is needed
Nadia had a sufficient amount of money to pay for her tickets.

underwater [un der WAW ter] *adj.* below the surface of the water
Jed likes swimming long distances underwater.

wondrous [WUHN druhs] *adj.* remarkable and amazing
Lisa thought that the shooting star she saw was wondrous.

Name _____ Date _____

Prologue *from* **The Whale Rider** by Witi Ihimaera
Vocabulary Warm-up Exercises

Exercise A *Fill in each blank in the paragraph below with an appropriate word from Word List A. Use each word only once.*

It was a hot day. The [1] _____ sun shone brightly in the sky. Mina looked [2] _____ at the flowers below her in the public garden. She inhaled and smelled their sweet [3] _____. She was so happy, she said a [4] _____ in thanks for the beautiful park. There were so many flowers it felt as if the colors had started [5] _____ in circles around her. She was [6] _____ by the seemingly endless variety of different flowers and the amazing number of them. They inspired her to greatness. She wanted to do [7] _____ deeds. Mina walked to the little pool at the center of the garden and saw that the flowers were [8] _____ in the water's surface.

Exercise B *Revise each sentence so that the underlined vocabulary word is used in a logical way. Be sure to keep the vocabulary word in your revision.*

Example: Airplanes fly high underwater.
Airplanes fly high in the sky. Submarines go deep underwater.

1. Wrinkled, brown leaves had fallen off most of the plants in the lush garden.
   _____

2. The two friends were similar because they had no interests in common.
   _____

3. The gigantic skyscraper looked small next to the tiny cottage.
   _____

4. Sandra found the wondrous experience to be rather boring.
   _____

5. The depths of the ocean are easy to navigate because they are near the surface.
   _____

6. Three million books were sufficient to supply the classroom.
   _____

7. Martin was hurling himself against the door because he wanted to open it gently.
   _____

Prologue *from* The Whale Rider by Witi Ihimaera
Reading Warm-up A

Read the following passage. Pay special attention to the underlined words. Then, read it again, and complete the activities. Use a separate sheet of paper for your written answers.

Natane walked <u>downward</u> toward the river. She always enjoyed going down the hill to the valley. It had been a full year since the last time Natane walked this way. She was once again going to the valley to meet with the great Chief Tahtonka. Like many others, she would receive his <u>blessing</u> for the year. This trip to see the chief was one of the most special and sacred events of the year for Natane.

It was the longest day of the year. This was a holy day according to the elders in Natane's tribe. Finally, the sun was setting, and pink and lavender clouds were gathering along the horizon. That meeting of earth and sky always looked so far away to Natane. She imagined a <u>noble</u> man on a horse, a good and true soul, carrying her toward it, away from her troubles.

Soon, Natane reached the river. She gathered with the others from her tribe to listen to the great chief. Before he started to speak, Natane's thoughts drifted to the river. She gazed down into its <u>swirling</u> waters. As the water spun in circles down the river's rapids, Natane could see the colors of the sky <u>reflected</u> in it. The river acted as a strange mirror for the sky, taking its colors and twisting them. She saw the last slivers of the <u>brilliant</u> sun shine brightly before they finally disappeared.

Raising his arms to the sky, Chief Tahtonka began to speak. He spoke of the importance of the sun and the river and the valley. Natane closed her eyes. She could smell the <u>perfumes</u> of the landscape around her. Their pleasing odors rose into Natane's nose. Natane focused on the sounds of the rushing river. Suddenly, the blessing was finished. Natane was <u>dazzled</u> by the nature around her and filled with a sense of amazement.

1. Underline the sentence that explains what the word <u>downward</u> means. Write a sentence using the word *downward*.

2. Underline the words that tell you why Natane went to receive the chief's <u>blessing</u>. Then, write a sentence with the word *blessing*.

3. Circle the words that tell you what <u>noble</u> means. Would you like to be *noble*? Explain.

4. Underline the words that tell you what the <u>swirling</u> water did. Explain what *swirling* means in your own words.

5. Circle the words that tell you what Natane saw <u>reflected</u> in the water. Do you like to see your own image *reflected* in a mirror? Why or why not?

6. Circle the words that describe what <u>brilliant</u> means. Then, write a sentence using the word *brilliant*.

7. Underline the words that tell you what Natane could smell in the <u>perfumes</u>. Then, write a sentence using the word *perfumes*.

8. Underline the words that describe what it means to be <u>dazzled</u>. Describe an experience that *dazzled* you.

Name _____ Date _____

Prologue *from* The Whale Rider by Witi Ihimaera
Reading Warm-up B

Read the following passage. Pay special attention to the underlined words. Then, read it again, and complete the activities. Use a separate sheet of paper for your written answers.

Whales are some of the world's most <u>gigantic</u> creatures. Some adult whales can grow to be more than one hundred feet long. They can weigh as much as 220 tons. These extremely large sea creatures live <u>underwater</u>. They spend most of their lives below the surface of the ocean.

Whales are mammals. They share <u>similar</u> traits with other mammals. Among these related traits are being warm-blooded, breathing in oxygen from the air, and giving birth to live young. Because they must breathe air, whales continuously rise to the surface of the ocean. A whale takes in air through a blowhole on its back. The animal must take in a <u>sufficient</u> amount of air to stay deep in the ocean for a long time. If the whale does not breathe in enough air, it cannot stay in the <u>depths</u> of the ocean. It must leave the deep and remote areas of the sea to return to the surface to breathe.

Another surprising trait of some large whale species is that they don't have teeth. Humpback whales, for example, have baleen. These giant comb-like plates filter out small animal life from seawater. These whales actually feed on some of the tiniest forms of life in the ocean. They eat by swallowing huge amounts of coastal waters. Their baleen captures the organisms that grow in these <u>lush</u>, life-filled, rich waters.

Smaller whales, such as killer whales, do have teeth. The fierce reputation of the killer whale comes from its skill as a hunter. Killer whales attack by <u>hurling</u> themselves against their prey. They forcefully throw themselves against their prey until it can be eaten. Killer whales, however, are also very protective. They have been known to risk their lives to help other whales in their families.

Whales are <u>wondrous</u> animals. There are many ways to continue learning about these remarkable and impressive creatures of the deep.

1. Circle the words that explain how whales are <u>gigantic</u>. What is something that you think is *gigantic*?

2. Underline the sentence that tells you what it means to live <u>underwater</u>. Then, write a sentence using the word *underwater*.

3. Circle the words that tell you what the word <u>similar</u> means. Then, define *similar* in your own words.

4. Underline the sentence that explains why a whale needs <u>sufficient</u> air. Circle the synonym for the word. Then, write a sentence with the word *sufficient*.

5. Circle the words that explain the word <u>depths</u>. Would you like to see the *depths* of the ocean? Explain.

6. Underline the words that describe what <u>lush</u> means. Define *lush* in your own words.

7. Circle the words that tell you what kind of action <u>hurling</u> is. Then, write a sentence with the word *hurling*.

8. Underline the words that describe the word <u>wondrous</u>. Then, write a sentence using the word *wondrous*.

Prologue *from* **The Whale Rider** by Witi Ihimaera
Writing About the Big Question

How much do our communities shape us?

Big Question Vocabulary

common	community	connection	culture	family
generation	group	history	influence	involve
isolate	participation	support	values	belief

A. *Use one or more words from the list above to complete each sentence.*

1. Meg loves to _____ her sisters in her musical projects, since they are talented and fun to work with, and they always improve on her ideas.

2. _____ in a nature walk is one of our Thanksgiving Day traditions, as we collect leaves and pinecones to decorate the table and wait for dinner to finish cooking.

3. Jorge's favorite season is the spring, when the new plant life and warmer weather _____ him to be more hopeful and think about new projects for himself.

4. Kendra has done research into her grandparents and great-grandparents in order to create a _____ tree as an anniversary present for her parents.

B. *Follow the directions in responding to each of the items below.*

1. List two different experiences when you felt a strong link with nature.

_____.

_____.

2. Write two sentences explaining one of the preceding experiences, and describe what you learned and how you felt about it. Use at least two of the Big Question vocabulary words.

_____

_____

C. *Complete the sentence below. Then, write a short paragraph in which you connect this experience to the Big Question.*

If I could be an animal for one day, I would be a _____ because I would be able to _____

_____

_____

_____

Name _____ Date _____

Reading: Ask Questions to Analyze Cause-and-Effect Relationships

A **cause** is an event, an action, or a feeling that makes something happen. An **effect** is what happens. Sometimes, an effect can become the cause of another event. For example, seeing litter in the park can cause you to pick it up. The good example you set might then cause someone else to help keep the park clean. As you read, look for clue words such as *because, as a result, therefore,* and *so* to signal a cause-and-effect relationship. Then, **ask questions** such as "What happened?" and "Why did this happen?" to help you follow the cause-and-effect relationships in a literary work.

DIRECTIONS: *Look at the organizer below. Some of the causes and effects and the questions you might ask about them in the Prologue have been listed for you. Fill in the missing causes, questions, and effects. Notice as you work that events may follow each other without one causing the next. Also, notice that an effect can become the cause of another event.*

CAUSE		EFFECT
1. Land and sea feel a great emptiness.	**2.** Why?	**3.** They are waiting for the gift of mankind.
4. _____ _____	**5.** _____	**6.** _____ _____
7. A man rides high on the back of a gigantic whale.	**8.** What happened?	**9.** _____ _____
10. _____ _____	**11.** _____	**12.** The spears turn into living creatures.

Name _____ Date _____

Prologue *from* The Whale Rider by Witi Ihimaera
Literary Analysis: Myths

Myths are fictional tales that describe the actions of gods or heroes. Every culture has its collection of myths. A myth can do one or more of the following:

- tell how the universe or a culture began
- explain something in nature, such as the return of spring after winter
- teach a lesson
- express a value, such as courage or honor

DIRECTIONS: *As you read the Prologue from* The Whale Rider, *look for examples of each characteristic of a myth. Use the examples to fill in the chart below. If you do not find an example of a particular characteristic, write "None" in the second column.*

A Myth Can . . .	How Prologue from *The Whale Rider* Shows This
1. Describe the actions of gods or heroes	
2. Tell how the universe or a culture began	
3. Explain something in nature	
4. Teach a lesson	
5. Express values and traditions that are important to the culture	

Name _____ Date _____

Prologue *from* The Whale Rider by Witi Ihimaera
Vocabulary Builder

Word List

    apex   clatter   reluctant   splendor   teemed   yearning

A. DIRECTIONS: *Complete each sentence below. Use examples or details from the story to show that you understand the meaning of the underlined vocabulary word. You may write additional sentences if necessary.*

    Example: The lizard was a *sentinel* that _____
    The lizard was a sentinel that watched, guarded, and waited for what might happen.

1. The forest was filled with <u>clatter</u> as _____

    _____

2. The fairy people were <u>reluctant</u> to welcome people because _____

    _____

3. The flying fish saw <u>splendor</u> in the whale rider's _____

    _____

4. His political career reached its <u>apex</u> when he _____

    _____

5. Adele's <u>yearning</u> for her old home was finally satisfied when _____

    _____

6. Yesterday the music store <u>teemed</u> with autograph seekers because _____

    _____

B. WORD STUDY: The Latin root *-splend-* means "to shine." Answer each of the following questions using one of these words containing *-splend-*.

1. If a house is noted for its <u>splendor</u>, what would you expect to find in it?

    _____

2. What might cause a sky to be described as *resplendent*? _____

    _____

Prologue *from* The Whale Rider by Witi Ihimaera
Enrichment: Myths and Science

Myths reveal what was important to the people who created them and passed them down from generation to generation. These fictional stories came from the imagination, but they were often based on the wish to identify causes and effects. People used myths to explain their history and the natural world around them. Myths contain their own kind of truth. They provide ideas and values that are still important today.

Science, on the other hand, provides facts about real-life events. Scientists use logical reasoning to find connections between causes and effects. They observe, measure, research, review, challenge, and test information to describe and explain the natural world.

DIRECTIONS: *Read each of the following passages from the Prologue from* The Whale Rider. *Then, write* **S** *if you think it is a scientific fact or* **M** *if you think the passage came from someone's imagination.*

_____ 1. "In the old days, in the years that have gone before us, the land and sea felt a great emptiness, a yearning."

_____ 2. "The sky was iridescent, swirling with the patterns of wind and clouds; sometimes it reflected the prisms of rainbow or southern aurora."

_____ 3. "Within the warm stomach of the rainforests, kiwi, weka, and the other birds foraged for huhu and other similar succulent insects."

_____ 4. "The first of the Ancients were coming, journeying from their island kingdom beyond the horizon."

_____ 5. "The only reluctant ones were the fairy people, who retreated with their silver laughter to caves in glistening waterfalls."

_____ 6. "The sun rose and set, rose and set."

_____ 7. "For the sacred sign was on the monster, a swirling tattoo imprinted on the forehead."

Choose one of the passages that you marked **S**. How might a scientist decide if this passage contains factual information?

_____

_____

_____

_____

Name _____ Date _____

Prologue *from* **The Whale Rider** by Witi Ihimaera
"Arachne" by Olivia E. Coolidge
Integrated Language Skills: Grammar

Sentences: Simple, Compound, and Complex Sentence Structure

Sentences can be classified according to the number and kinds of their **clauses**—groups of words with their own subjects and verbs.

- A **simple sentence** has one independent clause.

  The sun came out. Sam and Al raced. Priya stayed inside and played.

- A **compound sentence** has two or more independent clauses. Independent clauses are usually joined by a comma and a conjunction such as *and, but, or, nor,* or *yet.*

  We packed our bags, Mom made lunch, and Dad put gas in the car.

- A **complex sentence** has one independent clause and one or more subordinate clauses. Some words that begin subordinate clauses are *after, because, before, if, when, where,* and *who.*

  I have a cousin who is a performer.

A. PRACTICE: *Identify each sentence below. Write* **S** *if it is a simple sentence,* **CP** *if it is a compound sentence, or* **CX** *if it is a complex sentence.*

_____ 1. Nobody knows who first made up myths and folk tales.

_____ 2. Myths, folk tales, and fables are usually stories from oral tradition.

_____ 3. In some myths, when humans are too proud, they are punished by the gods.

_____ 4. Good behavior is rewarded, and bad behavior has serious consequences.

B. Writing Application: *Imagine that you are at an amusement park with friends. Write a paragraph about the things you might see and do there. Use at least one of each type of sentence in your paragraph.*

_____

_____

_____

_____

_____

_____

_____

_____

_____

Unit 6 Resources: Themes in Folk Literature

"**Arachne**" by Olivia E. Coolidge
Prologue *from* **The Whale Rider** by Witi Ihimaera
Support for Writing a Compare-and-Contrast Essay

Writing: "Arachne"

Use the following chart to take notes for your **compare-and-contrast essay**. In the first column, write down lessons learned from "Arachne." In the second column, write down lessons learned from your own experience.

Lessons learned from "Arachne"	Lessons learned from my own experience

Now, use your notes to draft your essay. As you write, remember to compare the difference between learning lessons from a myth and learning lessons from your own experience.

Writing: Prologue *from* **The Whale Rider**

Use the following chart to take notes for your **compare-and-contrast essay**. In the first column, write down the feelings expressed in Prologue. In the second column, write down your own experience of waiting for something exciting to happen.

Feelings the myth expresses	Your feeling of yearning for something

Now, use your notes to draft your esay. As you write, focus on the difference between the feelings expressed in the Prologue and your real-life feelings.

"Arachne" by Olivia E. Coolidge
Prologue *from* **The Whale Rider** by Witi Ihimaera
Support for Extend Your Learning

Research and Technoloy: "Arachne"

Use a library catalog or the Internet to find two reliable sources that provide information about the values and cultures of ancient Greece. Use this form to help you organize information for an **annotated bibliography.**

Source 1: _____

Publication Information: _____
_____
_____

Summary: _____
_____
_____

Source 2: _____

Publication Information: _____
_____
_____

Summary: _____
_____
_____

Research and Technoloy: Prologue *from* The Whale Rider

Use a library catalog or the Internet to find two reliable sources that provide information about the values and cultures of the Maori people of New Zealand. Use this form to help you organize information for an **annotated bibliography.**

Source 1: _____

Publication Information: _____
_____
_____

Summary: _____
_____
_____

Source 2: _____

Publication Information: _____
_____
_____

Summary: _____
_____
_____

Prologue *from* **The Whale Rider** by Witi Ihimaera
Open-Book Test

Short Answer *Write your responses to the questions in this section on the lines provided.*

1. How does the first sentence of *The Whale Rider* help you understand that the story is a myth?

_____

_____

2. In the prologue to *The Whale Rider*, the "clatter of tree bark" and other sounds hid something. What was hidden and why? Explain the meaning of *clatter* in your answer.

_____

_____

3. In the prologue to *The Whale Rider*, what causes the land and sea to sigh with gladness?

_____

_____

4. Myths describe the actions of gods or heroes. Are the Ancients in the prologue to *The Whale Rider* gods? Explain how you know.

_____

_____

5. The man comes riding on the back of a whale in the prologue to *The Whale Rider*. How do the Maori feel about whales? Use details from the selection to support your answer.

_____

_____

6. Personification is giving human characteristics to nonhuman subjects. In the chart below, list three examples of personification in *The Whale Rider*. On the line below, tell how the personification affects your understanding of the story.

What Is Personified	Language From Story

Name _____ Date _____

7. When the whale rider arrived, the land and sea were happy. How did the rider feel? Use details from the selection to explain.

_____

_____

_____

_____

8. At the end of the prologue to *The Whale Rider*, the last spear does something unusual. Explain what it does and what it shows about Maori beliefs.

_____

_____

_____

_____

9. At the end of the prologue, the whale rider says a prayer over the last wooden spear. What causes him to do this, and what is the effect of his prayer?

_____

_____

_____

_____

10. What does the whale rider seem to understand about the future? Use details from the story to explain.

_____

_____

_____

_____

Essay

Write an extended response to the question of your choice or to the question or questions your teacher assigns you.

11. A myth is about gods or heroes and can explain things in nature or tell how something began. In a brief essay, discuss why the prologue from *The Whale Rider* is a myth. Use details from the story for support.

12. Think about how the land, sea, and creatures are described in the prologue from *The Whale Rider*. In a brief essay, explain what these descriptions show about the Maori's relationship with nature. Use details from the selection.

13. At the beginning of the prologue to *The Whale Rider*, "the land and sea felt a great emptiness, a yearning." The yearning is finally satisfied when man arrives. In a brief essay, discuss whether the arrival of man was a good thing. Consider the shape of the land and sea today. Use details from the selection and from your own knowledge.

14. **Thinking About the Big Question: How much should our communities shape us?** In what ways do myths like the one in *The Whale Rider* shape members of a community? Explain your answer in a brief essay, using details from the selection. Include in your answer your opinion about whether these myths are important.

Oral Response

15. Go back to question 4, 5, or 9 or to the question your teacher assigns you. Take a few minutes to expand your answer and prepare an oral response. Find additional details in the selection that support your points. If necessary, make notes to guide your oral response.

Prologue *from* The Whale Rider by Witi Ihimaera
Selection Test A

Critical Reading *Identify the letter of the choice that best answers the question.*

_____ 1. The Prologue from *The Whale Rider* tells a story that the Maori people of New Zealand handed down for hundreds of years. Why is this story called a myth?
   A. It tells how the Maori culture began.
   B. It is about the Maori religion.
   C. It is a very old story.
   D. It describes where the Maori live.

_____ 2. What is one of the things that the myth in the Prologue explains?
   A. why the Maori are excellent swimmers
   B. how war came to the Maori
   C. why the Maori value whales
   D. why the Maori fear whales

_____ 3. In the Prologue, which of the following emotions do the land and sea feel?
   A. calmness
   B. anger
   C. gladness
   D. fear

_____ 4. At the beginning of the Prologue, everything is waiting for the gift from the gods. Finally, the Ancients (the gods) send the gift. What is the gift?
   A. the first man, the whale rider
   B. a gigantic whale that will be killed for food
   C. magical spears and other tools
   D. myths and folk tales that the Maori can tell

_____ 5. How are the whale rider and the whale in the Prologue alike?
   A. They are brave and patient.
   B. They are gentle and skillful.
   C. They are large and angry.
   D. They are powerful and splendid.

_____ 6. In the Prologue, the whale rider stays on the whale's back as it leaps high out of the water. What does this let the rider do?
   A. bond with the whale for life
   B. tame the whale for his people
   C. test his bravery and skill
   D. see the land so he can travel toward it

_____ 7. In the Prologue, the whale rider throws spears at the land. What is the effect of his spear throwing?

A. The land becomes angry.

B. The spears hit and kill people on the land.

C. The spears change into birds and eels.

D. The spears change into Maori people.

_____ 8. In the Prologue, the whale rider says a prayer over his last spear. What question should you ask at that point to help you follow the cause-and-effect relationships in the story?

A. Who is the whale rider?

B. Why is this man riding a whale?

C. What happens to the spear?

D. Where will the whale rider go?

_____ 9. In the Prologue, what is the effect of the whale rider's prayer over the last spear?

A. The spear disappears forever.

B. The spear leaps into the future.

C. The spear hits and kills the whale.

D. The spear falls into the water.

_____ 10. In the Prologue, what does the whale rider show that he cares most deeply about?

A. how the people on land will greet him

B. the strength of his body

C. his relationship with the Ancients

D. the people of the future who may need help

Vocabulary and Grammar

_____ 11. Which sentence about the Prologue uses the underlined vocabulary word *incorrectly*?

A. The fairy people <u>retreated</u> quickly to meet the coming gift.

B. The sad fairy people were <u>reluctant</u> to have their perfect lives change.

C. The forest echoed with the <u>clatter</u> of noisy animals across tree bark.

D. The first man's eyes shown with <u>splendor</u>.

_____ 12. How are the words *effect, consequence, outcome,* and *result* alike?

A. They are all opposites.

B. They all have the same basic meaning.

C. They are often used in myths.

D. They explain how things work.

____ 13. Which of the following sentences uses the underlined Academic Vocabulary word *incorrectly*?
  A. No one knew the <u>cause</u> of the Ancients' journey.
  B. The <u>reason</u> for their trip was that the land was discovered.
  C. What was the <u>result</u> of the whale rider's journey?
  D. The man's <u>relationship</u> with the whale was very important.

____ 14. Which of the following sentences about the Prologue is a compound sentence?
  A. They have found us.
  B. We have been found, and our blessing will come soon.
  C. We have been found, although our blessing is not yet here.
  D. We waited and waited.

Essay

15. Imagine that you are part of the Maori culture. What do you like most about the myth in the Prologue from *The Whale Rider*? In an essay, tell three things that you like about this story and why you like them. If there is anything in the story that you do not like, tell about that, too.

16. A prologue is an introduction to the events in the rest of the book. Based on the Prologue, what do you think the book *The Whale Rider* will be about? What details in the story support your answer? If you have read the book or seen the movie, include only the details that you can find in the Prologue.

17. **Thinking About the Big Question: How much should our communities shape us?** Consider what you know about myths and what they can do. How can a myth like the one in *The Whale Rider* shape members of a community? Explain your answer in a brief essay, using details from the selection. Include in your answer your opinion about whether these myths are important.

Prologue *from* **The Whale Rider** by Witi Ihimaera
Selection Test B

Critical Reading *Identify the letter of the choice that best completes the statement or answers the question.*

____ 1. The Prologue from *The Whale Rider* tells a myth handed down by the Maori people. It is a myth because it
     A. tells how the Maori culture began.
     B. contains animal and human heroes.
     C. is a very old story from New Zealand.
     D. tells about the Maori religion.

____ 2. One of the purposes of the Prologue is to explain
     A. why swimming is important to the Maori.
     B. the beginning of military arts.
     C. why the Maori value whales.
     D. that everything came from the sea.

____ 3. In the Prologue, what does the author give the land and the sea?
     A. human religion
     B. human wars
     C. human emotions
     D. human fears

____ 4. In the Prologue, what causes the land and sea to sigh with gladness?
     A. They see the first people arrive.
     B. The Ancients have found them.
     C. They are filled with life.
     D. They are happy to be waiting.

____ 5. Which phrase best describes the world as it waits in the Prologue?
     A. seething with anger
     B. teeming with life
     C. filled with doubt
     D. jumping with joy

____ 6. In the Prologue, the gift of the gods is
     A. the whale rider.
     B. the whale.
     C. magical spears.
     D. the Ancients.

____ 7. In the Prologue, the whale symbolizes, or stands for,
     A. the promise of the future.
     B. the gods helping people.
     C. intelligence and survival.
     D. strength and greatness.

____ 8. In the Prologue, riding on the whale as it rises to the sky lets the man
  A. bond with the whale.
  B. tame the whale for his people.
  C. test his bravery and skill.
  D. see and travel toward the land.

____ 9. In the Prologue, what is the effect of the man's spear throwing?
  A. The spears turn into music.
  B. The spears turn into the first people.
  C. The spears turn into plants.
  D. The spears turn into birds and eels.

____ 10. In the Prologue, after the whale rider says a prayer over his last spear, what question could a reader ask to help follow the cause-and-effect relationships in the story?
  A. What did the whale rider do?
  B. Where will the whale rider go?
  C. What happens to the spear?
  D. What was the prayer?

____ 11. In the Prologue, what effect does the whale rider's prayer have?
  A. The last spear leaps back to the past.
  B. The last spear leaps into the future.
  C. The last spear returns to the Ancients.
  D. The last spear stays with the rider.

____ 12. In the Prologue, the whale rider obviously cares about what will happen to
  A. the story of his arrival.
  B. the land and sea.
  C. the whale.
  D. the people yet to come.

____ 13. The myth in the Prologue from *The Whale Rider* teaches that
  A. people are descended from the gods.
  B. when help is needed, it will come.
  C. people should pray to the gods.
  D. the whale is all-knowing.

____ 14. The Prologue shows that the Maori value
  A. nature.
  B. competition.
  C. respect.
  D. confidence.

Vocabulary and Grammar

____ 15. Which sentence about the Prologue uses the underlined vocabulary word *incorrectly?*
  A. The <u>clatter</u> of many branches echoed through the forest.
  B. The fairy people were <u>reluctant</u> to see change come to their perfect world.
  C. The fairies <u>retreated</u> boldly to meet the man they feared.
  D. The shimmering water on the body of the whale shown with <u>splendor</u>.

____ 16. An effect is basically the same as a
  A. cause.
  B. reason.
  C. consequence.
  D. connection.

____ 17. Which sentence about the Prologue uses the underlined Academic Vocabulary word *incorrectly?*
  A. The <u>cause</u> of the underwater thunder was the impact of the whale's dive.
  B. The <u>effect</u> of the dive was a great trembling in the sea.
  C. As a <u>result</u> of his journey, the man found the land.
  D. As a <u>reason</u> for his journey, the man brought joy to the land and sea.

____ 18. Which sentence about the Prologue is a complex sentence?
  A. When you looked into the sea, you felt you could see to the end of forever.
  B. The land and sea felt a great emptiness.
  C. Sometimes the forest grew quiet, and fairy laughter could be heard.
  D. The sun rose and set, rose and set.

Essay

19. The myth told in the Prologue from *The Whale Rider* reveals a great deal about the Maori culture. In an essay, identify three elements, characteristics, or values of Maori culture that you find in the Prologue. Use examples from the story in your writing.

20. Write a brief summary of the myth told in the Prologue from *The Whale Rider*. In your summary, include three events that show cause-and-effect relationships in the story. Tell about these events in the order that they happened. Use words such as *because, as a result,* and *therefore* to signal the cause-and-effect relationships.

21. **Thinking About the Big Question: How much should our communities shape us?**
  In what ways do myths like the one in *The Whale Rider* shape members of a community? Explain your answer in a brief essay, using details from the selection. Include in your answer your opinion about whether these myths are important.

Vocabulary Warm-up Word Lists

Study these words. Then, complete the activities that follow.

Word List A

comfortably [KUHM fuhr tuh blee] *adv.* done in a relaxed and easy way
Rosa read her book while <u>comfortably</u> sitting in her favorite chair.

horror [HAWR uhr] *n.* great fear, terror, or shock
Charlie jumped back in <u>horror</u> when the rat ran across the floor.

knelt [NELT] *v.* bent one's legs and put one's knees on the ground
Dena <u>knelt</u> down on the floor to search for her pen under the desk.

newly [NOO lee] *adv.* recently
Justin happily took his <u>newly</u> found puppy home from the pound.

pebbles [PEB uhlz] *n.* small round stones
The bottom of the stream was covered in small <u>pebbles</u>.

peculiar [pi KYOOL yuhr] *adj.* strange or odd
There was something <u>peculiar</u> in the strange old woman's behavior.

rejoicing [ri JOY sing] *v.* being very happy about something
Kara was <u>rejoicing</u> because her baby sister had just been born.

splendid [SPLEN did] *adj.* impressively beautiful or grand
The giant castle on the hill was a <u>splendid</u> sight.

Word List B

assuredly [uh SHOOR ed lee] *adv.* done with certainty
After days of practice, Ann <u>assuredly</u> gave her oral report.

behold [bee HOHLD] *v.* to look at something with great interest
Juan found the Statue of Liberty a beautiful sight to <u>behold</u>.

cunning [KUHN ing] *adj.* clever and able to trick others
The <u>cunning</u> fox managed to slip out of its trap.

extremely [ek STREEM lee] *adv.* greatly or to a high degree
David was <u>extremely</u> happy when he won a college scholarship.

forbids [fuhr BIDZ] *v.* orders not to do something
The law <u>forbids</u> teachers from hitting their students.

identify [eye DEN tuh fy] *v.* to recognize someone or something
Carla tried to <u>identify</u> the bird by its markings.

magnificent [mag NIF uh suhnt] *adj.* very impressive or beautiful
The queen lived in a <u>magnificent</u> palace.

withdraw [with DRAW] *v.* to drop out or go away
Robbie chose to <u>withdraw</u> from the race after he hurt his ankle.

Name _____ Date _____

"Mowgli's Brothers" by Rudyard Kipling
from **James and the Giant Peach** by Roald Dahl
Vocabulary Warm-up Exercises

Exercise A *Fill in each blank in the paragraph below with an appropriate word from Word List A. Use each word only once.*

Nora looked down and saw something [1] _____ on the sidewalk. She
[2] _____ down to get a closer look at the strange object. Sure
enough, there was something lying on the ground next to some small round
[3] _____. It was a different kind of stone, a beautiful piece of purple
amethyst. It was [4] _____ in its beauty. Nora picked up the stone and
placed it in the palm of her hand, where it fit [5] _____. She wondered if
the stone belonged to anyone, and if that person had lost it. If she had lost this stone,
she would have reacted with [6] _____. Instead, however, she had found
it. She put her [7] _____ found treasure away in her pocket,
[8] _____ at her great fortune. Suddenly, she was very happy.

Exercise B *Decide whether each statement below is true or false. Circle T or F, and then explain your answers.*

1. To <u>identify</u> something is to recognize it.
   T / F _____

2. If the law <u>forbids</u> you from doing something, you should go ahead and do it.
   T / F _____

3. A <u>cunning</u> person is likely to trick others.
   T / F _____

4. A beautiful building is an unpleasant sight to <u>behold</u>.
   T / F _____

5. To <u>withdraw</u> from a situation is to become completely involved in it.
   T / F _____

6. If someone does something <u>assuredly</u>, he or she does it without confidence.
   T / F _____

7. Something that is <u>extremely</u> pleasurable is not fun to do at all.
   T / F _____

8. A <u>magnificent</u> house is usually large and grand.
   T / F _____

Unit 6 Resources: Themes in Folk Literature
© Pearson Education, Inc. All rights reserved.
98

Name _____ Date _____

"Mowgli's Brothers" by Rudyard Kipling
from **James and the Giant Peach** by Roald Dahl
Reading Warm-up A

Read the following passage. Pay special attention to the underlined words. Then, read it again, and complete the activities. Use a separate sheet of paper for your written answers.

Chang loved insects, and he always wanted to know more about them. One day when he was looking for bugs, Chang <u>knelt</u> down on the grass. His bent knees were gently cupped by the soft ground. <u>Comfortably</u> settled, Chang decided he wanted to know what it felt like to be a bug. He wanted to see the earth from the position of a tiny insect. To do this, he put his face into the ground and peered into the grass. "This," he thought to himself, "is how a bug sees the world."

Suddenly, Chang sprang back in <u>horror</u>. A beetle had climbed onto his nose! The fear and shock soon passed, however. Chang decided he enjoyed the <u>peculiar</u> sensation of the beetle walking on his face. Once he realized what it was, the odd feeling was not so scary after all.

Chang took the beetle off his face and happily held it in his hands. <u>Rejoicing</u> in his find, he looked at the insect's body. He examined each part of the bug, from its short antennae to its six legs. He watched how the wings of the bug shimmered beautifully in the sunlight. The flickering light was <u>splendid</u> as it reflected off the beetle's blue wings.

For a moment, Chang thought about taking this beetle back home as a pet. However, he knew that it was not right to take the beetle away from its home. He saw a patch of <u>pebbles</u> in the grass. Carefully, Chang set his beetle on the group of small stones.

As he walked away, he gave one last glance at his beetle. He thought of what he had just learned about how a beetle looked up close. Chang was happy about this <u>newly</u> acquired knowledge. He decided he would go to the library to learn more about this interesting kind of bug.

1. Underline the words that give a clue to the meaning of <u>knelt</u>. Write a sentence using *knelt*.

2. Circle the sentence that tells you why Chang was <u>comfortably</u> settled. What is something that you do *comfortably*?

3. Underline the words that mean about the same thing as <u>horror</u>. Then, write a sentence using the word *horror*.

4. Circle the words that explain what Chang thought was <u>peculiar</u>. Define *peculiar* in your own words.

5. Underline the words that tell you what Chang was <u>rejoicing</u> in. Use the word *rejoicing* in a sentence.

6. Circle the word that helps you know what <u>splendid</u> means. Describe something you think is *splendid*.

7. Circle the words that describe what <u>pebbles</u> are. Then, write a sentence using the word *pebbles*.

8. Underline the words that describe Chang's <u>newly</u> gained knowledge. Then, write a sentence using the word *newly*.

Unit 6 Resources: Themes in Folk Literature
© Pearson Education, Inc. All rights reserved.
99

Name _____ Date _____

Reading Warm-up B

Read the following passage. Pay special attention to the underlined words. Then, read it again, and complete the activities. Use a separate sheet of paper for your written answers.

Tigers are <u>magnificent</u> animals. These impressive and beautiful creatures are the largest members of the cat family. They live in the jungles of India and Malaysia. Scientists <u>identify</u> tigers by examining their special markings. Tigers can be easily recognized by the narrow stripes that run up and down their bodies. Their coats are usually orange-brown in color.

Tigers are known for their <u>cunning</u> as hunters. They cleverly hide in the jungle until they discover their prey. Then they quickly attack. Tigers eat whatever animals they can find. They usually hunt deer, wild pigs, and buffalo. Most tigers do their hunting by night. Their sharp sense of smell allows them to <u>assuredly</u> chase after their prey. This sense of smell gives them the certainty they need to follow their prey in the dark.

Sadly, there are far fewer tigers today than there were decades ago. It is believed that there are only about 6,000 tigers alive in the world today. When humans build on a tiger's territory, the tigers <u>withdraw</u> into more remote jungle land. As more jungle is taken up by human use, tigers remove themselves ever farther in search of safety. There is not enough jungle today for tigers to live safely.

Fortunately, some changes have been made to protect tigers. A law in India now <u>forbids</u> hunters from killing tigers for sport. The lives of many tigers have been saved by ordering hunters not to shoot these animals.

Because there are so few tigers living today, it is <u>extremely</u> rare to see one in the wild. Scientists and tiger watchers spend months of their lives waiting for this very uncommon event. They want to <u>behold</u> one of these beautiful cats, and to observe a tiger's behavior in its natural habitat.

1. Circle the words that explain what it means to be <u>magnificent</u>. Then, write a sentence using the word *magnificent*.

2. Underline the words that tell you how scientists <u>identify</u> tigers. Define *identify* in your own words.

3. Circle the sentence that tells you how tigers are <u>cunning</u> hunters. Then, explain something or someone you know that is *cunning*.

4. Underline the words that tell you what allows tigers to <u>assuredly</u> chase their prey. Explain *assuredly* in your own words.

5. Underline the sentence that describes why tigers <u>withdraw</u>. Then, use the word *withdraw* in a sentence.

6. Circle the words that tell you what Indian law <u>forbids</u>. Do you think this is a good law? Explain.

7. Circle the phrase that tells you why it is <u>extremely</u> rare to see a tiger in the wild. Use the word *extremely* in a sentence.

8. Underline the words that tell you why scientists want to <u>behold</u> a tiger. Do you think a tiger is a sight to *behold*? Explain.

Name _____ Date _____

"Mowgli's Brothers" by Rudyard Kipling
from **James and the Giant Peach** by Roald Dahl
Writing About the Big Question

How much do our communities shape us?

Big Question Vocabulary

common	community	connection	culture	family
generation	group	history	influence	involve
isolate	participation	support	values	belief

A. *Use one or more words from the list above to complete each sentence.*

1. When his family moved to the United States from India, Siddhartha was a little nervous about living in a place with such a different _____ from his own, but he settled in very quickly.

2. LeeAnn loved watching the life going on in her ant farm, in which individuals worked together for the _____ good.

3. Jen's favorite fantasy is to time-travel to a different period in _____; her favorite time-travel destination would be Elizabethan England, where she could meet William Shakespeare.

4. Jaime is fascinated with the social behavior of wolves, especially the way they recognize different levels of status within their _____.

B. *Follow the directions in responding to each of the items below.*

1. List two different times when you were in a very unusual environment.

   _____.

   _____.

2. Write two sentences describing one of the preceding experiences. Tell what it was like and how you felt about it. Use at least two of the Big Question vocabulary words.

   _____

   _____

C. *Complete the sentence below. Then, write a short paragraph in which you connect this experience to the Big Question.*

If I could spend time in any other place in the universe, I would like to go to _____ because _____

_____

_____

Unit 6 Resources: Themes in Folk Literature
© Pearson Education, Inc. All rights reserved.
101

"Mowgli's Brothers" by Rudyard Kipling
from **James and the Giant Peach** by Roald Dahl
Literary Analysis: Elements of Fantasy

Fantasy is imaginative writing that contains elements not found in real life. Stories about talking animals, books that come to life, or time travel are all examples of fantasy. Many fantastic stories, however, contain **realistic elements**—characters, events, or situations that are true to life. In a fantastic story about a talking cat, for example, the cat might do many things that real cats do. She might purr, stretch, and flex her claws, all of which are real-life cat behaviors.

DIRECTIONS: *Read each passage below and answer the questions.*

from "Mowgli's Brothers" by Rudyard Kipling

It was the jackal—Tabaqui the Dishlicker—and the wolves of India despise Tabaqui because he runs about making mischief, and telling tales, and eating rags and pieces of leather from the village rubbish-heaps. . . .

"Enter, then, and look," said Father Wolf, stiffly, "but there is no food here."

"For a wolf, no," said Tabaqui, "but for so mean a person as myself a dry bone is a good feast. Who are we, the Gidur-log [the jackal-people], to pick and choose?" He scuttled to the back of the cave, where he found the bone of a buck with some meat on it, and sat cracking the end merrily.

1. List two details that are not found in real life.

   _____

2. List two details that are true to life.

   _____

from *James and the Giant Peach* by Roald Dahl

"Is that a Glow-worm?" asked James, staring at the light. "It doesn't look like a worm of any sort to me."

"Of course it's a Glow-worm," the Centipede answered. "At least that's what she calls herself. Although actually you are quite right. She isn't really a worm at all. Glow-worms are never worms. They are simply lady fireflies without wings. Wake up, you lazy beast!"

But the Glow-worm didn't stir, so the Centipede reached out of his hammock and picked up one of his boots from the floor. "Put out that wretched light!" he shouted, hurling the boot up at the ceiling.

3. List two details that are not found in real life.

   _____

4. List two details that are true to life.

   _____

"Mowgli's Brothers" by Rudyard Kipling
from **James and the Giant Peach** by Roald Dahl
Vocabulary Builder

Word List

colossal   dispute   fostering   intently   monotonous   quarry

A. DIRECTIONS: *Each sentence below features a word from the Word List. If the sentence makes sense, explain why. If it does not make sense, write a new sentence using the word correctly.*

1. I watched the *colossal* specks of dust drift through the ray of sun.

   _____

2. "Please stop *fostering* me!" Ella said to her little brother.

   _____

3. We ended our *dispute* by shaking hands and agreeing to disagree.

   _____

4. If you read the book *intently,* you will probably miss some important details.

   _____

5. The leopard eyed his *quarry* from a low tree branch and prepared to pounce.

   _____

6. True, the adventure movie was long, but it was also exciting and *monotonous*!

   _____

B. DIRECTIONS: *Use a word from the Word List to complete each analogy. Your choice should create a word pair whose relationship matches the relationship between the first two words given.*

1. *Run* is to *quickly* as *work* is to _____.
2. *Elf* is to *small* as *giant* is to _____.
3. *Idea* is to *thought* as *disagreement* is to _____.
4. *Detective* is to *clue* as *hunter* is to _____.

Name _____ Date _____

"**Mowgli's Brothers**" by Rudyard Kipling
from **James and the Giant Peach** by Roald Dahl
Writing to Compare Literary Works

Before you draft your essay comparing and contrasting each story's fantastic and realistic elements, complete the graphic organizers below. For each graphic organizer, decide which story best fits each sentence.

Animals
The animals in _____ seem more realistic because _____ _____.
In contrast, the animals in _____ do more fantastic things such as _____.

Human Character
The boy in _____ is more fantastic because he _____ _____.
In contrast, the boy in _____ does more realistic things such as ___ _____.

Setting
The setting in _____ seems more realistic because _____ _____.
In contrast, the setting in _____ seems more fantastic because ____ _____.

Situation
The situation in _____ *might* really happen because _____ _____.
In contrast, the situation in _____ could never happen because ____ _____.

Now, use your notes to write an essay comparing and contrasting the authors' use of fantastic and realistic elements in these two stories. Begin your essay by stating which story contains more fantastic elements overall.

Unit 6 Resources: Themes in Folk Literature
104

"Mowgli's Brothers" by Rudyard Kipling
excerpt *from* James and the Giant Peach by Roald Dahl
Open-Book Test

Short Answer *Write your responses to the questions in this section on the lines provided.*

1. In "Mowgli's Brothers," how do the wolves feel about humans? Support your answer with details from the story.

   _____

   _____

   _____

   _____

2. Father Wolf has no feelings for the man cub that appears. Why does he refuse to give it to Shere Khan? Use details from the story to support your answer.

   _____

   _____

   _____

   _____

3. Shere Khan is much bigger than Mother Wolf. Is she afraid of him? Use details from "Mowgli's Brothers" to explain.

   _____

   _____

   _____

   _____

4. In the excerpt from *James and the Giant Peach*, does James behave in a realistic way when he sees the bugs? Use details from the story for support.

   _____

   _____

   _____

   _____

5. In *James and the Giant Peach*, when James arrives, all the creatures look at him intently. Explain why, basing your answer on the meaning of the word *intently*.

   _____

   _____

   _____

   _____

6. The centipede from *James and the Giant Peach* has both realistic and fantastic qualities. Use the graphic organizer below to compare a real centipede to the one in the story. On the line below, tell what James likes about the Centipede.

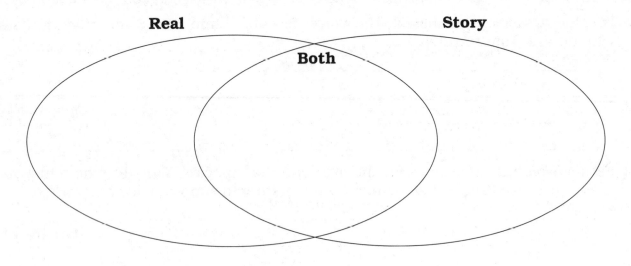

Real   **Both**   **Story**

_____

7. What element of fantasy do the excerpt from *James and the Giant Peach* and "Mowgli's Brothers" have in common?

_____

_____

8. Both the excerpt from *James and the Giant Peach* and "Mowgli's Brothers" contain realistic elements. List one example from each story, and tell why it is realistic.

_____

_____

_____

9. Think about the settings of *James and the Giant Peach* and "Mowgli's Brothers." Which one is more fantastic? Explain your answer.

_____

_____

10. Many of the characters in "Mowgli's Brothers" and in the excerpt from *James and the Giant Peach* are fantastic. Others are realistic. What do the realistic characters have in common?

_____

_____

Name _____ Date _____

Essay

Write an extended response to the question of your choice or to the question or questions your teacher assigns you.

11. Choose one element: setting, characters, or situation. In a brief essay, explain how that element is fantastic in "Mowgli's Brothers" and in the excerpt from *James and the Giant Peach*.

12. How are Mowgli and James alike? How are they different? In an essay, compare and contrast the characters. Include in your answer whether the characters are realistic or fantastic.

13. Think about the characters Baloo and Bagheera in "Mowgli's Brothers." Each one speaks for the man cub but for very different reasons. In an essay, describe each of these outsiders and their role at the Pack meeting. Include in your answer what each one seems to want.

14. **Thinking About the Big Question: How much should our communities shape us?** James and Mowgli have found new communities. Choose one of these characters, and in an essay discuss how he will be changed by his new community. Will these changes be positive or negative? Explain, using details from the selection to support your answer.

Oral Response

15. Go back to question 1, 8, or 9 or to the question your teacher assigns you. Take a few minutes to expand your answer and prepare an oral response. Find additional details in the selections that support your points. If necessary, make notes to guide your oral response.

"Mowgli's Brothers" by Rudyard Kipling
from **James and the Giant Peach** by Roald Dahl
Selection Test A

Critical Reading *Identify the letter of the choice that best answers the question.*

____ 1. In "Mowgli's Brothers," why do the wolves fear Tabaqui the jackal?
   A. because he steals their food
   B. because he sometimes goes mad
   C. because he makes trouble with the humans
   D. because he hunts their young

____ 2. Read this quote from "Mowgli's Brothers."
   "Man!" said Father Wolf, showing all his white teeth.

   Which statement is true about this quote?
   A. It contains only fantastic elements.
   B. It contains only realistic elements.
   C. It contains both fantastic and realistic elements.
   D. It does not contain fantastic or realistic elements.

____ 3. In "Mowgli's Brothers," the Law of the Jungle forbids killing humans. What reason do the animals give for this law?
   A. Humans are stronger than the animals.
   B. It is the duty of animals to protect humans.
   C. The cubs must be protected from humans.
   D. Humans are weak and defenseless.

____ 4. In "Mowgli's Brothers," Mother and Father Wolf like Mowgli right away. Why?
   A. He acts brave and bold.
   B. He seems lost and confused.
   C. He is very small.
   D. He is afraid of Shere Khan.

____ 5. In "Mowgli's Brothers," the tiger roars in anger when Mowgli is accepted into the Pack. Bagheera the panther says that one day Mowgli will make the tiger "roar to another tune." What does Bagheera mean by this?
   A. Mowgli will one day wound or kill the tiger.
   B. Mowgli will soon be roaring like a tiger.
   C. Mowgli will always remain a mystery to the jungle creatures.
   D. Mowgli will one day become the tiger's prey.

_____ 6. Where does the excerpt from *James and the Giant Peach* take place?
    A. in the Centipede's home
    B. in the center of a peach
    C. in an underground cave
    D. in the Earthworm's den

_____ 7. Read this sentence from *James and the Giant Peach.*

    There was an Old-Green-Grasshopper as large as a large dog sitting on a stool directly across the room from James now.

    What detail from the sentence tells you that you are reading fantasy?
    A. The grasshopper was old and green.
    B. The grasshopper was as large as a dog.
    C. The grasshopper was on a stool.
    D. The grasshopper was across the room from James.

_____ 8. Which phrase best describes the Centipede in *James and the Giant Peach?*
    A. slow to speak
    B. ready to help
    C. willing to lead
    D. quick to anger

_____ 9. Which detail from *James and the Giant Peach* is true to life?
    A. The Centipede asks James for help.
    B. The Centipede is boastful.
    C. The Centipede has many legs.
    D. The Centipede wears boots.

_____ 10. Which is true of both Mowgli in "Mowgli's Brothers" and James in *James and the Giant Peach?*
    A. They are scared by what is happening.
    B. Someone is planning to harm them.
    C. Some kind of magic is working on them.
    D. They accidentally wander into a strange place.

_____ 11. Which element of fantasy is in both "Mowgli's Brothers" and *James and the Giant Peach?*
    A. a natural setting
    B. boys who go exploring
    C. nonhuman creatures who speak
    D. a mysterious event

____ **12.** Which is true of the creatures in both "Mowgli's Brothers" and *James and the Giant Peach*?

    A. They do not trust the human who appears.

    B. They blame a human for their troubles.

    C. They accept a human into their group.

    D. They are confused by the human who appears.

Vocabulary

____ **13.** In *James and the Giant Peach*, Centipede says:

    Well, James, have you ever in your life seen such a marvelous colossal Centipede as me?

    What does *colossal* mean?

    A. hungry   **C.** friendly

    B. gigantic   **D.** grouchy

____ **14.** What does *fostering* mean in this sentence from "Mowgli's Brothers"?

    We will see what the Pack will say to this fostering of man-cubs.

    A. taking care   **C.** naming

    B. killing   **D.** lying down

Essay

15. The nonhuman creatures in both "Mowgli's Brothers" and *James and the Giant Peach* are similar to real creatures in some ways. They are different from real creatures in other ways. Choose one creature from each story. Write a brief essay that explains how each story creature is similar to and different from the same real-life creature.

16. **Thinking About the Big Question: How much should our communities shape us?** James and Mowgli have found new communities. James has found the insects, and Mowgli has found the wolves. Choose one of these characters. In an essay, discuss how he will be changed by his new community and whether these changes will be good or bad. Use details from the selection to support your answer.

"Mowgli's Brothers" by Rudyard Kipling
from **James and the Giant Peach** by Roald Dahl
Selection Test B

Critical Reading *Identify the letter of the choice that best completes the statement or answers the question.*

_____ 1. In "Mowgli's Brothers," what news does Tabaqui the jackal deliver to Father and Mother Wolf?
   A. Mowgli has been accepted as a member of the Wolf Pack.
   B. The tiger Shere Khan has changed his hunting grounds.
   C. The Wolf Pack is gathering on Council Rock.
   D. A human hunting camp has been disturbed by Shere Khan.

_____ 2. Which line from "Mowgli's Brothers" includes a realistic *and* a fantastic element?
   A. "Who speaks for this cub?" said Akela. "Among the Free People who speaks?"
   B. The bushes rustled a little in the thicket, and Father Wolf dropped with his haunches under him. . . .
   C. "Man!" said Father Wolf, showing all his white teeth.
   D. [Tabaqui] scuttled to the back of the cave, where he found the bone of a buck.

_____ 3. In "Mowgli's Brothers," the narrator explains that if a grown wolf kills one of his own pack's young, the punishment is death. He then says that "if you think for a minute, you will see that this must be so." Why must this be so?
   A. because the punishment for breaking any law is death
   B. because if young cubs are killed, the pack will die out
   C. because the cubs are needed to help the pack hunt
   D. because each wolf family wants to protect its own cubs

_____ 4. None of the wolves speaks in favor of accepting Mowgli into the Pack because
   A. the wolves are suspicious of humans.
   B. Mowgli does not show enough respect for Akela.
   C. the young wolves want the price Bagheera will pay for Mowgli.
   D. the Pack already has too many members.

_____ 5. Which words best describe Bagheera the panther in "Mowgli's Brothers"?
   A. cowardly but cruel
   B. beautiful but selfish
   C. honest but tricky
   D. charming but dangerous

_____ 6. Which element of "Mowgli's Brothers" is *most* realistic?
   A. the way the animals communicate
   B. the story situation
   C. the setting
   D. the animals' names

____ 7. In the excerpt from *James and the Giant Peach*, how do the creatures respond to James's arrival?
  A. They try to eat him.
  B. They grow fearful.
  C. They ignore him.
  D. They welcome him.

____ 8. Which line from *James and the Giant Peach* contains a realistic *and* a fantastic element?
  A. "I have a lot of legs," the Centipede answered proudly.
  B. The Centipede made a wriggling movement with his body. . . .
  C. The peach flesh was sweet and juicy, and marvelously refreshing.
  D. "I like it soft, thank you very much," James answered.

____ 9. In *James and the Giant Peach*, why does James decide to help the Centipede with his boots?
  A. because he finds the Centipede charming
  B. because he does not want to be disagreeable
  C. because everyone else is helping the Centipede
  D. because he hopes to earn a reward

____ 10. In *James and the Giant Peach*, the sleeping arrangement is realistic only for
  A. Centipede.
  B. Old-Green-Grasshopper.
  C. Earthworm.
  D. Spider.

____ 11. In *James and the Giant Peach*, Ladybug says to James, "You are one of us now, didn't you know that? You are one of the crew. We're all in the same boat." This suggests that
  A. something unusual has happened to all of them.
  B. the creatures have tricked James.
  C. James has crawled into a giant water craft.
  D. Ladybug is the leader of the group.

____ 12. Mowgli in "Mowgli's Brothers" and James in *James and the Giant Peach* both
  A. go looking for an exciting adventure.
  B. are frightened by the creatures around them.
  C. wander innocently into a strange situation.
  D. seem much older than they really are.

____ 13. The setting of *James and the Giant Peach* is
  A. less realistic than that of "Mowgli's Brothers."
  B. less fantastic than that of "Mowgli's Brothers."
  C. more realistic than that of "Mowgli's Brothers."
  D. as fantastic as that of "Mowgli's Brothers."

___ 14. What do the human characters in "Mowgli's Brothers" and *James and the Giant Peach* have in common?
   A. They are surrounded by realistic creatures.
   B. They behave realistically.
   C. They behave in fantastic ways.
   D. They are surrounded by totally fantastic creatures.

___ 15. Based on "Mowgli's Brother" and *James and the Giant Peach*, which is true of fantasy writing?
   A. It contains only elements that are not found in real life.
   B. It contains mostly real-life elements with one or two make-believe elements.
   C. It contains some make-believe elements and some real-life elements.
   D. It contains only elements that are true to real life.

___ 16. As the adventures of each boy unfold, what is most likely to happen?
   A. The creatures will turn against the boy.
   B. The boy will find a way to escape the creatures.
   C. The boy will turn into one of the creatures.
   D. The creatures will protect and help the boy.

Vocabulary

___ 17. What does the word *monotonous* mean in the following sentence?
   Akela never raised his head from his paws, but went on with the monotonous cry: "Look well!"

   A. unchanging   B. barely heard   C. extremely loud   D. terrifying

___ 18. In "Mowgli's Brothers," the tiger Shere Khan claims that Mowgli is his own *quarry*, or
   A. cub.   B. prey.   C. enemy.   D. leader.

___ 19. What does *intently* mean in this sentence?
   The creatures, some sitting on chairs, others reclining on a sofa, were all watching him intently.

   A. suspiciously   B. with great hope   C. with amusement   D. closely

Essay

20. Both "Mowgli's Brothers" and *James and the Giant Peach* contain fantastic and realistic elements. In an essay, identify two fantastic and two realistic elements from each story. Then explain why you think each author includes the realistic elements that he does.

21. The characters of James and Mowgli both behave in some surprising ways, but they also behave in some ways that are typical of children. In an essay, compare and contrast the characters. Which boy, in your opinion, is more realistic? Explain.

22. **Thinking About the Big Question: How much should our communities shape us?** James and Mowgli have found new communities. Choose one of these characters and discuss in an essay how he will be changed by his new community. Will these changes be positive or negative? Explain using details from the selection to support your answer.

Writing Workshop—Unit 6, Part 1
Research: Multimedia Report

Prewriting: Choosing Your Topic

To help create an interesting topic for your multimedia report, take the following self-interview.

What topics in my other classes interest me?	
What subjects do I know a lot about?	
What topic do I want to learn more about?	

Drafting: Writing a Script

Plan every word and action in your presentation by writing a script. In the left column, write the words in your script. In the right column, indicate sound effects, visuals, and other notes about the presentation.

Script	Presentation Notes

Writing Workshop—Unit 6, Part 1
Multimedia Report: Integrating Grammar Skills

Revising Sentence Fragments

Sentence fragments can make writing difficult to understand. A sentence fragment is a group of words that does not express a complete thought. To fix fragments, add more information to complete the idea.

Fragment	Corrected
After I heard about the celebration.	After I heard about the celebration, I started thinking about a gift.
Although I got hurt when I fell.	I really enjoyed the soccer game, although I got hurt when I fell.

Identifying Sentence Fragments

A. DIRECTIONS: *Identify each item below by writing* fragment *or* sentence *on the line.*

_____ 1. Because Celi likes jewelry, I want to get her a bracelet.

_____ 2. As long as Celi admired the display at the shop on Fifth Avenue.

_____ 3. Having planned the party for May 28 at four o'clock.

_____ 4. Since Celi couldn't come, we changed the date.

_____ 5. Shopped early for the favors, balloons, and snacks.

Fixing Sentence Fragments

B. DIRECTIONS: *On the lines, rewrite the fragments as complete sentences.*

1. Unless we invite everyone.

_____

2. Where to have the celebration.

_____

3. In order to use the clubhouse.

_____

4. If you don't have an idea for a gift.

_____

5. How to decorate for a party.

_____

Unit 6: Themes in Folk Literature
Benchmark Test 11

MULTIPLE CHOICE

Reading Skill: Cause and Effect

1. What do you call an event or an action that makes something else happen?
   A. a cause
   B. an effect
   C. a result
   D. a cause-and-effect relationship

2. Which of these words or phrases signals an effect?
   A. because
   B. since
   C. due to
   D. as a result

Read this selection. Then, answer the questions that follow.

The surface of the Earth is more than three-quarters water. This water—most of it oceans and seas—is exposed to the sun's heat and drying winds. As a result, some of the water slowly evaporates, or turns into water vapor, the gaseous state of water. Because it is less dense in this gaseous state, the water vapor rises into the atmosphere. Since the atmosphere is cool, the vapor cools down as it rises until it is cool enough to condense into water again. The tiny droplets of water in the atmosphere form clouds. As more and more water condenses, the droplets in the clouds become larger and heavier until they fall back down to the Earth as rain. The rain eventually gets back to the bodies of water on the Earth's surface, and the process starts all over again.

3. Which question best helps identify the cause-and-effect relationships in this selection?
   A. What is a cloud?
   B. What causes rain?
   C. What is water vapor?
   D. How much of the Earth's surface is water?

4. Which word or phrase signals an effect?
   A. as a result
   B. because
   C. since
   D. as

5. Based on the selection, what causes water to evaporate into water vapor?
   A. the weight of the water droplets
   B. drying winds and the cool atmosphere
   C. the sun's heat and drying winds
   D. the sun's heat and the cool atmosphere

6. How would you describe the cause-and-effect relationships in this selection?
   A. A single important event is the cause of many events.
   B. Many events are all causes of a single important event.
   C. There is a cycle of events in which one causes another, and so on.
   D. Events that are causes are completely unrelated to events that are effects.

Reading Skill: Create Outlines

Refer to the following outline of the selection to answer the questions.

Title: _____

  I. _____

    A. Put their own stamp on a song

    B. Might not reproduce the song exactly from memory

    C. _____

7. Which of these would be the best title for the outline?
   A. Why Folk Songs Have Anonymous Composers
   B. What Is Meant by the Oral Tradition of Folk Songs
   C. Where Folk Songs Got Their Start
   D. How Various Versions of Folk Songs Come to Exist

8. Which of these best belongs next to Roman numeral *I*?
   A. Composers' names are unknown
   B. Songs are passed along
   C. Singers make changes
   D. Common folk write songs

9. Which of these best belongs next to the letter *C*?
   A. Make changes to keep up with the times
   B. Have a problem with the oral tradition
   C. Sing about traveling on a horse
   D. Make a version about traveling in a car

Literary Analysis: Fables, Myths, Fantasy

10. Which term names the literature passed verbally from one generation to the next?
    A. fable
    B. myth
    C. cause-and-effect tradition
    D. oral tradition

Name _____   Date _____

Read this fable. Then, answer the questions that follow.

The Goose That Laid Golden Eggs

Once a poor farmer and his wife got a new goose on their farm. The new goose turned out to be special, for she laid eggs made of gold. Every day the goose laid one golden egg, which the couple sold for a nice chunk of money. However, the more money they had, the more they wanted. The farmer said to his wife, "Since our goose lays golden eggs, she must be made of gold inside. Instead of waiting for an egg each day, why don't we cut her open and get all the gold at once?" "No, no!" squawked the goose. "Do not kill me!" The wife, however, agreed with her husband's plan, and the goose was slain. Yet when they looked inside, the couple found no gold. What's more, once the goose was killed, there were no more golden eggs each day. So that was the end of the couple's money, and they went back to being poor. Too late they learned this lesson: Greedy people can lose everything.

11. What is the stated moral of this fable?
    A. The new goose turned out to be special.
    B. The more money they had, the more they wanted.
    C. Once the goose was killed, there were no more golden eggs each day.
    D. Greedy people can lose everything.

12. What is another lesson that the fable teaches?
    A. All that glitters may not necessarily be gold.
    B. It is better to have all your pleasure at once than to have a little each day.
    C. It is foolish to harm something or someone that benefits you.
    D. People need to learn to support themselves and not rely on others.

13. Which feature of this fable is typical of most fables?
    A. It includes a farmer and his wife as characters.
    B. It has an animal character that speaks and acts human.
    C. It has heroic characters admired in the cultures that produced them.
    D. It has a surprise ending.

14. Which element of the fable is fantasy that could not happen in real life?
    A. A goose could not speak and lay golden eggs.
    B. A farmer would not kill a goose that laid golden eggs.
    C. A goose could never lay an egg each day.
    D. Someone could not go from rich to poor so quickly.

15. For what main purpose did ancient peoples create myths?
    A. to create literature that would stand the test of time
    B. to explain natural events and express beliefs and values
    C. to show that gods and goddesses are just like human beings
    D. to honor the contributions of political leaders to the society

Name _____ Date _____

Read this short Greek myth. Then, answer the four questions about it.

Daedalus and Icarus

Daedalus was a clever builder. He and his son Icarus went to the island of Crete, where Daedalus worked for King Minos. There he built the famous labyrinth, or maze, to confine the bull-like monster known as the Minotaur. Then, Daedalus made King Minos angry, and the king had Daedalus and Icarus tossed into the labyrinth. Daedalus, however, knew how to escape what he had built. After he and Icarus fled the labyrinth, he cleverly used wax to glue bird feathers into two sets of wings for himself and his son. "Put these on," he told Icarus, "and we will fly away from Crete. But be careful, Icarus. Do not fly too close to the sun, or your wings will melt. And do not fly too close to the sea, or the moisture will weigh you down." So father and son put on the wings and escaped the island. Daedalus flew all the way to the island of Sicily. Icarus, however, enjoyed soaring through the sky so much that he forgot his father's advice. When he flew too close to the sun, the heat melted the wax in his wings, and he fell into the sea and drowned. To this day, the sea he fell into, west of the island of Samos, is known as the Icarian Sea.

16. What main lesson does the myth of Daedalus and Icarus teach?
    A. Do not work for a cruel leader.
    B. Avoid doing things to excess.
    C. Do not anger the gods.
    D. Birds of a feather flock together.

17. What does the myth of Daedalus and Icarus most clearly show about ancient Greek culture?
    A. Children usually obeyed their parents' instructions.
    B. Children usually did not obey their parents.
    C. The ancient Greeks admired harshness and cruelty in leaders.
    D. The ancient Greeks admired science and invention.

18. What does the myth of Daedalus and Icarus explain?
    A. how airplanes were invented
    B. why Minotaurs are extinct
    C. how to build a labyrinth
    D. how the Icarian Sea got its name

19. What details of the myth would best qualify as fantasy?
    A. the Minotaur and the characters' ability to fly
    B. King Minos and the labyrinth
    C. the labyrinth and the behavior and attitude of Icarus
    D. King Minos and the Minotaur

20. Which of these characters or situations is most clearly fantasy?
    A. Your best friend announces that he or she is moving to Japan.
    B. Human beings launch a space probe that travels to Mars.
    C. Someone says, "It's raining cats and dogs."
    D. A talented rooster wants to be an opera singer.

Vocabulary: Suffixes and Roots

21. Using your knowledge of the suffix *-ment*, what is the most likely meaning of *amendment* in the following sentence?

    Some treaties have provisions for amendment.

    A. the act of changing for the better
    B. the ability to be broken at a later time
    C. the quality of being flexible
    D. the state of instability

22. Using your knowledge of the suffix *-ous*, what is the most likely meaning of *hazardous* in the following sentence?

    His new job was hazardous.

    A. able to challenge
    B. full of danger
    C. involving no risk
    D. free of problems

23. What kind of word is formed by adding the suffix *-ous*?
    A. noun
    B. adverb
    C. verb
    D. adjective

24. What does the root *-mort-* mean?
    A. "death"
    B. "break"
    C. "throw"
    D. "stand"

25. How does the word *resplendent* reflect the meaning of the root *-splend-*?
    A. Something resplendent is very valuable.
    B. Something resplendent is envied.
    C. Something resplendent shines brightly.
    D. Something resplendent is easy to see.

26. Based on your understanding of the root *-mort-*, what does a *mortician* do?
    A. fixes things that are broken
    B. helps people find their seats
    C. takes care of funerals
    D. sells items to customers

Grammar

27. What is a clause?
    A. a group of words with its own subject and verb
    B. a group of words with either a subject or a verb but not both
    C. a group of words that interrupts a sentence to add information
    D. a group of words that restates the words that come before it

28. How is a subordinate clause different from an independent clause?
    A. A subordinate clause can stand alone as a complete sentence.
    B. A subordinate clause cannot stand alone as a complete sentence.
    C. A subordinate clause always comes at the beginning of a sentence.
    D. A subordinate clause always comes at the end of a sentence.

29. What is the independent clause in this sentence?

    When Matthew visited Florida last March, he went to the Kennedy Space Center.

    A. When Matthew visited Florida last March
    B. Matthew visited Florida
    C. he went to the Kennedy Space Center
    D. to the Kennedy Space Center

30. What is a compound sentence?
    A. a sentence with two subjects
    B. a sentence with one independent clause and one or more subordinate clauses
    C. a sentence with two verbs
    D. a sentence with two or more independent clauses

31. Which of these is a simple sentence?
    A. Ginnie was there, but we did not see her.
    B. She is the author whose book I read.
    C. In the morning we took a long walk to the marina.
    D. I will leave if I get sleepy.

32. Which of these groups of words is a sentence fragment?
    A. Until Caroline learned fluent Chinese
    B. If you go, I'll go.
    C. Please don't ask me that again!
    D. What were you doing yesterday?

33. Which of these groups of words is a complete sentence?
    A. It rained all night.
    B. The bus running on schedule.
    C. After the party ended.
    D. With a little luck and little elbow grease.

ESSAY

Writing

34. Recall an incident in which you learned something about life or human behavior. On your paper or a separate sheet, write a brief essay in which you recount the incident. Be sure to make the causes and effects clear.

35. Imagine that you are doing a multimedia report on fables from a particular culture or region of the world. On your paper or a separate sheet, jot down your ideas for what to include in the report and where to research your information.

Name _____

Unit 6: Themes in Folk Literature Skills Concept Map—2

How much do our communities shape us?

Words you can use
to discuss the
Big Question

Literary Analysis:
Folk Literature

Folk Literature	includes	personification

and

a universal theme

(demonstrated in this selection)

Selection name:

(demonstrated in this selection)

Selection name:

Reading Skills and Strategies:
Purpose for Reading

You can set a purpose
for reading

by

previewing the text

and by

making connections

(demonstrated in this selection)

Selection name:

Informational Text:
Street Map

You can read background information

to

connect and clarify main ideas

**Characteristics of
Folk Literature**
• Universal Theme
• Fantasy
• Personification
• Irony
• Dialect

Oral Tradition in Print
• Folk Tales
• Fables
• Myths
• Legends

Comparing Literary Works:
Foreshadowing and Flashback

are plot techniques

that

show something
about a past event
or a character's
past (flashback)

hint at
what might happen
later in the story
(foreshadowing)

(demonstrated in these selections)

Selection names:
1.
2.

Student Log

Complete this chart to track your assignments.

Writing	Extend Your Learning	Writing Workshop	Other Assignments

Vocabulary Warm-up Word Lists

Study these words from "Why the Tortoise's Shell Is Not Smooth." Then, complete the activities that follow.

Word List A

arrived [uh RYVD] *v.* reached a place
　　We <u>arrived</u> at the theater late, after the movie had already started.

compound [KAHM pownd] *n.* a group of buildings
　　Our house is one of the big ones in that <u>compound</u> over there.

custom [KUHS tuhm] *n.* habit; way of acting or doing things
　　Rick's family had a <u>custom</u> of eating dinner early on Sundays.

grumbled [GRUHM buhld] *v.* complained; made a growling unhappy noise
　　The kids <u>grumbled</u> after finding out that the field trip was cancelled.

hosts [HOHSTS] *n.* people who are having guests over
　　The hosts said <u>goodbye</u> to everyone who had come to their house.

invitation [in vuh TAY shuhn] *n.* a request to do something
　　I'm not going to the party because I didn't get an <u>invitation</u>.

preparations [prep uh RAY shuhnz] *n.* things a person does to get ready for something
　　The <u>preparations</u> were finished; we were ready to put on the show.

ungrateful [uhn GRAYT fuhl] *adj.* not thankful
　　Don't be <u>ungrateful</u>; thank your aunt for the gift.

Word List B

cunning [KUHN ing] *n.* cleverness
　　The tricky fox used his <u>cunning</u> to sneak up on the chicken.

dye [DYE] *n.* liquid used to change the color of something
　　Soak your white shirt in <u>dye</u> to make it turn black.

famine [FAM in] *n.* shortage of food
　　During the <u>famine</u>, people traveled hundreds of miles to find food.

feast [FEEST] *n.* a huge meal; party with food
　　We always eat a big <u>feast</u> on Thanksgiving Day.

plumage [PLOO mij] *n.* the feathers on a bird's body
　　Look at the feathers on that bird. What incredible <u>plumage</u> it has!

presented [pree ZENT id] *v.* shown, displayed, or offered
　　At the art show, Tim <u>presented</u> the paintings he had made.

tortoise [TAWR tis] *n.* type of turtle that lives on land
　　A <u>tortoise</u> has a round, dome-shaped shell.

yam [YAM] *n.* sweet potato-like vegetable
　　A <u>yam</u> tastes best when it is served with brown sugar.

"Why the Tortoise's Shell Is Not Smooth" by Chinua Achebe
Vocabulary Warm-up Exercises

Exercise A *Fill in each blank in the paragraph below with an appropriate word from Word List A. Use each word only once.*

Our family has a [1] _____. We always leave for vacation on the afternoon that school ends for summer. We go to a house in a beautiful [2] _____ of country homes. We begin travel [3] _____ a week before school ends. That way, we're ready to leave right away.

    This year, however, I got an [4] _____ to an end-of-school dinner. My parents [5] _____ about it, but said I could go for one hour. When I [6] _____ at the dinner, I told the [7] _____ why I had to leave early. I didn't want to seem [8] _____ when I left right after eating!

Exercise B *Revise each sentence so that the underlined vocabulary word is used in a logical way. Be sure to keep the vocabulary word in your revision.*

Example: During a <u>famine</u>, there is always plenty of food.
    During a <u>famine</u>, there is never enough food.

1. The <u>plumage</u> on the cow helps keep the cow warm.

   _____

2. Ron <u>presented</u> the award to me so I wouldn't be able to take a look at it.

   _____

3. A <u>tortoise</u>, like a lizard, has no shell.

   _____

4. A <u>yam</u> isn't something that you eat, it's something that you wear.

   _____

5. It was a real <u>feast</u>, so everyone felt hungry when they left.

   _____

6. If you like the color of the dress, dip it in <u>dye</u> to keep it the same.

   _____

7. Lee isn't known for her <u>cunning</u>; she's extremely clever.

   _____

"Why the Tortoise's Shell Is Not Smooth" by Chinua Achebe

Reading Warm-up A

Read the following passage. Pay special attention to the underlined words. Then, read it again, and complete the activities. Use a separate sheet of paper for your written answers.

In the United States, people drive on the right-hand side of the road. It's our <u>custom</u>, the way people do things. Customs, however, are not the same all over the world. In Ireland, India, and many other countries, people drive on the left-hand side of the road. The first time I visited Ireland, I found the difference hard to get used to. A friend offered to lend me his car. I turned him down. I wasn't being <u>ungrateful</u>. Driving on the left side just seemed too hard.

Japan has many customs that are different from those in the United States. While visiting Japan, I received an <u>invitation</u> to visit someone's home. I was surprised when the <u>hosts</u> offered me a pair of slippers. The slippers were for wearing while I was in their house. I was supposed to leave my shoes outside the door. That's the Japanese custom.

A few years ago I visited Mali, a country in West Africa. On the night I <u>arrived</u>, I was invited to someone's home for dinner. The person who invited me lived in the <u>compound</u> of buildings where I was staying.

As part of the <u>preparations</u> for eating, everyone washed his or her hands. Then, when it was time to eat, the dining custom surprised me. People didn't eat out of their own plates. Instead, there was one large shared bowl filled with food for everyone. At first, eating out of the shared bowl seemed odd. By the end of the meal, however, it felt completely normal.

I've never <u>grumbled</u> when coming across customs that seemed strange to me at first. I realize that in different places, things are done in different ways.

1. Underline the words that tell what a <u>custom</u> is. Then, name one holiday *custom* your family has.

2. Circle the sentence that explains why the writer wasn't being <u>ungrateful</u> by refusing the car. Then, tell what *ungrateful* means.

3. Underline the word that tells what kind of <u>invitation</u> was received. Then, use *invitation* in a sentence.

4. Circle the words that tell what the <u>hosts</u> offered. Then, explain what *hosts* are.

5. Circle the words that tell where the writer <u>arrived</u>. Then, tell what *arrived* means.

6. Underline the word that explains what you will find in a <u>compound</u>. Then, use the word *compound* in a sentence.

7. Circle the activity that was part of the <u>preparations</u> for eating. Then, tell what *preparations* are.

8. Underline the sentence that explains why the writer never <u>grumbled</u>. Then, tell what *grumbled* means.

Name _____ Date _____

Reading Warm-up B

Read the following passage. Pay special attention to the underlined words. Then, read it again, and complete the activities. Use a separate sheet of paper for your written answers.

The peacock is known for its beautiful <u>plumage</u>. When a male peacock spreads its tail feathers, the sight is amazing. The bright green feathers are decorated with blue "eyes," bright dots of color that look like they were created with <u>dye</u>.

The peacock is a good example of an animal with special markings. The natural world is filled with them. Some animals have distinctive markings on their feathers. Others have special markings on the fur, skin, or shell.

The red-back spider is an example from Australia. The spider is dark black, with a distinctive line marking down its back. Despite the name, the marking isn't always red. It often looks orange, the color of a <u>yam</u> or sweet potato. The red-back spider feeds on small insects that it catches in its web. If a red-back spider is hungry enough, it will eat its own kind. Better to eat another red-back, apparently, than give in to <u>famine</u>. Often, males are eaten by the larger female red-backs. A male red-back needs <u>cunning</u> in order to stay alive around the females.

The leopard <u>tortoise</u> is a good example of a reptile with decorative markings. The turtle comes from Africa. It can be found in many zoos and is sometimes kept as a pet. The turtle gets its name from the complex patterns that cover its shell. The bold patterns look something like those found on a leopard.

Often, animal markings serve a useful purpose. The four-eyed butterfly fish is a good example. To bigger fishes, the four-eyed butterfly fish is a delicious <u>feast</u>. However, the butterfly fish's markings, when <u>presented</u> to bigger fish, create a puzzle. The fish seems to have eyes at both ends of its body. One set is real; the others are just decorative markings. When bigger fish attack the tail, thinking it is the head, a four-eyed butterfly fish can often get away.

1. Underline the nearby word that has a similar meaning to <u>plumage</u>. Then, name two other animals that have *plumage*.

2. Circle the words that tell what looks like they were created with <u>dye</u>. Then, tell what *dye* is.

3. Circle the word that tells the color a <u>yam</u> is. Then, explain what a *yam* is.

4. Underline the words that explain how red-back spiders handle <u>famine</u>. Then, explain what *famine* means.

5. Underline the words that tell what a male red-back needs <u>cunning</u> for. Then, tell what *cunning* means.

6. Circle the word that has a similar meaning to <u>tortoise</u>. Then, name two places you might see a *tortoise*.

7. Underline the words that tell who considers butterfly fish a <u>feast</u>. Then, tell what *feast* means.

8. Circle the items that create a puzzle when <u>presented</u> to bigger fish. Then, use the word *presented* in a sentence.

"Why the Tortoise's Shell Is Not Smooth" by Chinua Achebe
Writing About the Big Question

How much do our communities shape us?

Big Question Vocabulary

common	community	connection	culture	family
generation	group	history	influence	involve
isolate	participation	support	values	belief

A. *Use one or more words from the list above to complete each sentence.*

1. Rob plays funny tricks, but his tricks tend to _____ him a little because we don't trust him completely.

2. Because she had been on the wrong end of some practical jokes, Marina identified with stories that _____ the idea that playing tricks is wrong.

3. In a popular story, a _____ ignores a boy's genuine cries for help because he had tricked everyone before by crying "wolf" when there was no wolf.

4. Glenna learned the hard way that playing tricks, even harmless ones, could break an important _____ between her and her best friends.

B. *Follow the directions in responding to each of the items below.*

1. List two different times when someone played a trick on you.

   _____.

   _____.

2. Write two sentences explaining one of the preceding experiences, and describe what happened and how you felt about it. Use at least two of the Big Question vocabulary words.

   _____

   _____

C. *Complete the sentence below. Then, write a short paragraph in which you connect this experience to the Big Question.*

   I played a trick on _____ when I _____

   _____

   _____

   _____

   _____

Name _____ Date _____

Reading: Preview the Text to Set a Purpose for Reading

Your **purpose** for reading is the reason you read a text. Sometimes, you may choose a text based on a purpose you already have. Other times, you may set a purpose based on the kind of text you have in front of you. **Setting a purpose** helps you focus your reading. You might set a purpose to learn about a subject, to gain understanding, to take an action, or simply to read for enjoyment.

Preview the text before you begin to read. Look at the title, the pictures, and the beginnings of paragraphs to get an idea about the literary work. This will help you set a purpose or decide if the text will fit a purpose you already have.

DIRECTIONS: *Answer the following questions as you preview "Why the Tortoise's Shell Is Not Smooth." You can use questions like these as you preview any text.*

1. Look at the title. What ideas or feelings do you have about the title? _____

   _____

2. Who is the author? What do you know about this author? _____

   _____

3. Look at any photographs, drawings, or artwork in the text. How does the artwork help you set a purpose for reading? _____

   _____

4. Read the beginning of several paragraphs in the text. What kind of text does this seem to be? _____

   _____

5. Think about the clues you picked up during your preview. What purpose will you set to help you focus your reading of this text? _____

   _____

Unit 6 Resources: Themes in Folk Literature
128

Name _____ Date _____

"Why the Tortoise's Shell Is Not Smooth" by Chinua Achebe
Literary Analysis: Personification

Personification is the representation of an animal or an object as if it had a human personality, intelligence, or emotions. In folk literature, personification is often used to give human qualities to animal characters. The actions of these animal characters can show human qualities, behavior, and problems in a humorous way.

DIRECTIONS: *As you read, think about the human and animal qualities shown by the tortoise, the birds, and the parrot in the story. Next to each name below, write two of that character's animal qualities on the lines at the left and two of that character's human qualities on the lines at the right. Treat the group of birds as one character.*

Animal Qualities   **Human Qualities**

_____   _____

_____   _____

1. Tortoise

_____   _____

_____   _____

2. the birds

_____   _____

_____   _____

3. Parrot

"Why the Tortoise's Shell Is Not Smooth" by Chinua Achebe
Vocabulary Builder

Word List

compound   cunning   custom   eloquent   famine   orator

A. DIRECTIONS: *Write your answer in a complete sentence using a Word List word.*

1. What might happen to people who live in a place where there is a *famine*?

   _____

2. What kind of job might require someone to be a skilled *orator*? Why?

   _____

3. Imagine that you have been asked to write an *eloquent* article for the paper. What will you write about?

   _____

4. Why is being <u>cunning</u> helpful in a competition?

   _____

5. How could a single house be turned into a <u>compound</u>?

   _____

6. What is your favorite family <u>custom</u>?

   _____

B. DIRECTIONS: *Choose the word or words that mean almost the same as the bold vocabulary word. Write the letter for your answer choice on the line.*

____ 1. When Tortoise spoke at the party, his speech was **eloquent.**
   A. humorous   C. long
   B. expressive   D. illogical

____ 2. The rains ended the drought that had caused years of **famine.**
   A. food abundance   C. food shortage
   B. flooding   D. rebellion

____ 3. A child whose mother is a famous storyteller might want to be a great **orator.**
   A. doctor   C. writer
   B. leader   D. speaker

C. WORD STUDY: The suffix *-ary* means "related to or connected with." Change each of the italicized words in parentheses to a word that ends in *-ary.*

1. It is a *(custom)* _____ practice in many societies to celebrate an adolescent's passage to manhood or womanhood.
2. A sensitive child might have an *(imagine)* _____ friend.
3. My mother was given the *(honor)* _____ title of professor emeritus.

Name _____ Date _____

"Why the Tortoise's Shell Is Not Smooth" by Chinua Achebe
Enrichment: Telling a Story

In "Why the Tortoise's Shell Is Not Smooth," Chinua Achebe retells a story that was passed down for hundreds of years in Nigeria. The story offers an explanation for something found in nature: a tortoise's cracked, bumpy shell. Within his story, Achebe includes details, such as the Nigerian names of the mother and daughter, and specific foods, such as yam pottage, that reflect ancient Nigerian customs and culture.

DIRECTIONS: *Create and tell a brief folk tale that will be handed down for generations and which explains something you see in nature today. In your tale, include details about your world today: what people eat, how they dress, how they communicate with each other. Use this page to plan your story.*

1. What is the title of your story?

   _____

2. What does your story explain in nature?

   _____

3. What is the basic plot of your story?

   _____

   _____

   _____

   _____

4. What words, phrases, and names from the story will you use to place your story in the United States in the twenty-first century? What details can you use to reflect the customs and culture?

   _____

   _____

When you have planned your story, practice telling it orally in front of a mirror. You may want to make notes to help you practice the first few times. Remember that you don't need to memorize the story exactly. When you present a story orally, use the most exciting or interesting events. Tell them in a way that will entertain your listeners. Change the tone and loudness of your voice. Try speaking in different voices when you say the words of the various characters. Use hand gestures that will help dramatize the story.

When you are ready to present your story, tell it to an audience. If possible, tell it to a group of younger children in your school.

Name _____   Date _____

"**Why the Tortoise's Shell Is Not Smooth**" by Chinua Achebe
Open-Book Test

Short Answer *Write your responses to the questions in this section on the lines provided.*

1. When you preview "Why the Tortoise's Shell Is Not Smooth," the title can help you set a purpose for reading. What purpose might you set? Explain.

   _____

   _____

   _____

2. As you preview "Why the Tortoise's Shell Is Not Smooth," you read this sentence: "Once upon a time . . . all the birds were invited to a feast in the sky." What does this tell you about the kind of story you will read?

   _____

   _____

3. In the beginning of "Why the Tortoise's Shell Is Not Smooth," how is Tortoise personified? Use two examples from the selection.

   _____

   _____

   _____

4. When Tortoise asks the birds if he can go to the feast, they say no. But then they agree. What does the change show about Tortoise and about the birds? Use details from the story.

   _____

   _____

   _____

5. Tortoise is very eloquent when he gives a speech at the party. The birds are glad they brought him. Why might the birds have been glad? Base your answer on the definition of *eloquent*.

   _____

   _____

6. Tortoise is described as a great orator. How does he use this talent to get what he wants? Use the definition of *orator* in your answer.

   _____

   _____

   _____

7. At the feast in the sky, what human characteristic does Tortoise show when he begins to eat? Use details from the story.

_____

_____

8. As the birds watch Tortoise eat, what human quality do they show? Use details from the story.

_____

_____

_____

9. What lesson is taught by "Why the Tortoise's Shell Is Not Smooth"? Support your answer with details from the story.

_____

_____

_____

10. Parrot's actions show his human qualities in "Why the Tortoise's Shell Is Not Smooth." The first column shows Parrot's actions. In the second column, write the characteristic he displays with each action. On the line below, explain whether you think Parrot's actions were appropriate.

Parrot's Action	Human Characteristic
Agrees to take message	
Changes message	

_____

Essay

Write an extended response to the question of your choice or to the question or questions your teacher assigns you.

11. In "Why the Tortoise's Shell Is Not Smooth," Tortoise is a very good speaker. In a brief essay, explain how Tortoise's words get him what he wants—except in one important moment. Use details from the story to support your answer.

12. In "Why the Tortoise's Shell Is Not Smooth," the birds get tricked several times. Do you think the birds could have avoided going home hungry? In a brief essay, explain how the birds were tricked and where along the way they could have avoided their problems. Include details from the story for support.

13. At the end of "Why the Tortoise's Shell Is Not Smooth," Tortoise crashes into the pile of hard things his wife has assembled. He does not, however, die. In a brief essay, explain what happens to Tortoise and offer an opinion as to why the story ends that way. Use details from the story and what you know about the oral tradition to support your opinion.

14. **Thinking About the Big Question: How much should our communities shape us?** Think about what happens to Tortoise. He is literally shaped by his community. Did the community of the birds go too far? In an essay, discuss whether you think what happens to Tortoise is fair. Use details from the story to support your answer.

Oral Response

15. Go back to question 3, 4, or 5 or to the question your teacher assigns you. Take a few minutes to expand your answer and prepare an oral response. Find additional details in the story that support your points. If necessary, make notes to guide your oral response.

"Why the Tortoise's Shell Is Not Smooth" by Chinua Achebe
Selection Test A

Critical Reading *Identify the letter of the choice that best answers the question.*

_____ 1. Previewing "Why the Tortoise's Shell Is Not Smooth" helps you set a purpose for reading. When do you preview a story?

    A. after you read it

    B. before you read it

    C. after you set a purpose for reading

    D. before you take a test

_____ 2. Setting a purpose for reading "Why the Tortoise's Shell Is Not Smooth" helps you do what?

    A. focus your thoughts about what you will read

    B. know what questions will be asked about the story

    C. finish reading the story by giving you clues about how it will end

    D. understand why some stories are better than others

_____ 3. What role does Ekwefi play in "Why the Tortoise's Shell Is Not Smooth"?

    A. She is the wife of Tortoise.

    B. She gives the feast in the sky.

    C. She teaches Tortoise how to fly.

    D. She is the storyteller.

_____ 4. Chinua Achebe gives human qualities, such as personality and feelings, to animal characters. What do you call this?

    A. tradition

    B. exaggeration

    C. personification

    D. conflict

_____ 5. Why do the birds believe Tortoise's lies?

    A. They think he has changed and that he is no longer a bad person.

    B. He has always told the truth before, and they think he is telling the truth now.

    C. They have never known anyone who tells lies.

    D. They feel sorry for him because he's so hungry, and they want to help him.

___ 6. Tortoise asks the birds to call him *All of You.* That name turns out to be very convenient for him at the feast. Based on what happens at the feast, what human quality is Tortoise showing when he takes that name?
   A. cleverness
   B. politeness
   C. pride
   D. foolishness

___ 7. Why do the birds become angry at Tortoise?
   A. He takes a feather from each bird.
   B. He steals their eggs.
   C. He tricks them into making him king.
   D. He eats most of the food at the feast.

___ 8. Why does Tortoise jump from the sky?
   A. He feels sick from eating too much.
   B. He has practiced flying.
   C. He thinks his wife has made a soft landing.
   D. He thinks it is not too far to fall.

___ 9. What human trait does Parrot show in "Why the Tortoise's Shell Is Not Smooth"?
   A. loyalty
   B. anger
   C. jealousy
   D. friendship

___ 10. "Why the Tortoise's Shell Is Not Smooth" is a folk tale that teaches a lesson. Which of these sentences best states the lesson in the story?
   A. A trickster may end up paying for his tricks.
   B. Hard work and patience are always rewarded.
   C. Never judge a person by his or her appearance.
   D. Everyone respects a person who is a smooth talker.

Vocabulary and Grammar

___ 11. Which of the following sentences about "Why the Tortoise's Shell Is Not Smooth" uses an italicized vocabulary word <u>incorrectly</u>?
   A. Because of the *famine,* everyone had enough to eat.
   B. Everyone went hungry during the *famine.*
   C. The birds loved to listen to fine speeches given by an *orator.*
   D. Tortoise was an *eloquent* speaker who was good at convincing listeners.

____ 12. An antonym is a word that means the opposite of another word. What is the antonym of *empty*, as in *an empty stomach*?

    A. sad

    B. plenty

    C. full

    D. lost

____ 13. Which sentence uses an italicized Academic Vocabulary word <u>incorrectly</u>?

    A. Reading will *enable* you to broaden your vocabulary.

    B. *Adapt* and narrow your search to find specific information.

    C. Previewing the text helps you *establish* a purpose for reading.

    D. When you read with a *purpose,* you get more confused.

____ 14. Which of the following sentences uses all of the commas correctly?

    A. They ate, soup, meat fish, and yams.

    B. They ate soup, meat, fish, and yams.

    C. They ate soup, meat, fish and yams.

    D. They ate soup, tasted the meat, and fish, and ate the yams.

Essay

15. In "Why the Tortoise's Shell Is Not Smooth," all of the characters are animals. The storyteller gives the animals human qualities. In an essay, identify the human qualities in Tortoise and the birds. Then tell how the story would have been different if the storyteller had used *human* characters instead of animals.

16. In "Why the Tortoise's Shell Is Not Smooth," the birds believe Tortoise when he tells them that everyone needs to take a new name for the feast. In an essay, tell whether you would have believed Tortoise about the need to take a new name. What would you have said and done that might have led to a happier ending to the story? If the story did have a happy ending, what else would be different about the story?

17. **Thinking About the Big Question: How much should our communities shape us?** Think about what happens to Tortoise. He is shaped by his community—the birds' actions give him his bumpy shell. Did the birds treat Tortoise badly, or did he get what he deserved? In an essay, discuss whether you think what happens to Tortoise is fair. Use details from the story to support your answer.

"Why the Tortoise's Shell Is Not Smooth" by Chinua Achebe
Selection Test B

Critical Reading *Identify the letter of the choice that best completes the statement or answers the question.*

_____ 1. The title and pictures in "Why the Tortoise's Shell Is Not Smooth" suggest that the text is
   A. a mystery story.
   B. a scientific article.
   C. a true story.
   D. a folk tale.

_____ 2. Reading the title of "Why the Tortoise's Shell Is Not Smooth" is part of what process?
   A. identifying where the text came from
   B. previewing the text
   C. deciding if the text is poetry or prose
   D. reviewing the text

_____ 3. Before you read "Why the Tortoise's Shell Is Not Smooth," the purpose you set for reading is
   A. to learn facts about turtles.
   B. to find out what you can do to protect an endangered species.
   C. to read for enjoyment.
   D. to understand the importance of speaking skills.

_____ 4. Which beginning of a paragraph from "Why the Tortoise's Shell Is Not Smooth" gives you the best idea about the kind of story it will be?
   A. Low voices, broken now and again by singing, reached Okonkwo. . . .
   B. "Once upon a time," she began, "all the birds were invited to a feast in the sky."
   C. "You do not know me," said Tortoise. "I am a changed man."
   D. He began to eat and the birds grumbled angrily.

_____ 5. In "Why the Tortoise's Shell Is Not Smooth," the animals are given human qualities. This strategy is called
   A. fictionalization.
   B. personification.
   C. imagination.
   D. tradition.

_____ 6. Which detail suggests Tortoise's mastery of speaking skills?
   A. Nothing that happened in the world of the animals ever escaped his notice. . . .
   B. . . . he went to the birds and asked to be allowed to go with them.
   C. His body rattled like a piece of dry stick in his empty shell.
   D. Tortoise had a sweet tongue. . . .

____ 7. The birds believe Tortoise's lies because
   A. they are too trusting.
   B. he has always told the truth before.
   C. they don't know anyone who lies.
   D. they feel sorry for him.

____ 8. Tortoise asks the birds to call him *All of You.* Based on what happens at the feast, you know that Tortoise is showing the human trait of
   A. cleverness.
   B. courtesy.
   C. arrogance.
   D. foolishness.

____ 9. The birds become angry at Tortoise because
   A. he says he is more beautiful than they are.
   B. he steals their eggs.
   C. he tricks them into crowning him king.
   D. he eats most of the food at the feast.

____ 10. The characters in "Why the Tortoise's Shell Is Not Smooth" act like humans, but they are still animals. Which quotation shows *both* human and animal qualities combined in one character?
   A. Some of them were too angry to eat.
   B. He asked the birds to take a message for his wife, but they all refused.
   C. Parrot promised to deliver the message, and then flew away.
   D. And then like the sound of his cannon he crashed on the compound.

____ 11. Tortoise jumps out of the sky because
   A. he has eaten enough and is ready to go home.
   B. he thinks that the birds have taught him to fly.
   C. he thinks his wife has created a soft landing for him.
   D. he has wings made of one feather from each bird.

____ 12. What human traits does Parrot show in "Why the Tortoise's Shell Is Not Smooth"?
   A. responsibility and patience
   B. loyalty and friendship
   C. intelligence and envy
   D. anger and deception

____ 13. Which sentence best describes the lesson in "Why the Tortoise's Shell Is Not Smooth"?
   A. A trickster may get tricked in return.
   B. Hard work is often rewarded.
   C. No one likes a smooth talker.
   D. Never judge a book by its cover.

____ 14. "Why the Tortoise's Shell Is Not Smooth" is a part of oral tradition. Which of these also is oral tradition?
A. a play based on a popular detective story
B. a novel written in the 1800s
C. a jump-rope rhyme chanted by children
D. a cartoon in today's newspaper

____ 15. The story of Tortoise and the birds explains
A. how to treat animals.
B. one small part of nature.
C. a scientific matter.
D. animal relationships.

Vocabulary and Grammar

____ 16. Which sentence uses a vocabulary word <u>incorrectly</u>?
A. Bad weather caused a *famine* in much of the world.
B. There was no food during the *famine.*
C. The *orator* spoke softly and not very well.
D. An *eloquent* speech can change people's minds.

____ 17. The antonym of *smooth* is
A. bumpy.   B. soft.   C. polished.   D. flat.

____ 18. Which sentence uses one or more Academic Vocabulary words <u>incorrectly</u>?
A. When you read with a *focus,* you are reading with a *purpose.*
B. Reading with a *purpose* will *enable* you to read more effectively.
C. A *purpose* will let you *establish* missing details in a text.
D. You can *adapt* a computer search by changing the key words.

____ 19. Which sentence uses commas correctly?
A. Tortoise, and the birds flew off to the feast in the sky.
B. He was full of kola nuts, soup, meat, fish and yams.
C. He fell, and fell, and fell, until he began to fear, that he would never stop falling.
D. She brought out his hoes, machetes, spears, guns, and even his cannon.

Essay

20. The animal characters in "Why the Tortoise's Shell Is Not Smooth" are personified; that is, the storyteller has given them human characteristics. Write an essay in which you identify the human qualities in Tortoise, the birds, Parrot, and Tortoise's wife. Tell which of the characters seems most human to you, and why. Support your answer with details from the story.

21. Write an essay in which you explain why you think it is important for writers and scholars to collect and preserve traditional tales such as "Why the Tortoise's Shell Is Not Smooth." Support your reasons with examples from the story.

22. **Thinking About the Big Question: How much should our communities shape us?** Think about what happens to Tortoise. He is literally shaped by his community. Did the community of the birds go too far? In an essay, discuss whether you think what happens to Tortoise is fair. Use details from the story to support your answer.

Vocabulary Warm-up Word Lists

Study these words from "He Lion, Bruh Bear, and Bruh Rabbit." Then, complete the activities that follow.

Word List A

awhile [uh WYL] *adv.* for a short time
  After looking through the bookstore <u>awhile</u>, Sheila went home.

dangerous [DAYN jer uhs] *adj.* likely to cause harm or injury
  It was <u>dangerous</u> to drive on the icy road.

distance [DIS tuhns] *n.* the amount of space between two places
  Steve walked the <u>distance</u> between school and his home.

drags [DRAGZ] *v.* pulls something along the ground
  The wounded dog <u>drags</u> its hurt leg along the ground.

fellow [FEL loh] *n.* a man or boy
  Most people thought that Louis was a very nice <u>fellow</u>.

lair [LAIR] *n.* a place where a wild animal rests and sleeps
  The fox returned to his <u>lair</u> after a day of hunting.

thunder [THUHN der] *n.* the loud, rumbling sound after lightning
  During the storm, lighting flashed and <u>thunder</u> rumbled.

whatever [hwut EV er] *pron.* anything or any
  Alex enjoyed the summers because he could do <u>whatever</u> he wanted to.

Word List B

anyhow [EN ee how] *adv.* no matter what the situation is
  Jackie didn't want to go to soccer practice <u>anyhow</u>.

figured [FIG yuhrd] *v.* understood or solved
  Aaron <u>figured</u> out how to solve the riddle.

hare [HAIR] *n.* a large wild rabbit with strong back legs
  The <u>hare</u> hopped through the field.

mumble [MUHM buhl] *v.* to speak quietly and unclearly
  Alicia thought she heard her friend <u>mumble</u> something softly.

ninety [NYN tee] *n.* the whole number between 89 and 91
  Pablo's grandfather is <u>ninety</u> years old.

scrawny [SCRAW nee] *adj.* unhealthily thin or small
  When Anna saw the <u>scrawny</u> kitten, she wanted to feed it.

sunshine [SUHN shyn] *n.* the light from the sun
  Anna loved to sit in the <u>sunshine</u> on bright days.

thicket [THIK it] *n.* a dense growth of plants, bushes, or small trees
  The mouse crawled among the plants in the <u>thicket</u>.

Name _____   Date _____

"He Lion, Bruh Bear, and Bruh Rabbit" by Virginia Hamilton
Vocabulary Warm-up Exercises

Exercise A *Fill in each blank in the paragraph below with an appropriate word from Word List A. Use each word only once.*

As a young man, Ricardo was the type of [1] _____ who always enjoyed an adventure. He liked to hike in the woods by himself, even though he knew this could be [2] _____. Once, he became lost in the woods for quite [3] _____. It started to rain, and lightning and [4] _____ filled the sky. Soon he found himself standing next to the [5] _____ of a wild animal. "Wow," he thought. "What if I'm standing here when that animal [6] _____ its prey home for dinner? It won't be very happy to see me." Ricardo knew that he needed to do [7] _____ it took to get out of the woods. So he began walking. He walked a great [8] _____. Finally, he found his way home.

Exercise B *Decide whether each statement below is true or false. Circle T or F, and then explain your answers.*

1. A riddle that has been <u>figured</u> out needs to be solved.
   T / F _____

2. When you <u>mumble</u>, you speak softly and are hard to understand.
   T / F _____

3. <u>Ninety</u> is a smaller number than one hundred.
   T / F _____

4. A <u>hare</u> has wings and a long tail.
   T / F _____

5. A <u>scrawny</u> animal is large and muscular.
   T / F _____

6. If you do something <u>anyhow</u>, you must not want to do it at all.
   T / F _____

7. A <u>thicket</u> is filled with closely growing plants.
   T / F _____

8. A day with lots of <u>sunshine</u> is bright and warm.
   T / F _____

Name _____ Date _____

Read the following passage. Pay special attention to the underlined words. Then, read it again, and complete the activities. Use a separate sheet of paper for your written answers.

Black bears live throughout North America. They live in forests from Mexico to Canada. Most bears live in national parks. There, they are protected from hunters and other humans.

Black bears eat a mixture of fruit, nuts, acorns, and meat. These bears will generally eat <u>whatever</u> food they can find. They search through the woods and will eat anything that they can. Often, bears will follow the smell of food to campsites. Black bears have surprised more than one <u>fellow</u> as they enter a man's tent, searching for food.

Many people believe that black bears are <u>dangerous</u> animals, but this is not really true. Most bears are not actually likely to harm people. A black bear will attack only if it is threatened. An angry bear will let out a booming roar. This shout can be so loud that it sounds like <u>thunder</u>.

Most bears hibernate during the winter. During this time, a bear will sleep for months, but it will wake up and leave its home for <u>awhile</u> every few days. It is important for the bear to move around for these short periods of time. A bear will sleep in its <u>lair</u>. This home may be created out of the hollow in a tree. It may also be created out of a group of logs that a bear <u>drags</u> together into a pile.

Adult black bears are excellent swimmers. In fact, one black bear was recorded swimming the <u>distance</u> of nine miles in the Gulf of Mexico. Bears can also run as fast as thirty miles an hour. Bears have an extremely sensitive smelling ability. Also, their sense of hearing is twice as strong as humans'.

Today, many black bear habitats are threatened as humans move into the forests where bears live. Hopefully, people will respect the territory of North American black bears and the animals will be allowed to thrive.

1. Underline the words that explain the meaning of <u>whatever</u>. Then, use *whatever* in a sentence.

2. Circle the words that tell why bears have surprised a <u>fellow</u> or two. Then, define *fellow* in your own words.

3. Circle the sentence that tells you why black bears are not <u>dangerous</u>. What is something that you know is *dangerous*?

4. Underline the words that describe the word <u>thunder</u>. Then, use the word *thunder* in a sentence.

5. Underline the words that tell you what <u>awhile</u> means. What is something that you would like to do for *awhile*?

6. Circle the nearby word with a meaning similar to <u>lair</u>. Then, define *lair* in your own words.

7. Circle the words that tell you what a bear <u>drags</u> to make its home. Then, write a sentence using the word *drags*.

8. Circle the words that tell what <u>distance</u> the bear swam. Then write a sentence with the word *distance*.

Name _____   Date _____

"He Lion, Bruh Bear, and Bruh Rabbit" by Virginia Hamilton
Reading Warm-up B

Read the following passage. Pay special attention to the underlined words. Then, read it again, and complete the activities. Use a separate sheet of paper for your written answers.

Jessica was happy to be outside in the warmth of the sunshine. The weather had been good all summer and the light from the sun had helped her garden grow. Jessica looked over her garden with pride. The peppers were ripening and the lettuce was almost ready to be eaten. The tomato plants had produced a bumper crop this year, and Jessica lovingly counted the number of fruits growing on the vines. There were actually ninety tomatoes in the garden! She remembered how happy she had been when she saw the first tomato. She couldn't believe that she was only ten shy of a hundred tomatoes now.

The only problem with the garden was the thicket right next to it. The dense growth of plants and bushes was home to a number of animals that often figured out how to get into the garden. It didn't seem to matter what kind of fence Jessica put around her garden. The animals always found their way inside.

While Jessica was weeding around the tomatoes, a hare jumped over the fence. It started to eat the lettuce. When Jessica first saw the hare, she could barely believe the size of the large, rabbit-like animal. Soon, another hare jumped from the thicket over the fence and into the garden. This one was smaller and so thin it looked downright scrawny.

Jessica started to shout, thinking the noise would frighten the hares away. Strangely, they were not frightened by the noise. They just kept on eating anyhow. The hares seemed determined to keep eating no matter how loud Jessica was.

Jessica was just as determined to protect her plants from being eaten by these unwelcome visitors. She stood up and ran towards the two hares, and they ran away as she got closer. When they had finally gone, she started to mumble to herself. "Good riddance!" she said softly, under her breath.

1. Underline the words that tell what sunshine is. Then use the word *sunshine* in a sentence.

2. Circle the words that explain how many ninety is. Then, write a sentence with the word *ninety*.

3. Underline the words that tell what a thicket is. Describe a *thicket* in your own words.

4. Underline the words that tell what the animals figured out. Then, use the word *figured* in a sentence.

5. Circle the words that tell you what the hare did. Then, define *hare* in your own words.

6. Underline the words that explain the word scrawny. What is something you would describe as *scrawny*?

7. Underline the words that explain why the hares kept eating anyhow. Then use the word *anyhow* in a sentence.

8. Circle the words that describe the word mumble. Define *mumble* in your own words.

"He Lion, Bruh Bear, and Bruh Rabbit" by Virginia Hamilton
Writing About the Big Question

How much do our communities shape us?

Big Question Vocabulary

common	community	connection	culture	family
generation	group	history	influence	involve
isolate	participation	support	values	belief

A. *Use one or more words from the list above to complete each sentence.*

1. Because Sandra had very good judgment but didn't talk very much, whatever she did say always had a lot of _____ among her friends.

2. Stefan was the oldest and hardest-working of six brothers, and all the members of his _____ knew they could always count on him.

3. My Aunt Charlotte became prominent in her _____ when she organized a food drive, and later on she was elected to the school board.

4. Rachel often became the second-in-command in any organization she joined because she preferred not to be the one in charge, but she did like to _____ other people's ideas.

B. *Follow the directions in responding to each of the items below.*

1. List two times when you asked for advice.

   _____.

   _____.

2. Write two sentences describing one of the preceding experiences. Tell what happened, what you learned, and how you felt about it. Use at least two of the Big Question vocabulary words.

   _____

   _____

C. *Complete the sentence below. Then, write a short paragraph in which you connect this experience to the Big Question.*

   If I had to classify myself as a leader or a follower, I would say that I am a _____ because _____

   _____

   _____

   _____

"He Lion, Bruh Bear, and Bruh Rabbit" by Virginia Hamilton

Reading: Preview the Text to Set a Purpose for Reading

Your **purpose** for reading is the reason you read a text. Sometimes, you may choose a text based on a purpose you already have. Other times, you may set a purpose based on the kind of text you have in front of you. **Setting a purpose** helps you focus your reading. You might set a purpose to learn about a subject, to gain understanding, to take an action, or simply to read for enjoyment.

Preview the text before you begin to read. Look at the title, the pictures, and the beginnings of paragraphs to get an idea about the literary work. This will help you set a purpose or decide if the text will fit a purpose you already have.

DIRECTIONS: *Answer the following questions as you preview "He Lion, Bruh Bear, and Bruh Rabbit." You can use questions like these as you preview any text.*

1. Look at the title. What ideas or feelings do you have about the title? _____

   _____

2. Who is the author? What do you know about this author? _____

   _____

3. Look at any photographs, drawings, or artwork in the text. How does the artwork help you set a purpose for reading? _____

   _____

4. Read the beginning of several paragraphs in the text. What kind of text does this seem to be? _____

   _____

5. Think about the clues you picked up during your preview. What purpose will you set to help you focus your reading of this text? _____

   _____

"He Lion, Bruh Bear, and Bruh Rabbit" by Virginia Hamilton
Literary Analysis: Personification

Personification is the representation of an animal or an object as if it had a human personality, intelligence, or emotions. In folk literature, personification is often used to give human qualities to animal characters. The actions of these animal characters can show human qualities, behavior, and problems in a humorous way.

DIRECTIONS: *As you read, think about the human and animal qualities shown by the lion, the bear, and the rabbit in the story. Next to each name below, write two of that character's animal qualities on the lines at the left and two of that character's human qualities on the lines at the right.*

Animal Qualities   **Human Qualities**

_____   _____

_____   1. He Lion   _____

_____   _____

_____   2. Bruh Bear   _____

_____   _____

_____   3. Bruh Rabbit   _____

Name _____ Date _____

Vocabulary Builder

Word List

    cordial   lair   olden   peaceable   scrawny   thicket

A. DIRECTIONS: *Write your answer on the lines following each item. Use complete sentences for each answer.*

1. Give an example of a *cordial* comment you might make to someone.

   _____

   _____

2. What is one creature you might find in a *lair*?

   _____

3. How would someone who is <u>peaceable</u> act during an argument?

   _____

4. Why would a <u>thicket</u> be a good place to hide?

   _____

5. How could a <u>scrawny</u> person change his appearance?

   _____

6. What are people's memories of <u>olden</u> times like?

   _____

B. DIRECTIONS: *Think about the meaning of the italicized vocabulary words and answer the questions. Use the vocabulary word in your answer.*

1. Imagine that you are walking in the woods and you find a *lair*. What would you do?

   _____

   _____

2. Imagine that you are camping in the woods. There is a bear outside your tent. How *cordial* would you be in greeting the bear? Why? What would you do?

   _____

   _____

C. WORD STUDY: The suffix *-en-* means "to become, to cause to be, or to be made of." Change each of the italicized words in parentheses to a word that ends in *-en*.

1. As I heard the words of praise, I felt my face *(red)* _____

2. As they grew tired, their efforts started to *(weak)* _____

3. Movies set in graveyards always *(fright)* me. _____

Name _____ Date _____

"He Lion, Bruh Bear, and Bruh Rabbit" by Virginia Hamilton
Enrichment: Telling a Story

Virginia Hamilton's story uses the kind of language that the original tellers of the tale might have used. **Dialect** is the special variation of language spoken by people of a particular region or group. Virginia Hamilton uses words and phrases that help you imagine how early African American storytellers spoke. For example, she uses "Bruh" instead of "Brother." She begins her story with "Say that he Lion would get up each and every mornin" instead of "Mr. Lion woke up every morning."

DIRECTIONS: *Tell a folk tale to an audience. To begin, think about a folk tale that you have heard at home or in your community. If you can't come up with a story you have heard, find a folk tale in the book section for young children at a library. Try to find a tale that includes clever dialogue with some use of dialect, interesting characters, vivid language, and some humor. Write your answers to the following questions on the lines provided.*

1. What is the title of your story? (You may need to make up a title.)

   _____

2. What happens in the story?

   _____

   _____

   _____

   _____

3. What words and phrases will help listeners know how the original tellers of the tale spoke?

   _____

   _____

Practice telling your story in front of a mirror or by retelling it several times to a friend or family member. You may need notes the first or second time, but you should eventually be able to tell the story without notes. Remember that you don't need to memorize the story exactly as it was written. When you present a story orally, use the most exciting or interesting events. Tell them in a way that will entertain your listeners. Change the tone and loudness of your voice. Try speaking in different voices when you say the words of the various characters. Use hand gestures that will help dramatize the story.

When you are ready to present your story, tell it to an audience. If possible, tell it to a group of younger children in your school.

"He Lion, Bruh Bear, and Bruh Rabbit" by Virginia Hamilton
"Why the Tortoise's Shell Is Not Smooth" by Chinua Achebe
Integrated Language Skills: Grammar

Punctuation: Commas

A **comma** is a punctuation mark used to separate words or groups of words. Commas signal readers when to pause. They also help prevent confusion in meaning. One important use for commas is to separate items in a series—three or more items written one after the other.

Words in a series: In February we saw sparrows, blue jays, and cardinals in the garden.

Phrases in a series: Before I leave for school, I have to feed the cats, take the dog for a walk, put birdseed out for the birds, and take the garbage to the garbage can.

A. Practice: *Insert commas where they belong in the following sentences.*

1. Bears rabbits wild pigs and foxes are all creatures of the forest.

2. They came out of the woods crept closer to the farmhouse and scared away the cat.

3. We drove to the park the river my school and the store before we came home.

B. Writing Application: *Write three sentences that tell about things you do on the weekend. In every sentence, use correctly punctuated words or phrases in a series.*

_____

_____

_____

_____

_____

_____

_____

_____

_____

_____

_____

_____

_____

150

"Why the Tortoise's Shell Is Not Smooth" by Chinua Achebe
"He Lion, Bruh Bear, and Bruh Rabbit" by Virginia Hamilton
Support for Writing an Invitation

Use the graphic organizer below to record details for an invitation to a gathering described in one of these stories. Review the story to find details you can use. Begin your invitation with a paragraph that describes the purpose of the gathering. Make up additional details, such as time and date, that are not provided in the story. You may also want to add artwork that you can copy when you create your invitation.

Come to _____

Purpose: _____

_____

_____

_____

Place: _____

Date: _____

Time: _____

Now create your invitation.

Name _____   Date _____

"Why the Tortoise's Shell Is Not Smooth" by Chinua Achebe
"He Lion, Bruh Bear, and Bruh Rabbit" by Virginia Hamilton
Support for Extend Your Learning

Listening and Speaking: "Why the Tortoise's Shell Is Not Smooth"

To prepare for your dramatic reading, list the person in your group who will read each part. If possible, ask your teacher to make copies of the text so each student can mark up his or her own copy to show who will say which words and how the words should be said. You may want to have three group members read together as the birds.

Ekwefi the storyteller (reads the parts that are not dialogue): _____

The Birds: _____

Tortoise: _____

Answer the following questions about the part you will be reading.

What are the most important lines I have? _____

_____

How should I say them? _____

_____

Which words should I stress for effect? _____

_____

Listening and Speaking: "He Lion, Bruh Bear, and Bruh Rabbit"

To prepare for your dramatic reading, list the person in your group who will read each part. If possible, ask your teacher to make copies of the text so each student can mark up his or her own copy to show who will say which words and how the words should be said.

Narrator (reads the parts that are not dialogue): _____

He Lion: _____

Bruh Rabbit: _____

Bruh Bear: _____

Answer the following questions about the part you will be reading.

When should I speak loudly? _____

_____

When should I speak softly? _____

_____

Which words should I stress for effect? _____

_____

Name _____ Date _____

"He Lion, Bruh Bear, and Bruh Rabbit" by Virginia Hamilton
Open-Book Test

Short Answer *Write your responses to the questions in this section on the lines provided.*

1. When you preview a text, you set a purpose for reading. Explain what setting a purpose helps you do and what purpose you set for reading "He Lion, Bruh Bear, and Bruh Rabbit."

   _____

   _____

   _____

   _____

2. At the beginning of the story, the little animals ask Bruh Bear and Bruh Rabbit for help. Compare the two characters. Tell how they are alike and how they are different. Then, on the line below, tell why Bruh Rabbit is more helpful in solving the problem of he Lion.

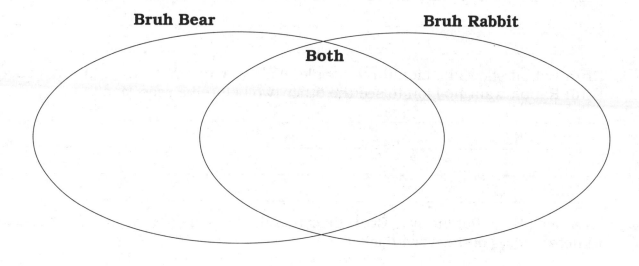

   _____

3. When Bruh Bear and Bruh Rabbit go to see he Lion, they act "cordial." Explain why they act this way. Use the meaning of *cordial* in your answer.

   _____

   _____

   _____

4. In the first half of "He Lion, Bruh Bear, and Bruh Rabbit," what human personality trait best describes he Lion? Explain your answer.

   _____

   _____

   _____

153

5. Which animal in "He Lion, Bruh Bear, and Bruh Rabbit" can be described as clever? Use details from the story to support your answer.

_____

_____

_____

6. In "He Lion, Bruh Bear, and Bruh Rabbit," animals are given human personality traits. Based on the story, what human traits are valued most? Explain, using support from the story.

_____

_____

_____

7. Why does Bruh Rabbit think that Man is the real king of the forest? Use details from the story to explain your answer.

_____

_____

8. Bruh Rabbit shows he Lion three people: Will Be, Once Was, and Man. Why does Bruh Rabbit want he Lion to see the other two before he sees Man?

_____

_____

_____

_____

9. Why does Bruh Rabbit drag Bruh Bear to a thicket when Man comes? Show your understanding of the word *thicket*.

_____

_____

_____

10. The author uses personification to give he Lion human qualities. Does he Lion have any animal qualities? Explain.

_____

_____

_____

Essay

Write an extended response to the question of your choice or to the question or questions your teacher assigns you.

11. All of the characters in "He Lion, Bruh Bear, and Bruh Rabbit" are personified—
    they are given human characteristics. Choose the character from the story that you
    find most human. In a brief essay, explain why you chose that character. Use
    details from the story to support your choice.

12. Choose the character that you admire most from "He Lion, Bruh Bear, and Bruh
    Rabbit." In a brief essay, explain why you chose that character. Be sure to describe
    the character's personality and explain what can be learned from the character.
    Use details from the story to support your answer.

13. Do you think "He Lion, Bruh Bear, and Bruh Rabbit" teaches it is better to be smart
    or better to be powerful? Answer the question in a brief essay. Use support from the
    selection, and explain whether you agree or disagree with the lesson.

14. **Thinking About the Big Question: How much do our communities shape us?**
    Consider how he Lion is shaped or changed by the community of animals. In a brief
    essay, explain what happens to he Lion and whether or not you think it is a good
    thing. Use details from the story.

Oral Response

15. Go back to question 2, 6, or 8 or to the question or questions your teacher assigns
    you. Take a few minutes to expand your answer and prepare your oral response.
    Find additional details in the story that support your points. If necessary, make
    notes to guide your oral response.

Name _____ Date _____

Selection Test A

Critical Reading *Identify the letter of the choice that best answers the question.*

____ 1. Before you read a text, you should set a purpose for reading. What does setting a purpose for reading "He Lion, Bruh Bear, and Bruh Rabbit" help you do?
A. It helps you focus your reading.
B. It helps you know what books to take home.
C. It helps you finish reading the story.
D. It helps you understand why some stories are better than others.

____ 2. In "He Lion . . . ," the animal characters are personified. That means that the animals have human qualities. What kind of person would you say he Lion is most like?
A. someone who is cruel but smart
B. someone who is gentle and kind
C. someone who is conceited and boastful
D. someone who is everybody's friend

____ 3. In "He Lion . . . ," why is Bruh Rabbit not afraid of he Lion?
A. Bruh Rabbit has a gun.
B. Bruh Rabbit has more friends.
C. Bruh Rabbit knows how to handle he Lion.
D. Bruh Rabbit is meaner than he Lion.

____ 4. In "He Lion . . . ," how do all the animals think and behave?
A. like dangerous wild animals
B. like different kinds of people
C. like house pets
D. like criminals

____ 5. In "He Lion . . . ," previewing the text helps set a purpose for reading. You preview before you read to get an idea about the story you will read. What is one way to preview the text?
A. Read it quickly to younger students. Then ask them how they liked it.
B. Ask the teacher what it's about. Take notes on what he or she says.
C. Read the last paragraph of the story. See if you can guess what happened before it.
D. Look at the title. See what ideas and feelings you get about the story from the title.

_____ 6. In "He Lion . . . ," what human characteristic does Bruh Rabbit show?
   A. cleverness
   B. nervousness
   C. bossiness
   D. gentleness

_____ 7. In "He Lion . . . ," when he Lion meets Man, what happens?
   A. He Lion attacks and kills Man.
   B. He Lion scares away Man.
   C. He Lion roars and Man shoots him.
   D. He Lion and Man become friends.

_____ 8. As a result of what happens in "He Lion . . . ," what does he Lion learn to be?
   A. more clever and careful
   B. more cruel and patient
   C. more modest and humble
   D. more generous and friendly

_____ 9. In "He Lion . . . ," what does Bruh Bear learn by the end of the story?
   A. how to climb a tree
   B. where he Lion's lair is
   C. how to handle he Lion
   D. what Man looks like

_____ 10. Why might storytellers have handed down the story of "He Lion . . . "?
   A. to warn people to stay out of the forest
   B. to prove that the rabbit is king of the forest
   C. to amuse people while teaching that being too proud is dangerous
   D. to show people that it's important to shoot lions before they attack

Vocabulary and Grammar

_____ 11. An antonym is a word that is the opposite in meaning of another word. For example, *night* is the antonym of *day*. In this sentence, what is an antonym for the underlined word?

"I know lots," said Bruh Bear, <u>slow</u> and quiet-like.

   A. quick
   B. weak
   C. tired
   D. loud

___ **12.** Which sentence about "He Lion . . ." uses an italicized vocabulary word <u>incorrectly</u>?

    A. The lion slept soundly in his *lair*.

    B. Bruh Bear climbed up a *lair* when he Lion roared.

    C. The rabbit greeted each animal with a *cordial* smile.

    D. Man was not *cordial* or kind when he met he Lion.

___ **13.** Which sentence uses an Academic Vocabulary word <u>incorrectly</u>?

    A. Setting a *purpose* makes you a better reader.

    B. You may have to *adapt* your reading speed to find information.

    C. The *focus* of a preview is the conclusion of a story.

    D. Reading will *enable* you to increase your vocabulary.

___ **14.** Which sentence about "He Lion . . ." uses commas correctly?

    A. He Lion, Bruh Bear, and Bruh Rabbit are characters.

    B. The bear that rabbit, and the lion were friends.

    C. Squirrel leaped Possum played dead and he Lion, kept roaring.

    D. The bear, and the rabbit went off, together.

Essay

15. In "He Lion, Bruh Bear, and Bruh Rabbit," almost all the characters are animals. However, the animal characters are personified—they are given human qualities. Choose the animal character that seems most human to you. In an essay, explain why you chose that character. Give at least two examples of human qualities that the animal displays.

16. "He Lion, Bruh Bear, and Bruh Rabbit" is a folk tale that teaches a lesson. In an essay, tell how the storyteller answers this question: Is it better to be a very strong person or a very smart person? Then, tell whether or not you agree with the story. Support your opinion with at least one reason or example from the story or from your own life.

17. Thinking About the Big Question: How much should our communities shape us? Consider how he Lion is shaped or changed by the community of animals. In a brief essay, explain what happens to he Lion and whether you think it is a good thing. Use details from the story.

"He Lion, Bruh Bear, and Bruh Rabbit" by Virginia Hamilton
Selection Test B

Critical Reading *Identify the letter of the choice that best completes the statement or answers the question.*

_____ 1. When you look at the title of "He Lion, Bruh Bear, and Bruh Rabbit" before you begin to read the story, you are
A. previewing the text.
B. focusing on your experience.
C. deciding if you want to read more.
D. guessing who the author might be.

_____ 2. Which quotation from "He Lion . . ." shows the characters' human and animal qualities?
A. "Scare all the little animals so they were afraid to come outside in the sunshine."
B. "So they went to Bruh Bear and Bruh Rabbit."
C. "He'd seen enough not to be afraid of an old he Lion."
D. "Kept their distance. He watchin them and they watchin him. Everybody actin cordial."

_____ 3. In "He Lion . . . ," the human quality that he Lion best represents is
A. cruelty.
B. conceit.
C. trickery.
D. fear.

_____ 4. In "He Lion . . . ," Bruh Rabbit is not afraid of he Lion because
A. he has a secret weapon.
B. he has friends who will help him.
C. he knows how to handle him.
D. he knows that he Lion is not mean.

_____ 5. In "He Lion . . . ," he Lion wants to find Man because
A. Bruh Rabbit says Man is king of the forest.
B. Bruh Bear tells him Man is weak.
C. he wants to meet someone more intelligent.
D. he has never seen Man.

_____ 6. In "He Lion . . . ," Bruh Rabbit thinks that Man is the real king of the forest because Man is
A. more powerful than he Lion.
B. smarter than he Lion.
C. bigger than he Lion.
D. kinder than he Lion.

____ 7. The animals in "He Lion . . ." behave mostly
    A. like real animals.
    B. like people.
    C. in wild, uncivilized ways.
    D. in unpredictable ways.

____ 8. In "He Lion . . . ," Bruh Rabbit's most outstanding human characteristic is
    A. cleverness.
    B. eagerness.
    C. bossiness.
    D. gentleness.

____ 9. Bruh Rabbit lets he Lion meet Man face to face because
    A. he is hoping that Man will kill he Lion.
    B. he thinks that is the best way to teach he Lion a lesson he won't forget.
    C. there is not enough space in the thicket for he Lion to hide with them.
    D. he Lion is not as afraid of Man as he and Bruh Bear are.

____ 10. In "He Lion . . . ," what happens when he Lion meets Man?
    A. He Lion attacks and eats the man.
    B. He Lion roars and scares away the man.
    C. He Lion roars and the man shoots him with a gun.
    D. He Lion runs and hides in some bushes.

____ 11. In "He Lion . . . ," he Lion learns to be more
    A. modest.
    B. cautious.
    C. thrifty.
    D. generous.

____ 12. The reason why storytellers handed down "He Lion . . . " was to
    A. warn people about the dangers of living in the forest.
    B. show people that the lion is king of the forest.
    C. amuse people while teaching them that pride can be dangerous.
    D. show people that it's important to shoot lions before they can attack.

____ 13. The word that best describes the overall feeling of "He Lion . . ." is
    A. sad.
    B. amusing.
    C. mysterious.
    D. realistic.

____ 14. In "He Lion . . . ," the human qualities that are valued and admired are
    A. pride and strength.
    B. fair play and patience.
    C. athletic ability and good looks.
    D. intelligence and modesty.

Vocabulary and Grammar

___ 15. In "He Lion . . . ," the lion scares all the little animals with his roaring. The antonym of *roaring* is
A. booming.   C. whispering.
B. shouting.   D. laughing.

___ 16. Which sentence about "He Lion . . ." uses a vocabulary word <u>incorrectly</u>?
A. The lion had his *lair* up on the cliff where he was not easy to reach.
B. Bruh Bear scrambled up a *lair* when he Lion roared.
C. Bruh Rabbit greeted each animal with a warm and *cordial* smile.
D. Man was unkind and far from *cordial* in his treatment of he Lion.

___ 17. Which sentence uses at least one Academic Vocabulary word <u>incorrectly</u>?
A. Setting a *purpose* will *enable* you to read more effectively.
B. The *focus* of your reading may *enable* you to *adapt* the conclusion.
C. Using different key words can help you *adapt* your computer search.
D. You preview the text to *establish* a *purpose* for reading.

___ 18. Which sentence about "He Lion . . ." uses commas correctly?
A. The bear, and that rabbit went off through the forest to find he Lion.
B. Squirrel, leaped in the trees, Possum played dead, and he Lion kept roaring.
C. He Lion, Bruh Bear and Bruh Rabbit saw Man coming.
D. Every morning he Lion would get up, stretch, and walk around.

Essay

19. In "He Lion, Bruh Bear, and Bruh Rabbit," the animals are personified—they display human qualities. Write an essay in which you tell what kind of person each animal in the title represents. Then tell why you think it is or is not a good idea to use animal characters to teach human lessons. Support your opinion with details from the story.

20. "He Lion, Bruh Bear, and Bruh Rabbit," like many other folk tales, has two purposes: to entertain and also to teach an important lesson about life. Write an essay explaining how the story achieves both those purposes. Do you think humor is a good way to get a message across? Why or why not?

21. In an essay, explain how you previewed the text of "He Lion, Bruh Bear, and Bruh Rabbit." How did previewing the text help you set a purpose for reading? After you read the story, did you find that it was what you expected from your preview? Explain why it did or did not fit the purpose you had set.

22. **Thinking About the Big Question: How much should our communities shape us?** Consider how he Lion is shaped or changed by the community of animals. In a brief essay, explain what happens to he Lion and whether you think it is a good thing. Use details from the story.

Vocabulary Warm-up Word Lists

Study these words from "The Three Wishes." Then, complete the activities that follow.

Word List A

comfort [KUHM fert] *v.* to make someone feel better
The mother cuddled and tried to <u>comfort</u> her crying child.

forgiveness [fawr GIV nis] *n.* pardon for doing something wrong
I asked my brother's <u>forgiveness</u> after accidentally breaking his toy.

granted [GRAN tid] *v.* given
We were <u>granted</u> one more day by our teacher to finish our work.

kindness [KYND nis] *n.* niceness, caring
Matt showed <u>kindness</u> by lending his coat to the freezing girl.

knowledge [NAHL ij] *n.* understanding, information
Aaron used his <u>knowledge</u> of engines to fix the car.

reward [ri WAWRD] *n.* gift received for doing something good
The woman gave me a <u>reward</u> for returning her lost wallet.

scarcely [SKAIRS lee] *adv.* barely, hardly, just
I had <u>scarcely</u> folded up my umbrella when it began to rain again.

scolded [SKOHLD id] *v.* found fault with; spoke sharply to
The boss <u>scolded</u> all the workers for coming to work late.

Word List B

bestow [bee STOH] *v.* give
I hope that the future will <u>bestow</u> happiness upon you.

greed [GREED] *n.* desire to have more of something; selfishness
He grabbed every single piece of bacon; I've never seen such <u>greed.</u>

mere [MEER] *adj.* nothing more than; simple
Somehow, a <u>mere</u> boy was able to slay the monster.

nevertheless [nev er thuh LES] *adv.* in spite of this
The roads were icy, but we made it home safely <u>nevertheless.</u>

portion [PAWR shuhn] *n.* part, share, section, or serving
Lew's <u>portion</u> of the work was done, so he took the afternoon off.

poverty [PAHV er tee] *n.* the state of being poor
Tim grew up in <u>poverty</u>. Sometimes, he had very little to eat.

quarreled [KWAWR uhld] *v.* argued; had a fight
The two sisters <u>quarreled</u> over who could go first.

repentance [ri PENT uhns] *n.* sorrow for having done wrong
He showed <u>repentance</u> for his stinginess by donating money to charity.

Name _____ Date _____

"The Three Wishes" by Ricardo E. Alegría
Vocabulary Warm-up Exercises

Exercise A *Fill in each blank in the paragraph below with an appropriate word from Word List A. Use each word only once.*

During the summer I lived with my grandparents, I was always treated with

[1] _____. I [2] _____ missed my home, but when I did,

Grandma was quick to [3] _____ me. Grandpa spent hours sharing his

great [4] _____ of baseball. He rarely [5] _____ me,

even when I was bad. As long as I apologized, I was shown [6] _____

at once. One day, I found an important paper Grandpa had lost. He gave me a

[7] _____. I was [8] _____ a trip to the circus.

Exercise B *Decide whether each statement below is true or false. Circle T or F. Then, explain your answers.*

1. Sharing everything you have is an example of <u>greed</u>.
   T / F _____

2. It would be surprising if a <u>mere</u> boy became president.
   T / F _____

3. <u>Nevertheless</u> means "in spite of this."
   T / F _____

4. A spoonful is a very large <u>portion</u> of ice cream.
   T / F _____

5. People with a lot of money are living in <u>poverty</u>.
   T / F _____

6. It is impossible to show <u>repentance</u> if you've done nothing wrong.
   T / F _____

7. No one has ever <u>quarreled</u> with a friend.
   T / F _____

8. If you <u>bestow</u> a gift on someone, it's rude to ask for it back.
   T / F _____

"The Three Wishes" by Ricardo E. Alegría
Reading Warm-up A

Read the following passage. Pay special attention to the underlined words. Then, read it again, and complete the activities. Use a separate sheet of paper for your written answers.

Mel had worked on his model volcano for weeks, but it barely survived for a few minutes after he finished it. He had <u>scarcely</u> put on the final coat of paint when I destroyed it. I was trying to grab Mel's skateboard from a pile of boxes in his garage. One box fell down. It landed on Mel's volcano and smashed it into bits.

For a few minutes, I just stared at the ruined model. Mel was my best friend, and I had destroyed his work. His parents had given him the model as a <u>reward</u> for doing well in school.

When Mel walked in, he saw the box, the skateboard, and the volcano. He immediately realized what had happened. He could see I was upset by the horrified look on my face, so he tried to <u>comfort</u> me.

"It's just a model, Jared," he said in a tone full of <u>forgiveness</u>. "Don't worry about it."

Still, I felt terrible; I should have been the one trying to comfort him. When I returned home, I couldn't even do my homework. My mother <u>scolded</u> me and sent me to bed, but the <u>knowledge</u> that I had ruined Mel's model wouldn't let me sleep.

I got out of bed and looked inside my savings jar. My parents <u>granted</u> me an allowance of five dollars a week. Each week, I put the money they gave me inside the jar. I counted the money. It was almost a hundred dollars. The next day after school, I went straight to the hobby store. I had just enough to buy a volcano.

When I gave the new model to Mel, he thanked me for my <u>kindness</u>.

"Really, you didn't have to do it," he said. "It was lots of fun to build once, but this time will be even better!"

1. Underline the nearby word that has a similar meaning as <u>scarcely</u>. Then, write a sentence using the word *scarcely*.

2. Circle the words that explain why Mel got a <u>reward</u>. Then, tell what *reward* means.

3. Underline Mel's reason for trying to <u>comfort</u> Jared. Then, tell what *comfort* means.

4. Circle the words that tell what is full of <u>forgiveness</u>. Then, tell what *forgiveness* means.

5. Circle the words that explain why Jared is <u>scolded</u> by his mother. Then, use the word *scolded* in a sentence.

6. Underline the words that describe the <u>knowledge</u> that was upsetting Jared. Then, tell what *knowledge* is.

7. Circle the nearby word that has a similar meaning as <u>granted</u>. Then, use the word *granted* in a sentence.

8. Underline the words that tell what Mel did as a result of Jared's <u>kindness</u>. Then, tell what *kindness* means.

"The Three Wishes" by Ricardo E. Alegría
Reading Warm-up B

Read the following passage. Pay special attention to the underlined words. Then, read it again, and complete the activities. Use a separate sheet of paper for your written answers.

The theme of "three wishes" plays a large role in many fairy tales and folk tales. These stories come from different times and different places, but most have a lot in common. Usually, the main character is going through difficult times. He or she is living in complete <u>poverty</u>, with little food to eat or nowhere to live. Then in the darkest moment, a magical creature appears. This creature, perhaps a genie or a fairy, decides to <u>bestow</u> three wishes on the main character. Typically, these wishes can be used for anything. The main character can ask for food, money, gold, jewels, or whatever his or her heart desires.

This remarkable turn of events does not always result in happiness. Sometimes, the lucky character is overcome by <u>greed</u>, and the desire for too much wealth leads to ruin. In some stories, husbands and wives have <u>quarreled</u> over how to use the wishes. In others, characters have argued over who gets the bigger <u>portion</u> of any riches that result. Often, a character will "waste" a wish, using it for a <u>mere</u> trinket or something equally small.

Even worse, a character may harm a friend or loved one with one of the wishes. For example, a husband or wife is turned into an animal or object. This may occur by accident, or it may be done in anger. Afterwards, the character who did it is filled with <u>repentance</u>. To undo the harm, a second wish must be used. Now, three wishes are down to one.

A reader usually knows that something will go wrong with the wishes; <u>nevertheless</u>, it's fun to keep reading and learn the details. It's also enjoyable to put oneself in the character's place. A reader can spend a lot of time thinking: What would I do if I suddenly had three wishes?

1. Underline the words that explain what it's like to live in <u>poverty</u>. Then, write a sentence using the word.

2. Circle the words that tell what fairies or genies often <u>bestow</u>. Then, give a synonym for *bestow*.

3. Circle the nearby words that describe the meaning of <u>greed</u>. Then, use the word *greed* in a sentence.

4. Underline the words that tell what husbands and wives have <u>quarreled</u> over. Then, tell what *quarreled* means.

5. Rewrite the sentence with <u>portion</u>. Replace the word with its synonym.

6. Underline the words that describe what you are doing with a wish when you use it on a <u>mere</u> trinket. Then, write a sentence using the word *mere*.

7. Underline the words that explain who is filled with <u>repentance</u>. Then, use the word *repentance* in a sentence.

8. Circle the words that tell what is <u>nevertheless</u> fun to do. Then, use the word *nevertheless* in a sentence.

Name _____ Date _____

Writing About the Big Question

How much do our communities shape us?

Big Question Vocabulary

common	community	connection	culture	family
generation	group	history	influence	involve
isolate	participation	support	values	belief

A. *Use one or more words from the list above to complete each sentence.*

1. Meredith wanted to live in a less competitive society, in which people tended to _____ one another rather than compete with one another.

2. When Lonnie compared his age group to his parents' _____, he was surprised to see how many similarities there were.

3. T.J. liked literature courses that gave points for class _____, since he really enjoyed discussing the readings with other students.

4. When she planned her school's arts festival, Maggi displayed the exhibits to emphasize whenever there was a _____ between two artists' points of view.

B. *Follow the directions in responding to each of the items below.*

1. List two different times when you wished for something.

_____

_____

2. Write two sentences describing one of the preceding experiences. Tell whether you got your wish, what you learned, and how you felt about it. Use at least two of the Big Question vocabulary words.

_____

_____

C. *Complete the sentence below. Then, write a short paragraph in which you connect this experience to the Big Question.*

If I could make sure everyone knew one particular old story, it would be the story of _____ because _____

_____

_____

_____

_____

"The Three Wishes" by Ricardo E. Alegría
Reading: Adjust Your Reading Rate

Once you have set your purpose for reading, **adjust your reading rate** to help you accomplish that purpose. Specifically, you should adjust your reading rate by doing the following:

- When reading to remember information, your reaing rate should be slow and careful. Pause now and then to think about what you have read, and read difficult pages over again until you understand them. Descriptive passages with much detail should also be read slowly.
- When reading for enjoyment, you may read more quickly. Reading dialogue quickly imitates the flow of a conversation.

DIRECTIONS: *As you read "The Three Wishes," think about how you should adjust your reading rate for different sections of the folk tale. Complete the graphic organizer below by filling in passages that you read slowly, moderately, and quickly.*

Slowly	Moderately	Quickly
↓	↓	↓

"The Three Wishes" by Ricardo E. Alegría
Literary Analysis: Universal Theme

The theme of a literary work is its central idea or message about life or human nature. A **universal theme** is a message about life that is expressed regularly in many different cultures and time periods. Examples of universal themes include the importance of honesty, the power of love, and the danger of selfishness.

Look for a universal theme in a literary work by focusing on the story's main character, conflicts the character faces, changes he or she undergoes, and the effects of these changes. You can use a graphic organizer like the one shown to help you determine the universal theme.

DIRECTIONS: *Fill in the boxes with details from "The Three Wishes." What universal theme do the details of the story lead to?*

> **1. Main Character**
> _____
> _____

> **2. Conflicts Character Faces**
> _____
> _____

> **3. How Character Changes**
> _____
> _____

> **4. Effects or Meaning of Change**
> _____
> _____

> **5. Universal Theme**
> _____
> _____

"The Three Wishes" by Ricardo E. Alegría
Vocabulary Builder

Word List

  covetousness   embraced   greed   repentance   scarcely

A. DIRECTIONS: *Write a* **synonym** *for each vocabulary word. Use a thesaurus if you need one. Write a sentence that includes the synonym. Be sure that your sentence makes the meaning of the word clear.*

  Vocabulary word: gratitude

  Synonym: thankfulness

  Sentence: We expressed our thankfulness to those who had helped us during the fire.

1. Vocabulary word: **embraced**   Synonym: _____

   Sentence: _____

2. Vocabulary word: **greed**   Synonym: _____

   Sentence: _____

3. Vocabulary word: **covetousness**   Synonym: _____

   Sentence: _____

4. Vocabulary word: **scarcely**   Synonym: _____

   Sentence: _____

5. Vocabulary word: **repentance**   Synonym: _____

   Sentence: _____

B. WORD STUDY: The Latin root *-pen-* means pain or punishment. Rewrite each of the following statements containing a word based on this root to make it more logical.

1. I felt *repentant* because I had done something to help my friend.

   _____

2. The team cheered when the referee gave their star player a *penalty*.

   _____

3. The prisoner was given a longer sentence because he expressed *penitence* for his crime.

   _____

"The Three Wishes" by Ricardo E. Alegría
Enrichment: Creating a Wish Poster

Suppose that you get a visit from the old man in the story. He tells you that you have earned three wishes. You can wish for anything, but the old man suggests that you use at least one of your wishes for something that will have universal value—that is, something that might make the world a better place.

A. DIRECTIONS: *List below what you would wish for.*

1. _____

2. _____

3. _____

B. DIRECTIONS: *Now choose one of your wishes that has universal value. In the space below, design a poster that tells people about your wish. Use words, colors, and pictures that show what you wish for and what you and others could do to help make the wish come true.*

Name _____ Date _____

"The Three Wishes" by Ricardo E. Alegría
Open-Book Test

Short Answer *Write your responses to the questions in this section on the lines provided.*

1. How would you describe the first two wishes that the husband and wife make in "The Three Wishes"? Explain, using details from the story.

   _____

   _____

2. In "The Three Wishes," the woman and the man both react to the news about the wishes. What lesson do you learn from the way they react? Use details to explain.

   _____

   _____

   _____

3. In "The Three Wishes," the wife embraced the woodsman when he appeared. When in the story might he have embraced his wife? Your answer should demonstrate an understanding of the word *embraced*.

   _____

   _____

   _____

4. Reread the third wish in "The Three Wishes." Why could it be described as very clever?

   _____

   _____

   _____

5. What does the third wish made by the woodsman in "The Three Wishes" demonstrate? Support your answer with details from the story.

   _____

   _____

   _____

   _____

6. In "The Three Wishes," what might the woodsman have wished for as the third wish if he were acting out of greed? Your answer should reflect an understanding of the word *greed*.

   _____

   _____

7. Find a paragraph in "The Three Wishes" that seemed difficult the first time you read it. Name one way that adjusting your reading rate can help you better understand the text.

_____

_____

_____

8. A universal theme is a message about life that is shared by many cultures. What is the universal theme in "The Three Wishes"?

_____

_____

_____

9. What does "The Three Wishes" tell you about the value of children in the Puerto Rican culture? Explain, using details from the folk tale.

_____

_____

_____

10. Use the chart to show the husband's reaction to each wish in "The Three Wishes." Then, on the line below, tell at what point the husband understands the message of the story.

	Wish 1	Wish 2	Wish 3
Husband's Reaction			

_____

Essay

Write an extended response to the question of your choice or to the question or questions your teacher assigns you.

11. In "The Three Wishes," the conflict starts when the husband and wife are given the wishes. In an essay, tell who seems most affected by the conflict. Consider which character changes the most over the course of the story. Use details from the story to support your answer.

12. A universal theme is a message about life that is shared by many people. In a brief essay, explain the universal theme in "The Three Wishes" and how it connects to your own life. Use details from the story and from your life to support your answer.

13. Imagine it is twelve years after the old man appeared in "The Three Wishes." There is a knock at the door, and the couple's child, now twelve years old, opens the door to find the same old man. The man gives the boy three wishes. In an essay, tell what the boy wishes for. Consider what he has learned from his parents.

14. **Thinking About the Big Question: How much should our communities shape us?** What is your community's view of the importance of money and love? In an essay, explain what you see as your community, your community's view of love and money, and how you are shaped by it. Use details from "The Three Wishes" to support your ideas.

Oral Response

15. Go back to question 4, 8, or 9 or to the question your teacher assigns you. Take a few minutes to expand your answer and prepare an oral response. Find additional details in "The Three Wishes" that support your points. If necessary, make notes to guide your oral response.

"**The Three Wishes**" by Ricardo E. Alegría
Selection Test A

Critical Reading *Identify the letter of the choice that best answers the question.*

_____ 1. "The Three Wishes" is a folk tale from Puerto Rico. It shows what the people of Puerto Rico think is most important. According to the story, which of these four things do Puerto Ricans value most?

   A. love
   B. money
   C. work
   D. luck

_____ 2. In "The Three Wishes," why are the husband and wife given three wishes?

   A. The wife demands them as payment.
   B. They have been poor for too long.
   C. They have worked hard all their lives.
   D. They are always willing to share.

_____ 3. In "The Three Wishes," how do the husband and his wife use their first two wishes?

   A. They use them to help their friends.
   B. They waste them accidentally.
   C. They wish for money and for servants.
   D. They give them to the old man to use.

_____ 4. In "The Three Wishes," what does the husband's final wish show?

   A. He is jealous of his wife and wants ears to match hers.
   B. He is greedier than his wife and thinks he can get more wishes.
   C. He is sorry for what he has done and wants to be happy again.
   D. He is still angry with his wife and blames her for their problems.

_____ 5. In "The Three Wishes," the old man tells the couple they will receive the "greatest happiness a married couple could know." What is he talking about?

   A. extra wishes
   B. a baby
   C. more money
   D. a bigger house

___ 6. A universal theme is a message about life that is expressed in many different places and at different time periods. In "The Three Wishes," the universal theme is the lesson that the main characters in the story learn about life. Which of the following statements best tells the universal theme in this story?
  A. No one can predict the future, and it's foolish to try.
  B. Happiness comes from love, not from riches.
  C. It's better to be rich than to be poor.
  D. Never let a stranger into your home.

Vocabulary and Grammar

___ 7. Which sentence uses an italicized vocabulary word <u>incorrectly</u>?
  A. The wife lovingly *embraced* her husband.
  B. They kissed and *embraced* their child.
  C. The husband's *greed* was rewarded.
  D. *Greed* and selfishness cause sadness.

___ 8. Antonyms are words that have opposite meanings. Which of the following words is the closest antonym for the word *contrast*?
  A. compete   B. compare   C. difference   D. identify

___ 9. Which of the following sentences uses an Academic Vocabulary word <u>incorrectly</u>?
  A. Finding the universal theme helps you *establish* a story.
  B. *Adapt* your reading speed to your *purpose* for reading.
  C. Doing homework can *enable* you to do well in school.
  D. One *focus* for reading could be to enjoy a good story.

___ 10. Which of the following items shows the correct use of a colon?
  A. You need all those things: and more.
  B. What caused the earthquake:? Nobody knows.
  C. Warning; No trespassing!
  D. After 6:00 p.m., everyone goes home.

Essay

11. In "The Three Wishes," you see how having three wishes affects a poor couple. In an essay, tell how the couple feel about each other *before* they get the wishes. Then tell how they get into trouble with their first two wishes. What is the *final* wish? What does that last wish show about what is important to the couple?

12. **Thinking About the Big Question: How much do our communities shape us?** Think about your community. What does your community think about love and money? In an essay, compare your community's views on love and money to the views expressed in "The Three Wishes." Be sure to tell who is in your community, what they think about love and money, and what you think about their ideas. Use details from "The Three Wishes" for support.

Unit 6 Resources: Themes in Folk Literature

"**The Three Wishes**" by Ricardo E. Alegría
Selection Test B

Critical Reading *Identify the letter of the choice that best completes the statement or answers the question.*

_____ 1. Which detail from "The Three Wishes" shows qualities valued in Puerto Rican culture?
A. Poor as they were, they were always ready to share what little they had. . . .
B. . . . an old man came to the little house and said that he had lost his way. . . .
C. The desire for riches had turned his head, and he scolded his wife. . . .
D. No sooner had he said these words than the donkey ears disappeared.

_____ 2. In "The Three Wishes," the woodsman is angry with his wife because she
A. gave the old man their food.
B. wasted the first wish.
C. wished for him to have donkey ears.
D. did not let him make a wish.

_____ 3. In "The Three Wishes," the first two wishes the woman and her husband make are
A. cruel.
B. thoughtful.
C. mean-spirited.
D. accidental.

_____ 4. In "The Three Wishes," the last wish the woodsman makes shows that he
A. is as foolish as his wife.
B. is still angry with his wife.
C. loves his wife more than riches.
D. wants more and more riches.

_____ 5. At the end of "The Three Wishes," the couple is rewarded because
A. they have learned their lesson.
B. the old man knows they need money.
C. they still love each other.
D. they were generous to their guest.

_____ 6. To find the universal theme in "The Three Wishes," you need to focus on
A. its ideas about love and marriage.
B. what each character says to others.
C. the language in the text.
D. how the main character changes.

_____ 7. Which of the following best states the universal theme of "The Three Wishes"?
A. Money isn't everything, but it helps.
B. Happiness is more important than wealth.
C. Sharing what you have always earns you a big reward.
D. Think before you speak.

____ 8. How should you adjust your reading rate when reading dialogue in "The Three Wishes"?
  A. Read more slowly to be sure to understand every word.
  B. Read moderately as you would a descriptive passage with many details.
  C. Read more quickly to imitate the flow of a conversation.
  D. Use the same reading rate that you used for the rest of the folk tale.

Vocabulary and Grammar

____ 9. Which sentence uses an italicized vocabulary word <u>incorrectly</u>?
  A. The wife *embraced* her husband when he appeared in their little house.
  B. Generosity and *greed* earned the wife a reward for her kindness.
  C. Someone who acted out of *greed* might have wished for money.
  D. When a child was born to the couple, they lovingly *embraced* him.

____ 10. Antonyms are useful in writing because they
  A. are words that sound alike.
  B. help develop supporting details.
  C. can be used to show contrast.
  D. are words with almost the same meaning.

____ 11. Which sentence uses an Academic Vocabulary word <u>incorrectly</u>?
  A. Finding universal themes helps you *establish* the conflicts in the story.
  B. You can *adapt your reading speed* to your *purpose* for reading.
  C. Facts and details *enable* you to support your opinion.
  D. Setting a *purpose* for reading gives you a *focus* as you read.

____ 12. Which sentence uses one or more semicolons correctly?
  A. The husband and the wife lived together; in the little house.
  B. Some people wish for power; and others want servants.
  C. The wife served the old man bread; milk; and apples.
  D. You have one wish left; you may have anything you want.

Essay

13. In "The Three Wishes," the woodsman and his wife go through a life-changing experience. In an essay, tell how the couple is tested and what happens as a result of the test. Identify the universal theme in the story. Then explain how the universal theme relates to the way in which the major character in the story changes.

14. One purpose you may set for reading "The Three Wishes" is to make connections between the story and your own experience. In an essay, identify three connections that you can make between your own life and the ideas, values, or situations in the story.

15. **Thinking About the Big Question: How much do our communities shape us?** What is your community's view of the importance of money and love? In an essay, explain what you see as your community, your community's view of love and money, and how you are shaped by it. Use details from "The Three Wishes" to support your ideas.

Vocabulary Warm-up Word Lists

Study these words from "The Stone." Then, complete the activities that follow.

Word List A

astonishment [uh STON ish muhnt] *n.* great surprise or amazement
  On her first plane flight, Carmen felt <u>astonishment</u> at leaving the ground.

claim [KLAYM] *v.* to say something belongs to you
  Rajiv found a comic book and tried to <u>claim</u> it as his own.

clutched [KLUHCHT] *v.* held onto something tightly
  Dora <u>clutched</u> at her purse, hoping that no one would try to steal it.

flung [FLUHNG] *v.* threw something violently
  Michael <u>flung</u> the rock far out into the lake.

glee [GLEE] *n.* enjoyment and delight
  Nicole was filled with <u>glee</u> when she won the lead in the school play.

pouch [POWCH] *n.* a small leather or fabric bag
  Evan kept his coins in a <u>pouch</u>.

squinted [SKWINT id] *v.* half-closed one's eyes to see better
  Keisha <u>squinted</u> as she looked into the bright sun.

wits [WITS] *n.* the ability to think clearly and quickly
  Alex hoped to keep his <u>wits</u> about him during the exam.

Word List B

amazement [uh MAYZ muhnt] *n.* a strong feeling of wonder
  Maggie looked at the huge skyscraper with <u>amazement</u>.

cleverness [KLEV uhr nis] *n.* intelligence
  Tim showed off his <u>cleverness</u> by solving the difficult riddle.

feeble [FEE buhl] *adj.* very weak
  The old man was <u>feeble</u> and could barely walk without his cane.

heed [HEED] *v.* to pay close attention to something or someone
  Audrey will <u>heed</u> her parents' warning to come home before dark.

midst [MIDST] *n.* middle; center
  There was a small cottage in the <u>midst</u> of the forest.

reluctantly [ri LUHK tuhnt lee] *adv.* unwillingly or without enthusiasm
  Though he wanted to play outside, Steve <u>reluctantly</u> stayed in and studied.

revenge [ri VENJ] *n.* action taken to get back at someone
  Kara wanted to get <u>revenge</u> on the boy who stole her backpack.

ungrateful [uhn GRAYT fuhl] *adj.* not thankful or appreciative
  Craig did not want to seem <u>ungrateful</u>, so he wrote thank-you notes.

"The Stone" by Lloyd Alexander
Vocabulary Warm-up Exercises

Exercise A *Fill in each blank in the paragraph below with an appropriate word from Word List A. Use each word only once.*

Alexis [1] _____ down at the pavement, narrowing her eyes to see more clearly. Much to her great [2] _____, she saw a twenty-dollar bill on the ground. She wondered whose it was. Looking around the street, she tried to figure out who could have dropped the money. Seeing no one else around, and keeping her [3] _____ about her, she leaned down, grabbed the bill, and [4] _____ it in her hands. Unless someone came along to [5] _____ the bill, it was hers to keep. She was happy and laughed aloud with [6] _____. In her excitement, she [7] _____ her hat up in the air and caught it again. Then, she placed the money in the small [8] _____ that she used as a wallet.

Exercise B *Revise each sentence so that the underlined vocabulary word is used in a logical way. Be sure to keep the vocabulary word in your revision.*

Example: Dennis showed off his <u>cleverness</u> by giving the wrong answer to the question.
Dennis showed off his <u>cleverness</u> by giving the right answer to the question.

1. Kathy decided to <u>heed</u> her teacher's warning and do exactly what she was warned not to do.

   _____

2. The boat was in the <u>midst</u> of the ocean, miles away from water.

   _____

3. The <u>feeble</u> old man could run faster than anyone in the race.

   _____

4. The boy <u>reluctantly</u> went to the theater to see his favorite movie.

   _____

5. Fred wanted to get <u>revenge</u> on Jose for giving him a compliment.

   _____

6. The <u>ungrateful</u> girl thanked her parents for the present.

   _____

7. Doing the same things day in and day out filled Jill with <u>amazement</u>.

   _____

"**The Stone**" by Lloyd Alexander
Reading Warm-up A

Read the following passage. Pay special attention to the underlined words. Then, read it again, and complete the activities. Use a separate sheet of paper for your written answers.

Tyrell loved to look at strange rocks and stones. When a new store selling special rocks opened in town, he was filled with glee. His excitement and delight grew when he got the chance to visit the store.

Tyrell looked over the selection of stones. There were clear yellow rocks and hollow rocks that were crusted with gems on the inside. Tyrell's eyes landed on one special rock that was blue with flecks of gold running through it. Tyrell looked carefully at the rock. He squinted, narrowing his eyes to get a better look at its details.

Tyrell decided to claim this rock as his own. As he went to the cash register to buy it, the shopkeeper eyed him.

"You know this is an unusual stone," the shopkeeper said mysteriously. "It has special powers, and you must be careful with it."

Tyrell clutched the rock, holding it tightly in his fist. After he bought the stone, he placed it carefully in a small leather pouch.

The next day, Tyrell carried the bag with the rock to school. He looked at the stone during recess. To his astonishment, it seemed larger than before. He was shocked and amazed that the rock had grown.

Later in the day, Tyrell looked again at the stone and noticed that it had grown even bigger! Tyrell struggled to keep his wits about him. He needed to be able to think quickly and clearly about what was going on. This certainly was an unusual stone.

Tyrell thought hard. What if the strange stone kept growing? It might get too big to deal with. Tyrell decided to get rid of it now. He went down to the lake and flung the stone into the water with all his might. Tyrell thought the stone seemed to get bigger as it sailed away. He was relieved to see it gone. Strange stones were interesting, but he would settle for a normal stone next time.

1. Underline the words that explain the meaning of glee. What makes you feel *glee*?

2. Circle the words that tell how and why Tyrell squinted. Then, use *squinted* in a sentence.

3. Circle the words that tell you what claim means. Then, define *claim* in your own words.

4. Underline the words that explain what Tyrell did when he clutched the rock. Then, write a sentence with the word *clutched*.

5. Underline the words that describe the word pouch. Use the word *pouch* in a sentence.

6. Underline the words that tell you what astonishment means. Define *astonishment* in your own words.

7. Circle the words that explain the word wits. Have you needed to use your *wits* lately? Tell why.

8. Circle the words that describe how Tyrell flung the stone in the water. Then, use the word *flung* in a sentence.

"The Stone" by Lloyd Alexander
Reading Warm-up B

Read the following passage. Pay special attention to the underlined words. Then, read it again, and complete the activities. Use a separate sheet of paper for your written answers.

Irish folk legends are rich with the stories of imaginary creatures. Leprechauns are the most famous of these special beings. To this day in Ireland, people share stories about the small, fairy-like leprechauns. In these stories, leprechauns are merry creatures who like to play tricks on humans.

Leprechauns live in the <u>midst</u> of people. They hide within everyday places such as farmhouses and cellars. There are two types of leprechauns. The first are simply called leprechauns. They are cheerful and known for their <u>cleverness</u>. Their sharp thinking abilities, though, can sometimes become <u>feeble</u>. When a leprechaun becomes weak like this, he can be spotted by humans. The second type of leprechauns are called cluricauns. These creatures are troublemakers. They often seek <u>revenge</u> by stealing from humans if they feel that they have been wronged.

According to legend, each leprechaun has a treasure. In most cases, this treasure is a pot of gold. A person who kidnaps a leprechaun can take the pot of gold. Leprechauns <u>reluctantly</u> give up their treasure to humans. Because they are unwilling to part with their treasure, the leprechauns try to trick humans. Irish legends are filled with the stories of <u>ungrateful</u> people who have been fooled by leprechauns. Few people in these stories are thankful for the experience of meeting a leprechaun.

Many people in Ireland still <u>heed</u> the warnings about leprechaun trickery. They pay close attention to the old legends. The stories are so well-loved and well-told that people visiting Ireland from all around the world are filled with wonder and surprise when they hear the stories. The art of Irish storytelling often fills tourists with <u>amazement</u>.

1. Underline the sentence that explains how leprechauns live in the <u>midst</u> of people. Then, write a sentence using the word *midst*.

2. Circle the words that explain the word <u>cleverness</u>. Then, tell what defines *cleverness* in your own words.

3. Underline the nearby word with a meaning similar to <u>feeble</u>. Then, write a sentence using the word *feeble*.

4. Underline the words that tell you why leprechauns seek <u>revenge</u>. Write a sentence using the word *revenge*.

5. Circle the words that tell you why leprechauns <u>reluctantly</u> give up their treasure. Have you done anything *reluctantly* lately?

6. Underline the nearby word that means the opposite of <u>ungrateful</u>. Then, define *ungrateful*.

7. Underline the words that explain <u>heed</u>. Then use the word *heed* in a sentence.

8. Circle the words that explain what <u>amazement</u> is. Use *amazement* in a sentence.

Name _____ Date _____

Writing About the Big Question

How much do our communities shape us?

Big Question Vocabulary

common	community	connection	culture	family
generation	group	history	influence	involve
isolate	participation	support	values	belief

A. *Use one or more words from the list above to complete each sentence.*

1. Emilio's father wanted to move to a new town to shorten his commute, but he worried about the effect of the move on his wife and children, who had strong ties to the _____.

2. When Raina tried out for her school's sketch-comedy team, she didn't think about how her new activity would _____ her from her old friends.

3. When Josh wrote an offbeat, funny story for his class, he had no idea that his story would _____ his classmates to see him as a comic genius.

4. Dania finally saw a _____ between her reading and her choice of friends when she realized that she was drawn to people who reminded her of certain characters.

B. *Follow the directions in responding to each of the items below.*

1. List two different times when a goal of yours conflicted with what someone else wanted.

_____.

_____.

2. Write two sentences describing one of the preceding experiences. Tell whether you got your wish, what you learned, and how you felt about it. Use at least two of the Big Question vocabulary words.

_____

_____

C. *Complete the sentence below. Then, write a short paragraph in which you connect this experience to the Big Question.*

If I could make one wish come true for my life, I would want _____ because _____

_____

_____

_____.

182

"The Stone" by Lloyd Alexander
Reading: Adjust Your Reading Rate

Once you have set your purpose for reading, **adjust your reading rate** to help you accomplish that purpose. Specifically, you should adjust your reading rate by doing the following:

- When reading to remember information, your reading rate should be slow and careful. Pause now and then to think about what you have read, and read difficult pages over again until you understand them. Descriptive passages with much detail should also be read slowly.
- When reading for enjoyment, you may read more quickly. Reading dialogue quickly imitates the flow of a conversation.

DIRECTIONS: *As you read "The Stone," think about how you should adjust your reading rate for different sections of the folk tale. complete the graphic organizer below by filling in passages that you read slowly, moderately, and quickly.*

Slowly	**Moderately**	**Quickly**
Passage	Passage	Passage
Passage	Passage	Passage

Name _____ Date _____

"The Stone" by Lloyd Alexander
Literary Analysis: Universal Theme

The theme of a literary work is its central idea or message about life or human nature. A **universal theme** is a message about life that is expressed regularly in many different cultures and time periods. Examples of universal themes include the importance of honesty, the power of love, and the danger of selfishness.

Look for a universal theme in a literary work by focusing on the story's main character, conflicts the character faces, changes he or she undergoes, and the effects of these changes. You can use a graphic organizer like the one shown to help you determine the universal theme.

DIRECTIONS: *Fill in the boxes with details from "The Stone." What universal theme do the details of the story lead to?*

Main Character

_____

↓

Conflicts Character Faces

_____

_____

↓

How Character Changes

_____

_____

↓

Effects or Meaning of Change

_____

_____

↓

Universal Theme

_____

_____

"The Stone" by Lloyd Alexander
Vocabulary Builder

Word List

feeble   jubilation   plight   rue   sown   vanished

A. DIRECTIONS: *Write a* **synonym** *for each vocabulary word. Use a thesaurus if you need one. Write a sentence that includes the synonym. Be sure that your sentence makes the meaning of the word clear.*

Vocabulary word: heartening

Synonym: encouraging

Sentence: The sales rep found the good response to the product very encouraging.

1. Vocabulary word: **plight**   Synonym: _____

   Sentence: _____

2. Vocabulary word: **feeble**   Synonym: _____

   Sentence: _____

3. Vocabulary word: **sown**   Synonym: _____

   Sentence: _____

4. Vocabulary word: **vanished**   Synonym: _____

   Sentence: _____

5. Vocabulary word: **jubilation**   Synonym: _____

   Sentence: _____

6. Vocabulary word: **rue**   Synonym: _____

   Sentence: _____

B. WORD STUDY: The Latin root *-van-* means "empty." Answer each of the following questions using one of these words containing *-van-: vanish, evanescent, vain*

1. What is a good way to make a rumor *vanish*?

   _____

2. Why would morning ground mist become *evanescent* as the day goes on?

   _____

3. How do you feel when your hard work has been in *vain*?

   _____

Name _____   Date _____

Enrichment: Be Careful What You Wish For

Dwarfs and fairies appear in folk tales from many countries. Many can grant wishes or bestow magical gifts. Imagine that you are one of the Fair Folk. You have in your bag something that all the humans want. Like Doli the dwarf, you hesitate to give the item to humans because it is a more powerful gift than they realize. In the space below, write a description of the magic item you have in your bag. Tell what it looks like, what power it has that makes the humans want it, and what power it has that the humans don't understand or don't know about.

_____

_____

_____

_____

_____

_____

_____

_____

_____

_____

_____

_____

_____

_____

_____

_____

_____

_____

_____

_____

_____

_____

"The Three Wishes" by Ricardo E. Alegría
"The Stone" by Lloyd Alexander

Integrated Language Skills: Grammar

Punctuation: Semicolons and Colons

A **semicolon** connects two independent clauses that are closely connected in meaning. (Remember that an independent clause can stand alone as a sentence.) A semicolon is also used to separate items in a series if those items have commas within them.

> Alice had never been given three wishes before; she was amazed at how the wishes might change her future.

> We visited some interesting places on our vacation, including New Bedford, Massachusetts; Providence, Rhode Island; and Danbury, Connecticut.

A **colon** is used after an independent clause to introduce a list of items, to show time, in the salutation of a business letter, and on warnings and labels.

> This is what he wished for: eternal youth, a new car, and an end to poverty in the world.

> Warning: Be careful what you wish for.

A. DIRECTIONS: *Rewrite each item below, inserting a colon or a semicolon wherever one is needed.*

1. We discussed three figures of speech simile, metaphor, and personification.

   _____

   _____

2. Warning No skateboarding here after 400 P.M.

   _____

   _____

3. My sister and I share a bedroom sometimes that room seems very small.

   _____

   _____

4. The train stops in Dallas, Texas St. Louis, Missouri and Chicago, Illinois.

   _____

   _____

B. Writing Application: *Imagine that you have three wishes, guaranteed to come true. Write three sentences about what you might wish for. Use at least one semicolon or one colon in each sentence.*

_____

_____

_____

"The Three Wishes" by Ricardo E. Alegría
"The Stone" by Lloyd Alexander
Support for Writing a Plot Proposal

A plot proposal is a plan of story events. Use this page to take notes for your plot proposal that illustrates a universal theme.

Universal theme: _____

_____

Conflict or situation that could be used to demonstrate that theme: _____

_____

Events that lead to the theme:

_____

_____

_____

_____

_____

_____

_____

_____

_____

_____

_____

_____

_____

_____

_____

_____

_____

_____

_____

_____

Now use your notes to write your plot proposal.

"The Three Wishes" by Ricardo E. Alegría
"The Stone" by Lloyd Alexander

Integrated Language Skills: Support for Extend Your Learning

Research and Technology: "The Three Wishes"

Use the lines below to take notes for your report on the land in Puerto Rico. You may want to research some of the following topics, using the key words listed.

Puerto Rico geography _____

_____

Puerto Rico climate _____

_____

Puerto Rico mountains _____

_____

Puerto Rico plants and animals _____

_____

Puerto Rico forests _____

_____

Research and Technology: "The Stone"

Use the lines below to take notes for your report on human aging. You may want to research some of the following topics, using the key words listed.

Gerontology (the study of aging) _____

_____

_____

Geriatrics (branch of medicine related to old age)_____

_____

_____

Aging _____

_____

Aging Skin/Human Skin _____

_____

Aging Changes _____

_____

_____

Name _____   Date _____

"**The Stone**" by Lloyd Alexander
Open-Book Test

Short Answer *Write your responses to the questions in this section on the lines provided.*

1. At the beginning of "The Stone," Maibon is upset with the idea of growing older. Based on your own experience, do you think growing older is a bad thing?

   _____

   _____

   _____

2. How does the message of "The Stone" relate to the modern world? Use details from the story and your own experience with how people feel about looking young.

   _____

   _____

   _____

3. When Maibon comes grumbling home at the beginning of "The Stone," his wife answers him. Explain what her answer shows about Modrona's personality.

   _____

   _____

   _____

4. What words would you use to describe Maibon based on his conversation with Doli? Use details from the story to support your answer.

   _____

   _____

   _____

5. In "The Stone," what does Doli think about humans? Support your answer with details from the story.

   _____

   _____

   _____

6. During his first meeting with Doli, how does Maibon's impatience influence what happens? Use details from the story to support your answer.

   _____

   _____

   _____

   _____

7. How does Maibon's attitude about growing old change from the beginning to the end of the story? Use the graphic organizer to record details from the story that show Maibon's attitude. Then, on the lines below, write how Maibon feels about being old at the very end of the story.

Beginning	Middle	End

_____

_____

8. A universal theme is a message about life that is shared by many cultures. What universal theme is demonstrated in "The Stone"? Support your answer with details from the story.

_____

_____

_____

9. How does the farm setting of the story contribute to the universal theme? Explain your answer using details from "The Stone."

_____

_____

_____

10. In "The Stone," Modrona does not share her husband's jubilation about the stone. How does Maibon show jubilation at the end of the story? Your answer should reflect an understanding of the word *jubilation*.

_____

_____

Essay

Write an extended response to the question of your choice or to the question or questions your teacher assigns you.

11. In "The Stone," Doli offers Maibon several choices of rewards, but Maibon chooses the stone that will keep him from growing any older. What choice do you think Maibon's wife would have made? Explain your answer in a brief essay. Include a description of Modrona's personality and details from the story.

12. Doli has quite a definite opinion of humans in "The Stone." In a brief essay, explain what his opinion is and whether he is right to have it. Use details from the story to support your response.

13. As you read, set a purpose to help you focus. Then, adjust your reading rate to help you accomplish that purpose. In an essay, tell how your purpose for reading changed as you read different parts of "The Stone". Explain how the changes in purpose affected your reading rate.

14. **Thinking About the Big Question: How much do our communities shape us?** In "The Stone," Maibon does not want to age. His wife calls him a fool. Does Maibon let his wife's opinion shape his own? Should he have paid more attention to her? In a brief essay, explain whether Maibon would have been better off being shaped by his wife or if he was right to stick to his own ideas. Use details from the story to support your answer.

Oral Response

15. Go back to question 1, 5, or 6 or to the question or questions your teacher assigns you. Take a few minutes to expand your answer and prepare an oral response. Find additional details in "The Stone" that support your points. If necessary, make notes to guide your oral response.

"The Stone" by Lloyd Alexander
Selection Test A

Critical Reading *Identify the letter of the choice that best answers the question.*

_____ 1. In "The Stone," Maibon often disagrees with his wife. At the beginning of the story, Maibon seems to be lazy and foolish. Which two words best describe his wife?
   A. lazy and foolish
   B. weak and nagging
   C. practical and clever
   D. mean and dishonest

_____ 2. At the beginning of "The Stone," what does Maibon fear most?
   A. being bored
   B. losing his farm
   C. losing his wife
   D. growing old

_____ 3. Maibon helps Doli the dwarf and earns a reward. Maibon can ask for anything. What does he ask for?
   A. a magic stone
   B. three wishes
   C. a bigger cottage
   D. a magic cook pot

_____ 4. In "The Stone," which word would Doli the dwarf use to describe humans?
   A. funny
   B. greedy
   C. clever
   D. scary

_____ 5. When you come to descriptive passages in "The Stone," you read more slowly. Which reading skill are you using?
   A. reading ahead to verify predictions
   B. adjusting your reading rate
   C. scanning for information
   D. distinguishing between important and unimportant details

_____ 6. In "The Stone," what unexpected power does the stone have?
   A. It kills everything Maibon dislikes.
   B. It causes Maibon's children to be older than Maibon.
   C. It stops everything on the farm from growing.
   D. It makes changes happen so quickly that life gets confusing.

    7. In "The Stone," Maibon refuses to get rid of the stone even though it is harming his family and his farm. Which word best describes Maibon's refusal?

       A. angry

       B. headstrong

       C. weak

       D. selfish

    8. How should the dialogue between the dwarf and Maibon be read in "The Stone"?

       A. quickly

       B. slowly

       C. carefully

       D. at the same rate as the descriptive passages

    9. A universal theme is a message about life that is expressed regularly in many different cultures and time periods. One way to find the universal theme in "The Stone" is to focus on how the main character changes. At the end of the story, Maibon has changed in several ways. What is the biggest change in Maibon at the end of the story?

       A. He loves his wife.

       B. He is happy about growing old.

       C. He and Doli are friends.

       D. He has lost the stone.

    10. Which of the following best states the universal theme of "The Stone"?

       A. The Fair Folk cannot be trusted.

       B. No one fears getting old.

       C. Human beings are ungrateful.

       D. Change is an important part of life.

Vocabulary and Grammar

    11. Which sentence uses an italicized vocabulary word <u>incorrectly</u>?

       A. Maibon wept in *jubilation* as he buried the stone.

       B. The Fair Folk welcomed Doli home with *jubilation.*

       C. Doli needed to be rescued from the *plight* he had gotten himself into.

       D. After he was no longer in a *plight,* Doli felt relieved.

____ 12. An antonym is a word that has the opposite meaning of another word. Antonyms are useful in writing because they show contrast. Which word is the best antonym to the word *young*?
   A. baby   C. old
   B. juvenile   D. youth

____ 13. Which sentence uses an italicized Academic Vocabulary word <u>incorrectly</u>?
   A. Setting a *purpose* gives you a *focus* for reading "The Stone."
   B. Reading will *adapt* you to increase your knowledge.
   C. Key words will *enable* you to do a computer search.
   D. You can *establish* a *purpose* for reading by previewing the text.

____ 14. Which sentence uses colons and semicolons correctly?
   A. We visited these places: Miami: Florida; Washington: D.C.; and New York City.
   B. We visited; these places; Miami; Florida, Washington; D.C., and New York: City.
   C. We visited these places; Miami; Florida; Washington; D.:C.; and New York City.
   D. We visited these places: Miami, Florida; Washington, D.C.; and New York City.

Essay

15. In "The Stone," Maibon learns an important lesson about life. This lesson is the central idea or theme of the story. It is a universal theme, an idea about life that is expressed regularly in many different cultures and time periods. In an essay, describe what Maibon fears at the beginning of the story. Then, tell what happens that changes his mind. Briefly describe the kind of person he is at the end of the story. How has he changed from the person he was when the story started? Finally, state what you think is the universal theme in "The Stone."

16. You should adjust your reading rate to help you accomplish your purpose for reading. Think of three different purposes for reading different parts of "The Stone." In an essay, discuss how the purpose for reading changes throughout the folk tale. Explain how changing your reading rate helped you to accomplish each of these three purposes. Use specific details from the folk tale to support your answer.

17. **Thinking About the Big Question: How much do our communities shape us?** In "The Stone," Maibon wants not to grow old. His wife calls him a fool. Does Maibon let his wife's opinion shape his own? Should he have paid more attention to her? In a brief essay, explain whether Maibon would have been better off listening to his wife or if he was right to stick to his own ideas. Use details from the story.

"**The Stone**" by Lloyd Alexander
Selection Test B

Critical Reading *Identify the letter of the choice that best completes the statement or answers the question.*

____ 1. In "The Stone," what do the disagreements between Maibon and Modrona show?
    A. They do not appreciate each other's strengths.
    B. They have opposite ideas about what is important.
    C. Modrona is wiser and more practical than her husband.
    D. Modrona is tired of the foolish decisions Maibon makes.

____ 2. In "The Stone," Maibon wishes to remain young forever because
    A. he is afraid of growing old and weak.
    B. he is afraid of death.
    C. he has so many things he wants to do.
    D. he believes that is the best wish.

____ 3. In "The Stone," Doli hesitates to give Maibon the magic stone because
    A. he thinks Maibon should ask for a practical kind of reward.
    B. he knows that Maibon will have a problem with it.
    C. he thinks it will not work and that Maibon will blame him.
    D. he is angry that human beings always ask for gifts.

____ 4. In "The Stone," Doli seems to believe that humans are
    A. greedy.
    B. comical.
    C. judicious.
    D. overbearing.

____ 5. In "The Stone," how does the stone affect humans, crops, and animals?
    A. by speeding up birth and growth
    B. by making everything sick or diseased
    C. by preventing growth and change
    D. by making everything younger

____ 6. When you read the descriptive passages in "The Stone" more slowly, you are
    A. adjusting your reading rate according to purpose.
    B. reading with care in order to verify previous predictions.
    C. scanning so that you can find a specific piece of information.
    D. gathering details in order to draw a conclusion.

____ 7. Maibon refuses to get rid of the stone even though he realizes that the stone is harming his farm and family. How would you characterize his refusal?
    A. vicious
    B. headstrong
    C. weak
    D. selfish

_____ 8. You can conclude that the stone keeps coming back to Maibon because
A. a magic stone must stay with its owner.
B. someone is playing a trick on him.
C. he has not accepted the need for change.
D. Doli wants to teach Maibon a lesson.

_____ 9. How does Maibon know the stone is truly gone?
A. He becomes old instantly.
B. Doli the dwarf disappears.
C. His wife tells him it is gone.
D. The fields and trees are suddenly full.

_____ 10. Think about how Maibon feels in the story. You can relate the text to your own life when
A. you have mixed feelings about keeping something or getting rid of it.
B. you think that adults don't understand you and your friends.
C. you think that life is unfair and you are not getting what you deserve.
D. you are able to help another person who is having problems.

_____ 11. In "The Stone," the universal theme is revealed mostly through
A. Maibon's relationship to Modrona.
B. the way Maibon changes in the story.
C. Maibon's attitude toward work.
D. the humor in the story.

_____ 12. In "The Stone," Maibon likes his gift until he realizes
A. he does not know what the future may hold for him.
B. only the elderly can acquire wisdom from experience.
C. his wife and children are getting older without him.
D. his life has become boring and without purpose.

_____ 13. Which of the following is the best description of what happens in "The Stone"?
A. Maibon and his wife quarrel, and she turns out to be right about everything.
B. Maibon gets his wish to stay young, but he learns that change is necessary.
C. Maibon's magic stone brings him bad luck, and he learns not to trust the Fair Folk.
D. Maibon does not change, and his children are soon older than their father.

_____ 14. In "The Stone," how does the farm setting help emphasize the theme?
A. The animals and crops are important to Maibon.
B. Events in a city would be more distracting.
C. Farms are filled with things that grow and change.
D. Maibon and his wife live on a farm.

_____ 15. Which is the biggest change in Maibon from the beginning to the end of the story?
A. how he feels about his wife
B. how he feels about growing older
C. how he feels about the Fair Folk
D. how he feels about magic

____ 16. Which of the following is the best statement of the universal theme of "The Stone"?
    A. Wishes can be dangerous.
    B. Everyone fears getting old.
    C. Human beings are ungrateful.
    D. Change is a natural part of life.

Vocabulary and Grammar

____ 17. Which sentence uses a vocabulary word *incorrectly*?
    A. Doli's *plight* started when he got his leg caught under a log.
    B. Maibon demanded a reward for releasing Doli from his *plight*.
    C. Crying miserably in *jubilation*, Maibon tried to bury the stone.
    D. There was much *jubilation* when Doli found his way home to the Fair Folk.

____ 18. Which sentence uses an italicized Academic Vocabulary word *incorrectly*?
    A. Reading will *enable* you to increase your knowledge.
    B. You can *adapt* your reading speed based on the *purpose* you set.
    C. Setting a *purpose* for reading gives you a *focus*.
    D. Key words *establish* you to do a computer search.

____ 19. Which sentence uses colons and semicolons correctly?
    A. We visited these places; Orlando, Florida: Raleigh, North Carolina: and New York City.
    B. We visited these places: Orlando, Florida; Raleigh, North Carolina; and New York City.
    C. We visited these places: Orlando, Florida, Raleigh, North Carolina and New York City.
    D. We visited these places; Orlando; Florida, Raleigh; North Carolina; and New York City.

Essay

20. Maibon learns an important lesson about life in "The Stone." In an essay, explain what you think Maibon learns. Use details that you remember from the story to tell how the character learns his lesson. Then explain why you think this lesson is a universal theme.

21. Suppose that you, like Maibon in "The Stone," are given a gift that lets you stop growing older. Unlike Maibon's gift, however, this magic would allow other life to continue to grow around you. In an essay, tell whether you would or would not accept the offer now or at any stage in your life, and give at least three reasons that support your answer.

22. **Thinking About the Big Question: How much should our communities shape us?** In "The Stone," Maibon wants not to age. His wife calls him a fool. Does Maibon let his wife's opinion shape his own? Should he have paid more attention to her? In a brief essay, explain whether Maibon would have been better off being shaped by his wife or if he was right to stick to his own ideas. Use details from the story.

Vocabulary Warm-up Word Lists

Study these words. Then, complete the activities that follow.

Word List A

accompanied [uh KUHM puh need] *v.* went along with
    The dog <u>accompanied</u> Carmen everywhere she went.

aware [uh WAIR] *adj.* knowing that something exists
    Because John was <u>aware</u> of the surprise party, he wasn't surprised at all.

condition [kuhn DISH uhn] *n.* the general state of a person or thing
    After jogging every day, Maria's muscles were in great <u>condition</u>.

expert [EK spert] *adj.* very skillful; highly trained
    Jackson listened to the doctor's <u>expert</u> advice.

intelligent [in TEL uh juhnt] *adj.* able to understand things quickly
    Because Johanna was <u>intelligent</u>, she quickly understood the solution to the problem.

prevented [pri VENT ed] *v.* stopped something from happening
    The new traffic light <u>prevented</u> many car accidents.

proper [PRAHP er] *adj.* appropriate or formal
    Deena tried to behave in a <u>proper</u> manner at the school assembly.

wrestling [RES ling] *v.* struggling; dealing with something difficult
    Miguel was <u>wrestling</u> with his decision to switch schools.

Word List B

assured [uh SHOORD] *v.* told positively; promised
    The teacher <u>assured</u> the students that they would pass the test.

breeding [BREED ing] *v.* raising animals to produce more of them
    Tom wanted to buy a stable so that he could begin <u>breeding</u> horses.

chirping [CHERP ing] *v.* twittering, peeping
    Gwen loved listening to the sound of crickets <u>chirping</u> at night.

discussion [dis KUHSH uhn] *n.* talk
    Chris enjoyed the class <u>discussion</u> about American history.

drafts [DRAFTZ] *n.* flows of cold air
    Julie shut the windows to prevent <u>drafts</u>.

fetch [FECH] *v.* to go after and bring something or somebody back
    I asked Nick to <u>fetch</u> me a carton of milk from the store.

injured [IN jerd] *adj.* harmed by something or someone
    Nicole's knee was <u>injured</u> after she fell in a bicycle accident.

local [LOH kuhl] *adj.* near your house, or in the area where you live
    The <u>local</u> store owners knew every customer in town.

"Lob's Girl" by Joan Aiken
"Jeremiah's Song" by Walter Dean Myers
Vocabulary Warm-up Exercises

Exercise A *Fill in each blank in the paragraph below with an appropriate word from Word List A. Use each word only once.*

Talisha had always admired Dr. Alvarez. As a college student, she was

[1] _____ with the decision of whether or not to become a doctor herself.

One day, Talisha [2] _____ Dr. Alvarez to work. His manner was very for-

mal and [3] _____. Still, he treated each of his patients with

[4] _____ care, showing his knowledge and training. Around noon, a

young man arrived with a broken leg. His left leg left him grumbling in pain, but he was

in good [5] _____ otherwise. "I was running on some ice," he said. "I

could have [6] _____ this injury so easily!" Talisha had read about bro-

ken legs and was [7] _____ that the patient needed a cast. She even

knew what type of cast he needed. Dr. Alvarez smiled. "You are smart!" he said. "Some-

day, you'll make a very [8] _____ doctor!"

Exercise B *Decide whether each statement below is true or false. Circle T or F. Explain your answers.*

1. If you went to a local store, you would have to travel far.
   T / F _____

2. A farmer who keeps cows for breeding expects to produce calves.
   T / F _____

3. If you fetch something for a friend, you plan to keep it for yourself.
   T / F _____

4. If people get injured, they would be hurt in some way.
   T / F _____

5. People open windows to prevent drafts from coming in.
   T / F _____

6. Chirping is the sound that wolves make.
   T / F _____

7. You can only have a discussion with yourself.
   T / F _____

8. If the doctor assured you that you were fine, it would mean that you are healthy.
   T / F _____

Name _____ Date _____

"Lob's Girl" by Joan Aiken
"Jeremiah's Song" by Walter Dean Myers
Reading Warm-up A

Read the following passage. Pay special attention to the underlined words. Then, read it again, and complete the activities. Use a separate sheet of paper for your written answers.

Imagine being trapped in a natural disaster, like an earthquake or an avalanche. You might be hurt and unable to move. You might be <u>wrestling</u> with your fears, struggling to stay calm. Suddenly, a German Shepherd appears. The dog notifies a rescue crew of your location. The crew arrives, and after judging your <u>condition</u>, or state, carries you to safety. You have just been saved by a rescue dog.

Rescue dogs are the heroes of the canine world. They go into disaster situations, but only after they have received the <u>proper</u> training. This includes learning how to seek out human smells.

Rescue dogs are chosen for their <u>intelligent</u> natures and keen senses of smell. They learn quickly. They use their <u>expert</u> sense of smell to find the survivors of many kinds of disasters. The dogs have been trained to focus on a human scent long enough to track down people that humans cannot find.

After a natural disaster, rescue crews are <u>aware</u> that some people may be trapped. These crews know that people caught in the disaster need to be saved. It is sometimes difficult for these crews to locate survivors. This is why rescue crews are often <u>accompanied</u> by rescue dogs. The dogs go along with the crew. They follow the smell of a trapped person. Then, they lead the crew toward the person. These dogs can track down a person in the dark. They can even find survivors underwater.

Rescue dogs work to save the survivors of earthquakes, avalanches, and mountain climbing accidents. These dogs have <u>prevented</u> the deaths of thousands of people. Rescue dogs are truly incredible for their ability to save lives.

1. Underline the word that means almost the same thing as <u>wrestling</u>. Then, use *wrestling* in a sentence.

2. Circle the word that means the same thing as <u>condition</u>. How would you describe your *condition* today?

3. Underline the words that describe one part of a rescue dog's <u>proper</u> training. Then, use *proper* in a sentence.

4. Circle the words that explain the word <u>intelligent</u>. Then, describe someone whom you think is *intelligent*.

5. Underline the sentence that tells why rescue dogs have an <u>expert</u> sense of smell. Then, use the word *expert* in a sentence.

6. Underline the words that tell you what rescue crews may be <u>aware</u> of. Define *aware* in your own words.

7. Circle the words that explain the word <u>accompanied</u>. Then, write a sentence with the word *accompanied*.

8. Circle the words that explain what rescue dogs have <u>prevented</u>. Then, use the word *prevented* in a sentence.

"Lob's Girl" by Joan Aiken
"Jeremiah's Song" by Walter Dean Myers
Reading Warm-up B

Read the following passage. Pay special attention to the underlined words. Then, read it again, and complete the activities. Use a separate sheet of paper for your written answers.

The sun was beginning to set as Elena finished her daily chores on the farm. She was covered in dirt from taking care of the pigs. Her father was <u>breeding</u> them, and soon the farm would be filled with piglets. Elena couldn't wait, since she loved to hear the squeals of the baby pigs as they rolled in the mud.

As she rushed into the house to clean up, Elena looked forward to the evening. Tonight, she was going to visit her favorite <u>local</u> person, Mr. Krebs. The older neighbor was like a grandfather to Elena. He had recently been <u>injured</u> in a farm accident, hurting his back, and Elena had been visiting him a lot while he recovered. The two would sit on his porch, having <u>discussions</u> about everything under the sun. They could talk for hours.

While Elena was getting ready to go, Mr. Krebs called up and asked for a favor.

"Would you <u>fetch</u> me some of your mother's mashed potatoes?" he asked.

"Don't worry, I'll bring you a big plate," Elena <u>assured</u> him. "Trust me."

Elena hurried out of her house, running along her usual path through the meadow as the sun went down. At that moment, the crickets began <u>chirping</u> and soon, their twittering noises filled the air.

When Elena arrived at Mr. Krebs's house, she found the old man sitting alone. She took her seat on Mr. Krebs's porch, swinging back and forth in a rocker. She felt <u>drafts</u> of cold air begin to blow across the porch as the temperature dropped. She buttoned her sweater against the chill of the wind.

"Now," she said, "what should we talk about tonight?"

"Whatever you want," Mr. Krebs said with a smile.

1. Circle the words that tell the effect of <u>breeding</u> pigs. Then, use **breeding** in a sentence.

2. Underline the word that is a clue to what <u>local</u> means. What is something *local* that you like?

3. Circle the phrase that tells you how Mr. Krebs was <u>injured</u>. Then, use *injured* in a sentence.

4. Circle the word that tells you what <u>discussion</u> means. Then, write a sentence with the word *discussion*.

5. Underline the words that tell you what it means to <u>fetch</u> something. Explain *fetch* in your own words.

6. Circle the phrase that gives a clue to the meaning of <u>assured</u>. Use the word *assured* in a sentence.

7. Underline the words that tell what the <u>chirping</u> of the crickets sounded like. Then, describe *chirping* in your own words.

8. Circle the words that explain what <u>drafts</u> are. Do you like to feel *drafts*?

Name _____ Date _____

"**Lob's Girl**" by Joan Aiken
"**Jeremiah's Song**" by Walter Dean Myers

Writing About the Big Question

How much do our communities shape us?

Big Question Vocabulary

common	community	connection	culture	family
generation	group	history	Influence	involve
isolate	participation	support	values	belief

A. *Use one or more words from the list above to complete each sentence.*

1. For her school project, Zoe started an online tutoring network, so that students could help and _____ one another.

2. Mikel found that his _____ in a service club helped him make new friends and feel good—without hurting his studies.

3. When Marilinda joined her neighbors in preparing for a hurricane, the experience _____ her to take a free class in disaster preparedness.

4. Last winter's bad weather taught TJ that a _____ can work together, when one of his neighbors organized teams to check on elderly neighbors shut in after each storm.

B. *Follow the directions in responding to each of the items below.*

1. List two different times when someone helped you through a difficult experience.

   _____.

   _____.

2. Write two sentences explaining one of the preceding experiences, and describe how it made you feel. Use at least two of the Big Question vocabulary words.

   _____

   _____

   _____

C. *Complete the sentence below. Then, write a short paragraph in which you connect this experience to the Big Question.*

One time, our neighbors helped _____ when _____

   _____

   _____

   _____

Unit 6 Resources: Themes in Folk Literature
203

Name _____ Date _____

"**Lob's Girl**" by Joan Aiken
"**Jeremiah's Song**" by Walter Dean Myers
Literary Analysis: Plot Techniques

Writers can use a range of **plot techniques** to help them tell the events in a story. Two common plot techniques are foreshadowing and flashback.

- **Foreshadowing** is the author's use of clues to hint at what might happen later in the story. For example, a story's narrator might describe a sign that reads *Danger* hanging on a fence. This detail might suggest that something dangerous will happen later in the story. It also helps the author build suspense, the quality that keeps you wondering what will happen next.
- A **flashback** is a scene that interrupts a story to describe an earlier event. Flashback is often used to show something about a character's past. For example, a flashback about the loss of a special pet might explain why a character dislikes the new family dog.

DIRECTIONS: *Read each of the following passages from "Lob's Girl" and "Jeremiah's Song." Then, complete the sentence that follows.*

1. **from "Lob's Girl"**

   A. [Aunt Rebecca] found the family with white shocked faces; Bert and Jean were about to drive off to the hospital where Sandy had been taken, and the twins were crying bitterly. <u>Lob was nowhere to be seen</u>.

   The underlined detail foreshadows _____ .

   B. The twins were miserably unhappy. They forgot that they had sometimes called their elder sister bossy and only remembered how often she had shared her pocket money with them, how she read to them and took them for picnics and helped with their homework.

   From the flashback in this paragraph, you learn that _____

   _____ .

2. **from "Jeremiah's Song"**

   A. Grandpa Jeremiah had been feeling poorly from that stroke, and one of his legs got a little drag to it. Just about the time Ellie come from school the next summer he was real sick.

   This description of Grandpa foreshadows _____ .

   B. When the work for the day was finished and the sows fed, Grandpa would kind of ease into one of his stories and Macon, he would sit and listen to them and be real interested.

   This flashback about Macon tells the reader that _____

   _____ .

"**Lob's Girl**" by Joan Aiken
"**Jeremiah's Song**" by Walter Dean Myers
Vocabulary Builder

Word List

decisively   diagnosis   melancholy   resolutions

A. DIRECTIONS: *Revise each sentence so that the underlined vocabulary word is used logically. Be sure to keep the vocabulary word in your revision.*

Sentence: After I told her every detail, Mom thanked me for the <u>summary</u>.

Revision: Mom thanked me for the brief <u>summary</u> of what had happened.

1. Unsure what to do with the ball, Aaron threw it <u>decisively</u> to first base.

_____

_____

2. Our club could not decide what to do, so we were able to make good <u>resolutions</u> for the coming year.

_____

_____

3. The story's funny, happy ending made Li feel <u>melancholy</u>.

_____

_____

4. After the vet's clear <u>diagnosis</u>, we still didn't know what was wrong with Spot.

_____

_____

B. DIRECTIONS: *Write the letter of the word that means the same or almost the same as the vocabulary word.*

_____ 1. melancholy
   A. depressed   C. sweet
   B. peaceful   D. mean

_____ 2. diagnosis
   A. speech   C. disease
   B. measurement   D. conclusion

_____ 3. resolutions
   A. apologies   C. promises
   B. guesses   D. chores

"Lob's Girl" by Joan Aiken
"Jeremiah's Song" by Walter Dean Myers

Writing to Compare Literary Works

Before you draft your essay comparing and contrasting the authors' use of foreshadowing and flashback in these stories, complete the graphic organizers below.

Foreshadowing	
Examples from "Lob's Girl"	**Examples from "Jeremiah's Song"**
Which story's foreshadowing creates greater suspense? Why?	

Flashback	
Examples from "Lob's Girl"	**Examples from "Jeremiah's Song"**
Which story's flashbacks reveal more about its characters? How?	

Now, use your notes to write an essay comparing and contrasting the authors' use of foreshadowing and flashback in these two stories. Remember to tell which story you enjoyed more and why.

Name _____ Date _____

"Lob's Girl" by Joan Aiken
"Jeremiah's Song" by Walter Dean Myers
Open-Book Test

Short Answer *Write your responses to the questions in this section on the lines provided.*

1. At the beginning of "Lob's Girl," there is a flashback to the time when Sandy was born. What is the purpose of that flashback?

   _____

   _____

   _____

2. Toward the beginning of "Lob's Girl," the author foreshadows Sandy's accident. What information does Joan Aiken provide to foreshadow the accident?

   _____

   _____

   _____

3. Why does the author of "Lob's Girl" say that Lob came to the family decisively? Base your answer on the definition of *decisively*.

   _____

   _____

4. In "Jeremiah's Song," the narrator remembers something about Ellie. His memory, in the form of a flashback, tells the reader how Ellie has changed. What is the memory, and what does it say about how Ellie has changed?

   _____

   _____

   _____

5. In "Jeremiah's Song," the author foreshadows events that may happen after the story ends. Predict one of those events. Support your answer with details in the story.

   _____

   _____

   _____

6. In "Jeremiah's Song," Ellie questions the doctor's diagnosis. Does the reader learn of the doctor's diagnosis? Explain. Base your answer on the definition of *diagnosis*.

   _____

   _____

   _____

7. The narrator of "Jeremiah's Song" talks a lot about Macon. In the middle of the story, when the narrator goes into his grandfather's room, he says that the room smells terrible and that his grandfather looks "scary." At that point, what is his attitude toward Macon? Support your answer with a detail from the story.

_____

_____

8. Both "Lob's Girl" and "Jeremiah's Song" contain flashbacks. What does this plot technique add to the stories? Support your answer with one detail from each story.

_____

_____

_____

9. In "Lob's Girl," an important character is Lob, a dog, and in "Jeremiah's Song," an important character is Macon, a young man. In what way are those two characters alike?

_____

_____

_____

10. Both "Lob's Girl" and "Jeremiah's Song" use foreshadowing. Complete this chart to analyze the event that is foreshadowed in each example. Then, on the lines below, describe how foreshadowing can increase the enjoyment of a story.

"Lob's Girl": "At the same time he [Lob] gave himself, though no one else was aware of this at the time."	**Event Foreshadowed:**
"Jeremiah's Song": "Macon had an old guitar he used to mess with, too."	**Event Foreshadowed:**

_____

_____

Essay

Write an extended response to the question of your choice or to the question or questions your teacher assigns you.

11. Both "Lob's Girl" and "Jeremiah's Song" contain foreshadowing and flashbacks. Choose one of the stories to write about. In an essay, describe an example of each plot technique as it is used in the story. Then, tell what purpose the plot technique serves. For example, does the flashback make the story more interesting? Does the foreshadowing add to the suspense?

12. In a brief essay, write about Grandpa Jeremiah's stories in "Jeremiah's Song." Consider what they mean to Grandpa, the narrator, Macon, Ellie, and the doctor.

13. Both "Lob's Girl" and "Jeremiah's Song" deal with devoted friendships. In an essay, compare and contrast the friendships in the two stories. Discuss how Lob and Sandy's relationship is similar to and different from Macon's relationship with Grandpa Jeremiah. Cite details from the stories to support your points.

14. **Thinking About the Big Question: How much should our communities shape us?** In "Lob's Girl," Lob leaves Liverpool, a city in the north of England, for a fishing village on the southern coast. In "Jeremiah's Song," Ellie has been changed by the experience of going away to college. She is now a member of two communities, one at college and one at home. In an essay, discuss the contrasts between the two communities in one of these stories. Explain, for example, why Lob might have preferred Cornwall to Liverpool. If you are writing about "Jeremiah's Song," consider how Ellie has changed. Consider also whether the changes are negative or positive. Cite details from the story to support your points.

Oral Response

15. Go back to question 1, 6, or 7 or to the question or questions your teacher assigns you. Take a few minutes to expand your answer and prepare an oral response. Find additional details in "Lob's Girl" or "Jeremiah's Song" that support your points. If necessary, make notes to guide your oral response.

Name _____ Date _____

"Lob's Girl" by Joan Aiken
"Jeremiah's Song" by Walter Dean Myers
Selection Test A

Critical Reading *Identify the letter of the choice that best answers the question.*

_____ 1. What does the following passage from "Lob's Girl" foreshadow?

The village was approached by a narrow, steep, twisting hill-road, and guarded by a notice that said LOW GEAR FOR 1 1/2 MILES, DANGEROUS TO CYCLISTS.

    A. Lob will travel many miles to find Sandy.

    B. An accident will happen on the hill.

    C. Lob will hike up the hill with Sandy.

    D. A person on a bike will be hurt.

_____ 2. In "Lob's Girl," why does Lob want to stay with the Pengelly family?

    A. He feels a connection to Sandy.

    B. The Pengellys feed him fish.

    C. He likes living near the sea.

    D. Mr. Dodsworth is cruel to him.

_____ 3. In "Lob's Girl," how does Lob die?

    A. He drowns at sea.

    B. He dies of old age.

    C. He gets hit by a truck.

    D. No one knows.

_____ 4. In "Lob's Girl," the hospital officials let Granny Pearce bring Lob to Sandy's bed even though it is against the rules. Why do they let this happen?

    A. They think Sandy is likely to die.

    B. They feel sorry for Lob.

    C. They think Lob is very smart.

    D. They are afraid of Granny Pearce.

_____ 5. Which word *best* describes Lob in "Lob's Girl"?

    A. brave

    B. old

    C. happy

    D. loyal

___ 6. Who tells the story "Jeremiah's Song"?

   A. a college student

   B. Macon

   C. a boy

   D. Grandpa Jeremiah

___ 7. In "Jeremiah's Song," why does Ellie dislike Grandpa Jeremiah's stories?

   A. She thinks they are too old and not true.

   B. She thinks they are too long and scary.

   C. She has heard them too many times.

   D. She thinks they are for children.

___ 8. In "Jeremiah's Song," why does Macon spend so much time with Grandpa Jeremiah?

   A. His mother has asked him to.

   B. He respects the older man.

   C. He thinks it is his duty.

   D. He wants to be near Ellie.

___ 9. What does this flashback from "Jeremiah's Song" suggest about Ellie?

   Before she went off to college she used to put cocoa butter on her arms and face
   and it would smell real nice. When she come back from college she put something
   else on, but that smelled nice too.

   A. She is pretty.

   B. She is vain.

   C. She loves college.

   D. She has changed.

___ 10. "Lob's Girl" and "Jeremiah's Song" both have examples of flashback and fore-
        shadowing. Why do the authors use flashbacks?

   A. to look forward in time

   B. to create suspense

   C. to tell more about a character

   D. to make the story exciting

___ 11. How are Lob in "Lob's Girl" and Macon in "Jeremiah's Song" alike?

   A. Both are devoted to their friends.

   B. Neither has good manners.

   C. Neither has a family.

   D. Both are easily scared.

___ 12. What story event occurs in both "Lob's Girl" and "Jeremiah's Song"?

    A. A mystery is solved.

    B. Someone is badly hurt.

    C. Something gets broken.

    D. A loved one dies.

Vocabulary

___ 13. What does the word *melancholy* mean in this passage from "Lob's Girl"?

    Then she saw the train slide away out of sight around the next headland, with a <u>melancholy</u> wail that sounded like Lob's last good-bye.

    A. loud   C. scary

    B. excited   D. sad

___ 14. What does *decisively* mean in this passage from "Lob's Girl"?

    Some people choose their dogs, and some dogs choose their people. The Pengelly family had no say in the choosing of Lob; he came to them in the second way, and very <u>decisively</u>.

    A. quietly   C. with hesitation

    B. with determination   D. gracefully

Essay

15. The authors of "Lob's Girl" and "Jeremiah's Song" both use foreshadowing and flashback in their stories. In an essay, define foreshadowing and flashback. Give an example of each plot technique from one of the stories. Then tell which plot technique you think makes a story more interesting. Explain why.

16. The titles "Lob's Girl" and "Jeremiah's Song" are similar: both contain an apostrophe-*s* ('*s*). Usually, an apostrophe-*s* shows ownership. Is that what the apostrophe-*s* in each story title shows? How does Lob "own" Sandy? What song does Grandpa Jeremiah "own"? Write a brief essay to explain the meaning of each title.

17. **Thinking About the Big Question: How much should our communities shape us?** In "Jeremiah's Song," Ellie has been changed by going away to college. She is now part of two communities, one at college and one at home. In an essay, discuss how Ellie has been shaped and changed by college and whether the changes are negative or positive. Use details from the story to support your points.

Name _____ Date _____

"Lob's Girl" by Joan Aiken
"Jeremiah's Song" by Walter Dean Myers
Selection Test B

Critical Reading *Identify the letter of the choice that best completes the statement or answers the question.*

____ 1. Which detail in this passage from "Lob's Girl" is an example of foreshadowing?

She picked up a bit of driftwood and threw it. Lob, whisking easily out of his master's grip, was after it like a sand-colored bullet. He came back with the stick, beaming, and gave it to Sandy. At the same time he gave himself, though no one else was aware of this at the time.

A. She picked up a bit of driftwood and threw it.
B. was after it like a sand-colored bullet
C. came back with the stick, beaming
D. At the same time he gave himself

____ 2. In "Lob's Girl," Sandy ends up in the hospital because
A. she catches the flu after a swim in the ocean.
B. Lob trips her as they are playing on the beach.
C. she is hit by a truck on the hill outside her house.
D. Lob runs away from her on the walk to Aunt Rebecca's.

____ 3. In "Lob's Girl," the character trait that Lob *best* represents is
A. bravery.
B. loyalty.
C. intelligence.
D. gentleness.

____ 4. What does this flashback from "Lob's Girl" reveal?

Sandy was really Alexandra, because her grandmother had a beautiful picture of a queen in a diamond tiara and a high collar of pearls. It hung by Granny Pearce's kitchen sink and was as familiar as the doormat. When Sandy was born, everyone agreed that she was the living spit of the picture. . . .

A. that there is something royal about Sandy's appearance
B. that Granny Pearce looked just like Sandy when she was young
C. that Sandy is actually a queen named Alexandra
D. that Sandy does not like her real name

____ 5. Which sentence about "Jeremiah's Song" best describes how Ellie has changed since she began attending college?
A. She no longer likes the people in her hometown.
B. She likes listening to Grandpa's stories more than she used to.
C. She thinks she knows more than everyone at home.
D. She appreciates her hometown more than she used to.

___ 6. Which sentence best tells Grandpa Jeremiah's feelings about his stories?
   A. They remind him of his childhood.
   B. They are good entertainment for his grandchildren.
   C. They help him pass the time during his illness.
   D. They tell about his past and his people.

___ 7. What does this flashback from "Jeremiah's Song" suggest about Macon?
   It was right after Ellie went back to school that Grandpa Jeremiah had him a stroke and Macon started coming around. I think his mama probably made him come at first, but you could see he liked it.

   A. He enjoys Grandpa's company.
   B. He does not respect his mother.
   C. He is not very healthy.
   D. He is trying to avoid Ellie.

___ 8. What story event is foreshadowed in this sentence from "Jeremiah's Song"?
   Macon had an old guitar he used to mess with, too.

   A. Grandpa giving Macon a new guitar
   B. Ellie changing her mind about Macon
   C. Macon writing a song for Grandpa
   D. the narrator learning to play the guitar

___ 9. How does the narrator in "Jeremiah's Song" feel about Macon?
   A. He feels safe with Macon around.
   B. He feels ignored by Macon.
   C. He feels speechless around Macon.
   D. He feels jealous of Macon.

___ 10. Which statement is true of the foreshadowing in "Lob's Girl" and "Jeremiah's Song"?
   A. The foreshadowing in "Jeremiah's Song" creates greater suspense.
   B. The foreshadowing creates equal suspense in both stories.
   C. The foreshadowing creates suspense in neither story.
   D. The foreshadowing in "Lob's Girl" creates greater suspense.

___ 11. How are Lob in "Lob's Girl" and Macon in "Jeremiah's Song" similar?
   A. They both travel many miles to find someone they love.
   B. They both express love through their actions.
   C. They both love someone who does not love them.
   D. They both love the feeling of freedom.

___ 12. How might Lob in "Lob's Girl" and Grandpa in "Jeremiah's Song" be considered similar?
   A. They both fear death and try to avoid it.
   B. They both try to protect loved ones from death.
   C. They both continue to give to their loved ones after they die.
   D. They both use a kind of magic to convince others they are not dead.

____ 13. Both "Lob's Girl" and "Jeremiah's Song" are about
      A. important companions who pass through people's lives.
      B. valuable advice passed from one person to another.
      C. overcoming obstacles to help someone in need.
      D. generous people whose experiences make them selfish.

____ 14. Why do the authors of "Lob's Girl" and "Jeremiah's Song" use flashbacks?
      A. to remind readers of what they have already learned in the story
      B. to show how one story event causes another story event
      C. to suggest what might happen after a story's action ends
      D. to give readers a better understanding of a character's past

Vocabulary

____ 15. What does the word *diagnosis* mean in this passage from "Jeremiah's Song"?
      "Are you sure of your diagnosis?" Ellie asked. . . .
      "Yes, I'm sure," he said. "He had tests a few weeks ago and his condition was bad then."
      A. explanation of a medical condition
      B. summary of test results
      C. person who works in a doctor's office
      D. illness that can be life-threatening

____ 16. What does *resolutions* mean in this sentence from "Lob's Girl"?
      So they dutifully took no notice of him the next day until he spoiled their resolutions by dashing up to them with joyful barks. . . .
      A. creations   C. intentions
      B. vacations   D. celebrations

Essay

17. The titles "Lob's Girl" and "Jeremiah's Song" both include an apostrophe-s, which usually indicates ownership or possession. In an essay, explain what each title means. Is the 's used to show ownership or some other kind of relationship? Why do you think the author chose that particular title? Which title do you find more surprising or moving, and why?

18. The authors of "Lob's Girl" and "Jeremiah's Song" both use the plot techniques of foreshadowing and flashback to add interest to their stories. In an essay, define *both* techniques. Then choose *either* technique and analyze its use in both stories. Which author relies more heavily on that technique? Why? To support your thinking, provide examples from both of the stories.

19. **Thinking About the Big Question: How much do our communities shape us?** In "Lob's Girl," Lob leaves Liverpool, a city in the north of England, for a fishing village on the southern coast. In "Jeremiah's Song," Ellie has been changed by the experience of going away to college. She is now a member of two communities, one at college and one at home. In an essay, discuss the contrasts between the two communities in one of these stories. Explain, for example, why Lob might have preferred Cornwall to Liverpool. If you are writing about "Jeremiah's Song," consider how Ellie has changed. Consider also whether the changes are negative or positive. Cite details from the story to support your points.

Name _____ Date _____

Research: Research Report

Prewriting: Choosing Your Topic

Answer the self-interview questions below to generate ideas for your report and choose one as your general topic.

What interesting people have I read about? Who would I like to learn more about?	
What places would I like to learn more about? What places would I like to visit someday?	
What historical events would I like to research?	

Drafting: Organizing Your Report

Use the following outline to organize your thesis statement, subtopics, and the facts and details related to each subtopic for your report.

I. Introduction:
II. Topic:
A. Supporting Details:
B. Supporting Details:
III. Topic:
A. Supporting Details:
B. Supporting Details:
IV. Conclusion:

Name _____ Date _____

Research Report: Integrating Grammar Skills

Punctuating Citations and Titles of Reference Works

When you cite sources, you must be sure to punctuate them correctly. Follow the guidelines in the charts.

Underlined / Italicized	Quotation Marks
Book Title: <u>Treasure Island</u> Play Title: <u>The Arkansas Bear</u> Long Poem: <u>The Song of Hiawatha</u> Magazine: <u>Kids Discover</u> Newspaper: <u>The News Sun</u>	Short Story: "Born Worker" Chapter from a Book: "All About Earth" Short Poem: "Winter Poem" Article: "How to Build a Birdhouse" Web Site Article: "Into Africa"

Direct Quotation	Example
Set off the exact words of another person with quotation marks.	In a speech, Abraham Lincoln said, "A house divided against itself cannot stand."

Identifying Errors in Citations

A. DIRECTIONS: *Some of the titles below are used correctly, but others are not. Look at the type of source in parentheses. Then write* yes *if the citation is correct or* no *if it is incorrect.*

_____ 1. "The Captain's Papers" (a chapter in the book <u>Treasure Island</u>)

_____ 2. "Lincoln: A Photobiography" (a book about Abraham Lincoln)

_____ 3. <u>Smithsonian</u> (a magazine)

_____ 4. "The New York Times" (a newspaper)

_____ 5. <u>How to Take a Great Photograph</u> (magazine article)

Fixing Errors in Citations

B. DIRECTIONS: *On the lines provided, correct the errors in the use of underlines or quotation marks for the quotes and their sources. There is one error in each sentence.*

1. "'Twas brillig, and the slithy toves" is a line in the short poem <u>Jabberwocky</u>.

_____

2. The White House Web site has an article titled <u>Abraham Lincoln</u>.

_____

3. <u>Snakes Alive</u> is an article in <u>Sports Illustrated for Kids</u>.

_____

4. "Abraham Lincoln: The Prairie Years and the War Years" is a book by Carl Sandburg.

_____

Unit 6 Vocabulary Workshop—1
Idioms

Many idioms are very commonly used in our everyday lives and are very familiar to native English speakers. To people who do not speak English well, these idioms can be very confusing.

DIRECTIONS: *Write a paragraph about an unusual day. Use three or more of the following idioms in your story. Use a dictionary if you are unsure of their meaning.*

"hit the nail on the head"

"got up on the wrong side of the bed"

"go the extra mile"

"over the top"

"put your best foot forward"

"till the cows come home"

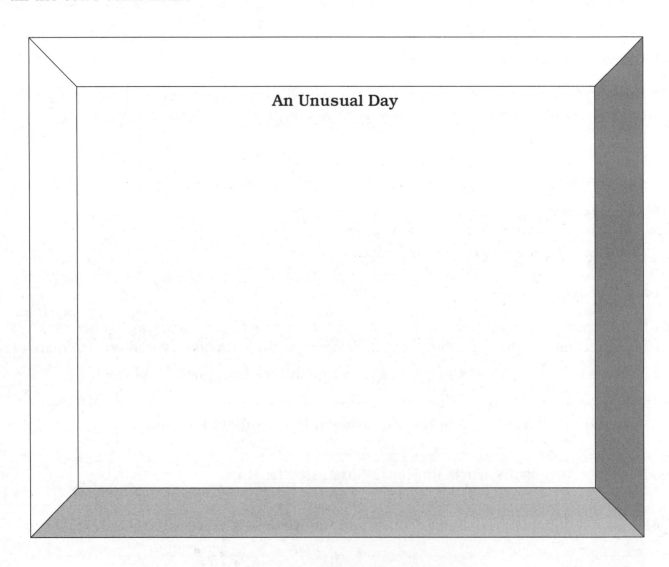

An Unusual Day

Name _____ Date _____

Unit 6 Vocabulary Workshop—2
Idioms

It is possible to be familiar with an idiom but misinterpret its meaning. When in doubt, use a dictionary or a reliable Internet source to clear up questions.

DIRECTIONS: *Answer each question. Make sure your answer shows that you understand the idiom(s) in the sentence.*

1. If a picture paints a thousand words, then why draw when you can write?

   _____

   _____

2. If Mary goes to the movies once in a blue moon, does she go every day?

   _____

   _____

3. If Kelly sees the handwriting on the wall, is she predicting that something wonderful will happen?

   _____

   _____

4. If Sally made no bones about it, did she beat around the bush?

   _____

   _____

5. If Margot made her speech off the cuff, did she work hard preparing it?

   _____

   _____

6. If your plans are simply pie in the sky, are they likely to happen?

   _____

   _____

7. After Charlie ran out of steam, did he run faster?

   _____

   _____

8. If Jason turned a blind eye on the fight, did he tell his friends about it?

   _____

   _____

Name _____ Date _____

Communications Workshop—Unit 6
Delivering an Oral Response to Literature

After listening to a book on tape, use the following chart to help you express your feelings and thoughts about the book you chose.

Title of book: _____

What is your interpretation of the book?
Give a brief summary of the important features of the book.
What quotations and relevant examples are you going to use for support?
What is your overall feeling or judgment about the book?

Unit 6: Themes in Folk Literature
Benchmark Test 12

MULTIPLE CHOICE

Reading Skill: Set a Purpose for Reading

1. When should you set a purpose for reading?
   A. before you read
   B. after you finish reading
   C. only when you read to be entertained
   D. only when you read to be informed

2. When your purpose for reading is to make connections, what do you connect?
   A. one character with another
   B. symbols with their meanings
   C. the characters with their setting
   D. the literature with your own experience

3. If no purpose for reading is assigned, what should you do to set a purpose for reading?
   A. Read the material twice and think carefully about the purpose.
   B. Preview the material before you begin reading it.
   C. Do research on the subject before reading the material.
   D. Read other works by the author before reading the material.

Read this selection. Then, answer the questions that follow.

(1) When rubber first comes out of a rubber tree, it is not waterproof and it melts easily. (2) In the 1830s, an American named Charles Goodyear decided to make rubber a useful product. (3) He spent his own life savings, trying for years to find the right formula. (4) Then, he found it quite by accident when he spilled sulfur on some rubber he was heating. (5) The resulting product had all the properties that make rubber useful—it was waterproof, pliable, resistant to heat and cold, and excellent insulation from electric currents. (6) However, the process was so easy to copy that Goodyear could not get a meaningful patent on it. (7) One of the copycats even gave the process a name—vulcanization—from Vulcan, the Roman god of fire and metalwork.

4. Which of these is the most likely purpose you would have for reading the selection?
   A. to learn about rubber trees and where they grow
   B. to learn about the Roman god Vulcan
   C. to learn about the development of vulcanized rubber
   D. to learn the laws and processes of chemistry

5. Which is a reasonable purpose you might have for reading this selection?
   A. to investigate products before buying them
   B. to escape into an imaginary world of adventure
   C. to be entertained with an interesting nonfiction account
   D. to get a better understanding of the business world

Name _____ Date _____

Read these selections. Then, answer the questions that follow.

A. Insects come in all shapes and sizes. Some insects damage crops and can harm humans. However, others, like dragonflies, are quite beneficial. The dragonfly is one of the largest insects. It feasts on around 600 insects per day, such as gnats, flies, and crop pests. It is also one of the main predators of mosquitoes. Despite old folk tales that claim dragonflies sew up your ears or lips, they do not attack humans.

B. Although insects are commonly thought of as pests, it is important to realize their helpfulness to our everyday lives. Without insects operating in their ecosystems, our world would be very different. Take the honeybee, for example. Without bees, there would be no honey or beeswax. Bees also help in the process known as pollination. Their bodies pick up pollen and transfer it so that seed plants can reproduce. While it is true that a bee can sting a human, the benefit this insect supplies far outweighs the risk.

6. What main idea do the two selections share?
   A. Certain insects damage crops and can harm humans.
   B. Insects can be very helpful to human beings.
   C. Old folk tales do not tell the truth about insects.
   D. Insects come in all shapes and sizes.

7. Selection B states, "Without insects operating in their ecosystems, our world would be very different." Based on Selection A, how would the statement be true if there were no dragonflies?
   A. Without dragonflies, pollination could not take place.
   B. Without dragonflies, there would be many more mosquitoes.
   C. Without dragonflies, there would be fewer folk tales.
   D. Without dragonflies, there would be no honey.

8. Based on the ideas in both selections, to whom would both the dragonfly and the bee probably be most helpful?
   A. doctors   C. construction workers
   B. folk tale writers   D. farmers

Literary Analysis: Personification and Universal Theme

9. What is personification?
   A. creating and developing characters in a work of literature
   B. adopting a special personality in telling a story
   C. using your own personal style in writing a story
   D. giving human qualities to an animal or an object

10. What is a universal theme?
   A. a theme that covers the whole work, not just part of it
   B. a theme about the skies or the heavens
   C. a theme expressed regularly in many cultures and eras
   D. any theme about life or human nature

11. What does foreshadowing usually help create?
    A. universal themes
    B. suspense
    C. flashbacks
    D. personification

Read this tale from folk literature. Then, answer the questions that follow.

The Frog and the Scorpion

Once a frog was about to cross a river when a scorpion addressed him from the river bank.

"Please help me, kind frog," said the scorpion. "Will you take me across the river on your back?"

"No," said the frog, "for scorpions always sting other creatures, and you will sting me."

"Why would I?" asked the scorpion. "I cannot swim, so if I stung you, we both would drown."

So the frog unwisely accepted the scorpion's promises and agreed to cross the river with the scorpion on his back. When they were halfway across, however, the scorpion stung the frog.

"Fool!" said the frog. "Now we both will drown! Why did you sting me when you promised not to?"

"I could not help it," said the scorpion. "It is my nature."

12. What are the main human qualities that the frog displays in this tale?
    A. kindness and bad judgment
    B. courage and gratitude
    C. helpfulness and wisdom
    D. anger and sorrow

13. What change occurs in the scorpion's behavior by the end of the tale?
    A. The scorpion grows friendlier and more talkative as the story progresses.
    B. The scorpion is shy at first but later becomes bold.
    C. The scorpion gets more and more frightened as the story progresses.
    D. The scorpion seems to treat others better but in fact does not.

14. Which of these universal themes does the tale most clearly convey?
    A. Anyone can change for the better if given encouragement.
    B. Those who treat others kindly will be treated kindly in return.
    C. Someone will not usually change his or her true nature.
    D. An act of kindness is its own reward.

15. What foreshadowing occurs in the tale?
    A. the scorpion addressing the frog from the river bank
    B. the scorpion calling the frog "kind frog"
    C. the frog's agreeing to carry the scorpion being called unwise
    D. the scorpion's final words, "It is my nature"

Read this story. Then, answer the questions that follow.

When Mindy asked her best friend Lena to help her study for a makeup Spanish test, Lena was too busy. "I can't help you study for a test I took last week," Lena explained, "especially since my brother promised to take me for a drive in his new car. You know how long I've been waiting to do that."

Mindy said nothing, but she was annoyed. She remembered all the help she had given Lena with schoolwork—like the time when Lena lost a paper and Mindy stayed up late helping her retype it.

A week later, Lena was out sick from school and asked Mindy to drop off the notes she took in math.

"I'd come if I could," said Mindy, "but I can't. I have to take my dog to the vet."

"But you don't have a dog!" Lena exclaimed.

"Yes I do," said Mindy. "I got one last week when I realized I needed a new best friend."

16. What big idea does the universal theme of this story explore?
   A. friendship
   B. courage
   C. education
   D. illness

17. What would you say is one universal theme of this story?
   A. True friendship means coming through for a friend in need.
   B. It takes courage to be someone's true friend.
   C. Illness often brings out the worst in people.
   D. Everyone needs some help with their education.

18. Which of these story incidents is a flashback?
   A. Mindy taking a makeup Spanish test
   B. Lena taking a promised drive in her brother's new car
   C. Mindy remembering the help she gave Lena with schoolwork
   D. Mindy getting a dog

Vocabulary

19. Using your knowledge of the suffix *-en*, what is the most likely meaning of *hearten* in the following sentence?

   I hope our words will hearten him.

   A. make peaceful   C. cause to cheer up
   B. fill with indignation   D. inspire to action

20. Using your knowledge of the suffix *-ary*, what is the most likely meaning of *momentary* in the following sentence?

   She had a momentary lapse of judgment.

   A. having trivial consequences   C. having ill effects
   B. lasting for only an instant   D. lasting for a long time

21. To which of the following words could you successfully add the suffix *-en*?
    A. convert
    B. vital
    C. astound
    D. quick

22. What does the root *-van-* mean?
    A. "empty"
    B. "order"
    C. "hold"
    D. "suffer"

23. How does the word *penitentiary* reflect the meaning of the root *-pen-*?
    A. People in a penitentiary cannot get out.
    B. People in a penitentiary are being punished.
    C. People in a penitentiary have committed crimes.
    D. People in a penitentiary are guarded.

24. Based on your understanding of the root *-van-*, what happens to something that *evanesces*?
    A. It increases in size.
    B. It takes on a different shape.
    C. It disappears slowly.
    D. It turns from a solid to a liquid.

Grammar

25. Which of these sentences is punctuated correctly?
    A. School will be closed on these days, Election Day, and Thanksgiving.
    B. School will be closed on these days: Election Day, and Thanksgiving.
    C. School will be closed on these days; Election Day and Thanksgiving.
    D. School will be closed on these days: Election Day and Thanksgiving.

26. Which of these sentences is punctuated correctly?
    A. The bus leaves at 7:30; everyone should be there on time.
    B. The bus leaves at 7:30, everyone should be there on time.
    C. The bus leaves at 7.30: everyone should be there on time.
    D. The bus leaves at 7-30; everyone should be there on time.

27. How should you correct the punctuation in this sentence?

    Last month we read "To Kill a Mockingbird," a famous novel by Harper Lee, "Charles," a funny story by Shirley Jackson, and *Annabel Lee,* a long, creepy poem by Edgar Allan Poe.

    A. Put the title of the first work in italics instead of quotation marks and change the commas after *Lee* and *Jackson* to semicolons.
    B. Put the titles of the first two works in italics instead of quotation marks and change the commas after *Lee* and *Jackson* to semicolons.
    C. Put the title of the poem in quotation marks instead of italics and change the commas after *Lee* and *Jackson* to semicolons.
    D. Put the title of the first work in italics instead of quotation marks but make no other changes.

28. When should you indent a quotation and introduce it with a colon?
    A. whenever you use one in a term paper
    B. when it is especially important
    C. when it is five or more lines long
    D. whenever you quote material exactly

Spelling

29. Which of these words is spelled correctly?
    A. telaphone
    B. television
    C. teliscope
    D. tellecast

30. In which sentence is the italic word spelled correctly?
    A. We drove through Beverly Hills in our new *automobile.*
    B. The car has *autamatic* windows and door locks.
    C. We stopped to ask a movie star to sign her *autegraph.*
    D. At the nearby bookstore, we bought the star's *auttobiography.*

31. In which sentence is the italic word spelled correctly?
    A. The *psyclone* practically blew the town away.
    B. Do your town *resycle* newspapers and cardboard?
    C. Stella and Steve were riding on a *bicycle* built for two.
    D. My four-year-old sister rides all over on her *trisicle.*

ESSAY

Writing

32. Imagine that you are a character in a fable or folk tale you have read. Write an invitation to an event in the tale. The invitation should be in the form of a letter. The person you send it to can be another character in the tale or someone else. If the tale does not provide all the details you need to include in your invitation, you can make some up.

33. Think of a universal theme that means a lot to you. It can be a moral message you believe in or any message that you think relates to your own life. Then, write a plot proposal, or story plan, for a story that teaches or illustrates the universal theme.

34. Think of something you encountered in your reading that you might want to research further. It could be an author whose work you like, a culture that produced a tale you enjoyed, or something in the background information or setting of a particular story. Write a plan for the research you will need to do to investigate the topic further. Include general information about where you will do your research as well as specific information about the sources you might consult to find out more about different aspects of your subject.

Diagnostic Tests and Vocabulary in Context
Use and Interpretation

The Diagnostic Tests and Vocabulary in Context were developed to assist teachers in making the most appropriate assignment of *Prentice Hall Literature* program selections to students. The purpose of these assessments is to indicate the degree of difficulty that students are likely to have in reading/comprehending the selections presented in the *following* unit of instruction. Tests are provided at six separate times in each grade level—a *Diagnostic Test* (to be used prior to beginning the year's instruction) and a *Vocabulary in Context,* the final segment of the Benchmark Test appearing at the end of each of the first five units of instruction. Note that the tests are intended for use not as summative assessments for the prior unit, but as guidance for assigning literature selections in the upcoming unit of instruction.

The structure of all Diagnostic Tests and Vocabulary in Context in this series is the same. All test items are four-option, multiple-choice items. The format is established to assess a student's ability to construct sufficient meaning from the context sentence to choose the only provided word that fits both the semantics (meaning) and syntax (structure) of the context sentence. All words in the context sentences are chosen to be "below-level" words that students reading at this grade level should know. All answer choices fit *either* the meaning or structure of the context sentence, but only the correct choice fits *both* semantics and syntax. All answer choices—both correct answers and incorrect options—are key words chosen from specifically taught words that will occur in the subsequent unit of program instruction. This careful restriction of the assessed words permits a sound diagnosis of students' current reading achievement and prediction of the most appropriate level of readings to assign in the upcoming unit of instruction.

The assessment of vocabulary in context skill has consistently been shown in reading research studies to correlate very highly with "reading comprehension." This is not surprising as the format essentially assesses comprehension, albeit in sentence-length "chunks." Decades of research demonstrate that vocabulary assessment provides a strong, reliable prediction of comprehension achievement— the purpose of these tests. Further, because this format demands very little testing time, these diagnoses can be made efficiently, permitting teachers to move forward with critical instructional tasks rather than devoting excessive time to assessment.

It is important to stress that while the Diagnostic Tests and Vocabulary in Context were carefully developed and will yield sound assignment decisions, they were designed to *reinforce*, not supplant, teacher judgment as to the most appropriate instructional placement for individual students. Teacher judgment should always prevail in making placement—or indeed other important instructional—decisions concerning students.

Name _____ Date _____

Diagnostic Tests and Vocabulary in Context
Branching Suggestions

These tests are designed to provide maximum flexibility for teachers. Your *Unit Resources* books contain the 40-question **Diagnostic Test** and 20-question **Vocabulary in Context** tests. At *PHLitOnline,* you can access the Diagnostic Test and complete 40-question Vocabulary in Context tests. Procedures for administering the tests are described below. Choose the procedure based on the time you wish to devote to the activity and your comfort with the assignment decisions relative to the individual students. Remember that your judgment of a student's reading level should always take precedence over the results of a single written test.

Feel free to use different procedures at different times of the year. For example, for early units, you may wish to be more confident in the assignments you make—thus, using the "two-stage" process below. Later, you may choose the quicker diagnosis, confirming the results with your observations of the students' performance built up throughout the year.

The **Diagnostic Test** is composed of a single 40-item assessment. Based on the results of this assessment, make the following assignment of students to the reading selections in Unit 1:

Diagnostic Test Score	Selection to Use
If the student's score is 0–25	more accessible
If the student's score is 26–40	more challenging

Outlined below are the three basic options for administering **Vocabulary in Context** and basing selection assignments on the results of these assessments.

1. For a one-stage, quicker diagnosis using the *20-item* test in the *Unit Resources:*

Vocabulary in Context Test Score	Selection to Use
If the student's score is 0–13	more accessible
If the student's score is 14–20	more challenging

2. If you wish to confirm your assignment decisions with a *two-stage* diagnosis:

Stage 1: Administer the 20-item test in the *Unit Resources*	
Vocabulary in Context Test Score	Selection to Use
If the student's score is 0–9	more accessible
If the student's score is 10–15	(Go to Stage 2.)
If the student's score is 16–20	more challenging

Stage 2: Administer items 21–40 from *PHLitOnline*	
Vocabulary in Context Test Score	Selection to Use
If the student's score is 0–12	more accessible
If the student's score is 13–20	more challenging

3. If you base your assignment decisions on the full 40-item **Vocabulary in Context** from *PHLitOnline:*

Vocabulary in Context Test Score	Selection to Use
If the student's score is 0–25	more accessible
If the student's score is 26–40	more challenging

Unit 6 Resources: Themes in Folk LIterature

Grade 6—Benchmark Test 11
Interpretation Guide

For remediation of specific skills, you may assign students the relevant Reading Kit Practice and Assess pages indicated in the far-right column of this chart. You will find rubrics for evaluating writing samples in the last section of your Professional Development Guidebook.

Skill Objective	Test Items	Number Correct	Reading Kit
Reading Skill			
Cause and Effect	1, 2, 3, 4, 5, 6		pp. 236, 237
Creating Outlines	7, 8, 9		pp. 238, 239
Literary Analysis			
Fables and Folk Tales	10, 11, 12, 13, 14		pp. 240, 241
Myths	15, 16, 17, 18, 19		pp. 242, 243
Elements of fantasy	20		pp. 244, 245
Vocabulary			
Suffixes and Roots -ment, -ous, -splend-, -mort-	21, 22, 23, 24, 25, 26		pp. 246, 247
Grammar			
Independent and Subordinate Clauses	27, 28, 29		pp. 248, 249
Simple, Compound, and Complex sentences	30, 31		pp. 250, 251
Revising Sentence Fragments (run-ons)	32, 33		pp. 252, 253
Writing			
Essay	34	Use rubric	pp. 256, 257
Multi-media Report	35	Use rubric	pp. 258, 259

Grade 6—Benchmark Test 12
Interpretation Guide

For remediation of specific skills, you may assign students the relevant Reading Kit Practice and Assess pages indicated in the far-right column of this chart. You will find rubrics for evaluating writing samples in the last section of your Professional Development Guidebook.

Skill Objective	Test Items	Number Correct	Remediation (Reading Kit)
Reading Skill			
Setting a Purpose	1, 2, 3, 4, 5		pp. 260, 261
Connect and Clarify Main Ideas	6, 7, 8		pp. 262, 263
Literary Analysis			
Personification	9, 12, 13		pp. 264, 265
Universal Theme	10, 14, 16, 17		pp. 266, 267
Foreshadowing and Flashback	11, 15, 18		pp. 268, 269
Vocabulary			
Suffixes and Roots -en, -ary, -van-, -pen-	19, 20, 21, 22, 23, 24		pp. 270, 271
Grammar			
Commas	25		pp. 274, 275
Semicolons and Colons	26, 27		pp. 272, 273
Punctuating Citations and Titles of Reference Works	28		pp. 276, 277
Spelling			
Word Families	29, 30, 31		pp. 278, 279
Writing			
Invitation	32	Use rubric	pp. 280, 281
Plot Proposal	33	Use rubric	pp. 282, 283
Research Report	34	Use rubric	pp. 284, 285

ANSWERS

Big Question Vocabulary—1, p. 1

1. Robert, Cindy, Glenn and Darcy are the names of people in my *family*.
2. Robert and Cindy are both 40, they are in the same *generation*. I am part of the younger *generation*, with my brother Glenn who is 12 and my sister Darcy who is 10. I am 11. I have three grandparents, all in their 80's.
3. My family and I have *common* ideas about how to spend Sunday morning. We sleep late and then eat a big, delicious breakfast.
4. My brother and sister *support* me when I have a lot of homework. Darcy brings me hot cocoa and Glenn helps me with my math problems.
5. My parents have *influenced* me to get lots of exercise and eat healthfully.

Big Question Vocabulary—2, p. 2

1. *community*
2. the way we are always there for each other and the deep *connection* we feel towards each other.
3. *belief*
4. the most important thing we can do for our friends
5. *participation* will be a valuable and fun part of your life.
6. *Values*

Big Question Vocabulary—3, p. 3

1. I feel *isolated* in the city. I miss the *culture* of a small town and I do not understand the *culture* of the people here.
2. Get *involved* with a *group* of people who like to play soccer like you do.
3. Thank you. It is nice to talk to you Steve, because we share a similar *history* and you really understand me.

"Black Cowboy, Wild Horses" by Julius Lester

Vocabulary Warm-up Exercises, p. 8

A. 1. distinct
2. scarcely
3. herd
4. corral
5. plains
6. grazed
7. presence
8. maintaining

B. Sample Answers

1. Yes, the air became cooler at <u>dusk</u>.
2. Yes, the lights <u>flickered</u> during the night.
3. Yes, I have climbed a <u>steep</u> mountain.
4. Yes, the warning lights were <u>faint</u>.
5. The students just <u>milled</u> around because the teacher had not arrived.
6. Yes, I was <u>peering</u> through the telescope.
7. Yes, that is a spider <u>suspended</u> over my plate.
8. Yes, I am amazed by the <u>vastness</u> of the universe.

Reading Warm-up A, p. 9

Sample Answers

1. (eat grass and plants); Buffalo also *grazed*.
2. <u>have some features that [others] do not have</u>; This shirt comes in three *distinct* colors—black, white, and striped.
3. (protect); You would most likely see a *corral* on a ranch.
4. (large groups of horses); Cattle, sheep, and goats also live in *herds*.
5. (open spaces); You would usually not find mountains on *plains*.
6. <u>Compared to that large number, there are now . . . any left</u>; *Scarcely* means "hardly any at all."
7. (keeping); The good condition of a car also needs *maintaining*.
8. (on the plains) and (America); Someone who asks for your *presence* wants you to appear before them, visit them, or be with them.

Reading Warm-up B, p. 10

Sample Answers

1. <u>only a few minutes of daylight left</u>; *Dusky* means "dark."
2. (Growing less and less bright); *Bright* means the opposite of *faint*.
3. <u>open space larger than anything I had ever seen</u>; The ocean and outer space also have the quality of *vastness*.
4. (sharply sloping); The road was so *steep* that the car could not make it to the top.
5. (light) and (faded); If a light bulb flickered, you would replace it.
6. <u>eyes straining</u>; When you are *peering*, you are using the sense of sight.
7. <u>hanging there in midair</u>; If a climber is *suspended*, he is hanging by a rope.
8. (moving around, not willing to leave); If students *milled* around after class, they might be waiting to speak to the teacher.

Julius Lester

Listening and Viewing, p. 11

Sample answers and guidelines for evaluation:

Segment 1: In his books, Julius Lester retells traditional folk tales for a young audience. Students may answer that it is important to continue sharing these stories so that they are preserved. Students may also suggest that they can learn more about American history and culture by reading traditional tales.

Segment 2: Bob Lemmons was a former slave turned cowboy who was able to corral wild horses. Julius Lester became fascinated with Lemmons after learning that he was able to round up horses by convincing the horses that he, himself, was a horse. Students may answer that details and vivid language are important because they make the story come alive, help put the reader into the world created in the story, and make the story more realistic.

Segment 3: By rewriting his drafts, Julius Lester learns more about his subject and develops his ideas further. Students may answer that they can learn more about their interests and what matters to them by writing.

Segment 4: Students may answer that Julius Lester's stories bridge past and present because he writes traditional tales of the past so that young readers can learn more about American history and culture. Students may suggest that stories have a beginning, a middle, and an end in which problems are resolved; stories can give readers faith that life's problems are solvable.

Learning About the Oral Tradition, p. 12

1. universal theme
2. myth
3. fable
4. personification
5. folk tale

"Black Cowboy, Wild Horses"
by Julius Lester

Model Selection: The Oral Tradition, p. 13

A. 1. hyperbole
2. Samples include "mountains made of fear," "as white as grief," "as hard and stinging as remorse."
3. personification
4. Samples include "the sun's round shoulders," "candle flames shivering," "the earth shuddered."
5. Answers may vary. Like other cowboys, Bob goes out to round up wild horses. He sleeps outdoors, and he has a great working relationship with his horse. Unlike other cowboys, Bob has an extremely keen, uncanny sense for the thoughts, fears, and movements of horses. He can make himself act like a horse in order to find the herd, overtake the lead stallion, and bring the herd into the corral.

B. Students may describe the story as a legend or a folk tale. It is based on facts about a real man, Bob Lemmons, and true events, but many details of the story make Bob seem almost magical and greater than life.

Open-Book Test, p. 14

Short Answer

1. It is an example of personification, giving human characteristics to a nonhuman subject.
   Difficulty: *Easy*   **Objective:** *Literary Analysis*

2. It contains a universal theme or message about life and fantasy, highly imaginative writing with elements not found in real life.
   Difficulty: *Average*   **Objective:** *Literary Analysis*

3. It is a fable, a short story with animal characters that teaches a lesson.
   Difficulty: *Average*   **Objective:** *Literary Analysis*

4. The stories stopped changing after they were written down. As they were told orally, each storyteller might add and change details.
   Difficulty: *Challenging*   **Objective:** *Literary Analysis*

5. The author uses personification to give human characteristics to the sky and the earth. For example, he says "the earth lay napping like a curled cat."
   Difficulty: *Easy*   **Objective:** *Literary Analysis*

6. Lester is using hyperbole. He is exaggerating what Bob could do.
   Difficulty: *Average*   **Objective:** *Literary Analysis*

7. He has to smell of the natural things the mustangs are used to. If he smells like a man, they will run from him.
   Difficulty: *Challenging*   **Objective:** *Interpretation*

8. *Remorse* means "guilt over a wrong." Remorse can come over you quickly and take over all your thoughts, just like a hard rain can come quickly and blot out everything else.
   Difficulty: *Challenging*   **Objective:** *Vocabulary*

9. The herd has just lost a colt. The leader is distracted by the death and "would not have the heart to fight fiercely."
   Difficulty: *Average*   **Objective:** *Interpretation*

10. They are both longing to be free to run and ride with the wild horses out on the open plains.
    Difficulty: *Average*   **Objective:** *Interpretation*

Essay

11. Students should state that Lemmons has amazing powers to understand and communicate with horses. He is able to read animal tracks to understand the size of the animals, how many there are, and where they are going. He respects and loves nature. Some students may say he is strong and brave because of the way he handles the horses. Others may say he is cruel because he uses violence with the horses.
    Difficulty: *Easy*   **Objective:** *Essay*

12. Students should use examples from the story to show how Lester brings to life the cowboy, the horses (including Warrior), and the plains of the American West. Their writing should include descriptive images and should make the point that Lester's imagination gives life to historical facts about black cowboys.

    Difficulty: *Average*   **Objective:** *Essay*

13. Answers will vary. Students may suggest some of the following themes: all animals yearn for freedom; all animals can communicate; animals and humans are connected. All suggested themes should be supported with details from the story.

    Difficulty: *Challenging*   **Objective:** *Essay*

14. Students may say Bob's decision is completely shaped by his community. It is his job to round up wild horses. His community of cowboys depends on his skill and his work. Students should state and support their opinion of whether he made the right choice.

    Difficulty: *Average*   **Objective:** *Essay*

Oral Response

15. Oral responses should be clear, well organized, and well supported by appropriate examples from the selection.

    Difficulty: *Average*   **Objective:** *Oral Interpretation*

Selection Test A, p. 17

Learning About the Oral Tradition

1. ANS: A	DIF: Easy	OBJ: Literary Analysis
2. ANS: B	DIF: Easy	OBJ: Literary Analysis
3. ANS: D	DIF: Easy	OBJ: Literary Analysis
4. ANS: D	DIF: Easy	OBJ: Literary Analysis
5. ANS: C	DIF: Easy	OBJ: Literary Analysis

Critical Reading

6. ANS: B	DIF: Easy	OBJ: Literary Analysis
7. ANS: D	DIF: Easy	OBJ: Comprehension
8. ANS: D	DIF: Easy	OBJ: Comprehension
9. ANS: A	DIF: Easy	OBJ: Comprehension
10. ANS: C	DIF: Easy	OBJ: Comprehension
11. ANS: A	DIF: Easy	OBJ: Comprehension
12. ANS: D	DIF: Easy	OBJ: Interpretation
13. ANS: C	DIF: Easy	OBJ: Interpretation
14. ANS: B	DIF: Easy	OBJ: Comprehension
15. ANS: B	DIF: Easy	OBJ: Interpretation

Essay

16. Students will probably say that Bob and Warrior want to be free, to run with the wild horses out in the lands that do not have fences and limits.

    Difficulty: *Easy*

    Objective: *Essay*

17. Students should present accurate summaries of their chosen portions of the story and provide reasons for their choices.

    Difficulty: *Easy*

    Objective: *Essay*

18. Students may say Bob's decision is completely shaped by his community. It is his job to round up wild horses. His community of cowboys depends on his skill and his work. He stays for them, not to please himself. Students should state and support their opinion of whether he made the right choice.

Selection Test B, p. 20

Learning About the Oral Tradition

1. ANS: B	DIF: Average	OBJ: Literary Analysis
2. ANS: C	DIF: Average	OBJ: Literary Analysis
3. ANS: D	DIF: Average	OBJ: Literary Analysis
4. ANS: A	DIF: Average	OBJ: Literary Analysis
5. ANS: A	DIF: Challenging	OBJ: Literary Analysis
6. ANS: C	DIF: Average	OBJ: Literary Analysis

Critical Reading

7. ANS: B	DIF: Average	OBJ: Literary Analysis
8. ANS: C	DIF: Average	OBJ: Comprehension
9. ANS: D	DIF: Average	OBJ: Comprehension
10. ANS: A	DIF: Average	OBJ: Comprehension
11. ANS: C	DIF: Average	OBJ: Comprehension
12. ANS: A	DIF: Average	OBJ: Comprehension
13. ANS: C	DIF: Average	OBJ: Literary Analysis
14. ANS: A	DIF: Challenging	OBJ: Interpretation
15. ANS: C	DIF: Challenging	OBJ: Comprehension
16. ANS: B	DIF: Challenging	OBJ: Interpretation
17. ANS: A	DIF: Average	OBJ: Interpretation
18. ANS: C	DIF: Challenging	OBJ: Interpretation

Essay

19. Students may suggest such themes as "all animals are related, physically and emotionally," "all animals yearn for freedom," "all animals can communicate at some level," and so on. All suggested themes should be supported by details from the story.

    Difficulty: *Average*

    Objective: *Essay*

20. Students should note that he is able to read animal tracks to tell the number and size of the animals as well as the direction in which they are moving. He has uncanny powers to understand and communicate with horses. He is strong, resilient, brave, and able to work alone. He has also been able to train his horse to be an extremely strong and capable partner. He respects nature and the rights of living things. He refuses to kill

the rattlesnake, even though it was lethal. The violence associated with the defeat of the stallion may make students have some negative thoughts about him as well. Some may say that he can be cruel in order to get the results that he needs.

Difficulty: *Average*

Objective: *Essay*

21. Students should effectively paraphrase the selected image and clearly explain how the image contributes to their understanding.

Difficulty: *Challenging*

Objective: *Essay*

22. Students may say Bob's decision is completely shaped by his community. It is his job to round up wild horses. His community of cowboys depends on his skill and his work. Students should state and support their opinion of whether he made the right choice.

"The Tiger Who Would Be King" by James Thurber
"The Ant and the Dove" by Leo Tolstoy

Vocabulary Warm-up Exercises, p. 24

A. 1. jungle
2. creature
3. stripes
4. cubs
5. den
6. prowled
7. greet
8. sake

B. Sample Answers

1. If I <u>inquired</u> about a topic, that means I asked about it and so would want to know more about it.

2. I would not choose to witness something that made me feel <u>horror</u> because it would scare me.

3. A <u>monarch</u>, such as a king or queen, is not elected.

4. I would want to <u>defend</u> those I love and protect them from harm.

5. If my vacation days are <u>numbered</u>, it means not many of them are left.

6. I would expect a <u>struggle</u> to be long, hard, and difficult.

7. After a person has <u>surveyed</u> a situation, he or she has learned more about that situation by looking at the whole thing closely.

8. I would not believe it because <u>imaginary</u> things are not real.

Reading Warm-up A, p. 25

Sample Answers

1. <u>living animals</u>; A *creature* is a living being like a person or an animal.

2. (narrow bands of color); My tabby cat has *stripes* on her fur.

3. (There, they are protected by the thick plant growth of these tropical areas.); The tree frogs lived among the plants in the *jungle.*

4. <u>meet, friendly manner</u>; I usually *greet* my friends by saying hello.

5. <u>young tigers</u>; The lioness looked after her newborn *cubs.*

6. (this home); A *den* is a place where certain types of animals live.

7. <u>hunting for prey</u>; The cat *prowled* through the barn, looking for mice.

8. (laws have been passed, benefit tigers); I studied hard for the *sake* of getting good grades.

Reading Warm-up B, p. 26

Sample Answers

1. <u>king or queen</u>; A *monarch* is the unelected single ruler of a country.

2. (great effort); The *struggle* for women's rights is still being fought.

3. <u>They have looked at the government.</u> The general *surveyed* the battlefield.

4. <u>There is only a small amount of time left.</u> My days as the shortest person in my family are *numbered* because I'm growing taller.

5. <u>to ask the proper questions</u>; This morning, I *inquired* about train schedules to the city.

6. (real); Something that is *imaginary* is made up and is not real.

7. <u>the injustices of the first government</u>; The civil rights worker wanted to *defend* his ideals.

8. (terror); The boy felt a sense of *horror* when he saw the victims of the crime.

Writing About the Big Question, p. 27

A. 1. community, culture, family, generation, group
2. belief
3. influence
4. history, values

B. Sample Answers

1. I didn't speak up when some friends were criticizing another girl; I joined a group of friends who were putting on a play.

2. When I did not defend the other girl, I felt **isolated** even though I was in a **group.** I realized that I didn't have anything in common with my friends, and their **influence** had made me **participate** in something I felt was wrong.

C. Sample Answer

Members of my community helped one another when the winter rainstorms caused the creek to flood and we piled sandbags around one another's houses. It was a great experience. I got to meet neighbors I had never spoken to before. I also felt good about helping people.

"The Tiger Who Would Be King"
by James Thurber
"The Ant and the Dove" by Leo Tolstoy

Reading: Reread to Analyze Cause-and-Effect Relationships, p. 28

Sample Answers
2. The tiger goes to the lion's den.
4. All the animals join the fight.
5. The tiger wins but is badly hurt.

Effect B. Everyone dies. OR There is no kingdom left to rule.

Literary Analysis: Fables and Folk Tales, p. 29

Sample Answers
1. The tiger and the lion are the main characters.
2. None of the characters is admirable.
3. They all get into trouble; they don't think before they act.
4. There's no point in being king if you have no subjects. (Students may find other lessons.)
5. An ant, a dove, and a man are the main characters.
6. The dove (or the ant) is admirable.
7. The dove saves the ant without thinking about a reward. The ant pays back the kindness that it owes the dove.
8. You never can tell how or when a good deed will be repaid. (Students may find other lessons.)

Vocabulary Builder, p. 30

Sample Answers
A. 1. surprised; Surprised by the sudden thunder, I ran for shelter.
2. sneaked; A skunk sneaked under the porch and waited quietly.
3. repel; The ant fought bravely to repel the enemy attacker.
4. asked; We asked about the location of the exhibit at the information desk.
5. gave back; My father gave his friend back all of the money he owed.
6. king; The crown prince became king when his father died.

B. 1. Possible response: give him a CD.
2. Possible response: a referee's call.
3. Possible response: she explained her views on the issue.

Enrichment: Cooperation, p. 31

A. Sample Answers
1. I could offer to lend her my bike or deliver her papers for her.
2. I could help him understand how to do long division.

3. I could help out by setting the table, offering to wash the dishes, or helping with some of the cooking.

B. Students should write about a situation in which one person helps another.

Open-Book Test, p. 32

Short Answer
1. The animals die because they join in the fight.
   Difficulty: *Easy* **Objective:** *Reading*
2. It is a fable. It has animal characters, and there is a moral at the end.
   Difficulty: *Easy* **Objective:** *Literary Analysis*
3. The tigress is practical. She tells the tiger he cannot be king because there is already a king.
   Difficulty: *Average* **Objective:** *Interpretation*
4. Effect boxes: all the animals are killed; tiger is king
   Tiger does get what he wants, to be king, but he is dying and all the animals are dead.
   Difficulty: *Average* **Objective:** *Reading*
5. *Prowled* means "moved quietly and secretly." He moved this way because he wanted to sneak up on lion and defeat him.
   Difficulty: *Average* **Objective:** *Vocabulary*
6. Students should explain the moral in their own words. Some examples: be careful what you wish for, think before you act, your actions are important.
   Difficulty: *Challenging* **Objective:** *Literary Analysis*
7. The people valued kindness. The dove saved the ant from drowning, and the ant saved the dove from being captured.
   Difficulty: *Easy* **Objective:** *Interpretation*
8. It is both grateful and surprised that the ant was able to save it from the hunter.
   Difficulty: *Challenging* **Objective:** *Interpretation*
9. The ant bites the hunter's foot, which surprises the hunter and causes him to drop his net.
   Difficulty: *Average* **Objective:** *Reading*
10. It is entertaining, and it teaches a lesson about being kind.
    Difficulty: *Average* **Objective:** *Literary Analysis*

Essay
11. Students should explain the lesson of each story. They may say that "The Tiger Who Would Be King" teaches you to think before you act or to be careful what you wish for. The lesson of "The Ant and the Dove" is to be kind. Students should support their opinions on which lesson is more important.
    Difficulty: *Easy* **Objective:** *Essay*
12. Students should make a case for either lesson. Some will say that it is just to be kind. The dove saved the ant with no thought of being repaid. Only at the end does the dove think about its kindness being returned. Others may say that the dove's thoughts at the end show the real lesson and that the ant saved the dove in return

for being saved. Most students will say the better lesson is just to be kind.

Difficulty: *Average* **Objective:** *Essay*

13. Students who say that "The Tiger Who Would Be King" would change the most should explain that the battle between the animals would be a war scene and probably more upsetting. They may say the story would be more effective in warning against the dangers of war, but it may be less effective because it would be less entertaining. Students who say "The Ant and the Dove" would change the most should explain that human characters would make the story more realistic. They may say the story would be more effective because of the realism.

Difficulty: *Challenging* **Objective:** *Essay*

14. Students should explain that the animals were shaped by the community as they jumped into the battle between the tiger and the lion. Most of them acted without thinking about their actions or even knowing why they were fighting. Most students will say the animals acted unwisely in allowing themselves to be shaped in this way.

Difficulty: *Average* **Objective:** *Essay*

Oral Response

15. Oral responses should be clear, well organized, and well supported by appropriate examples from the selections.

Difficulty: *Average* **Objective:** *Oral Interpretation*

Selection Test A, p. 35

Critical Reading

1. ANS: A	DIF: Easy	OBJ: Comprehension
2. ANS: C	DIF: Easy	OBJ: Reading
3. ANS: B	DIF: Easy	OBJ: Literary Analysis
4. ANS: D	DIF: Easy	OBJ: Reading
5. ANS: B	DIF: Easy	OBJ: Interpretation
6. ANS: C	DIF: Easy	OBJ: Literary Analysis

Vocabulary and Grammar

7. ANS: A	DIF: Easy	OBJ: Vocabulary
8. ANS: B	DIF: Easy	OBJ: Vocabulary
9. ANS: D	DIF: Easy	OBJ: Vocabulary
10. ANS: A	DIF: Easy	OBJ: Grammar

Essay

11. If students choose "The Tiger Who Would Be King," they may state either Thurber's lesson ("You can't very well be king of beasts if there aren't any"), or they may say that war is bad for everyone, or that no one wins a war. If they choose "The Ant and the Dove," they may identify the lesson as "Kindness pays off," or "Help others because they will be there for you when you need help." Students may explain that either lesson could easily apply to human society, where war and unkindness are common.

Difficulty: *Easy*

Objective: *Essay*

12. Students should explain that the animals were shaped by the community as they jumped into the battle between the tiger and the lion. Most of them acted without thinking about their actions or even knowing why they were fighting. Most students will say the animals acted unwisely in allowing themselves to be shaped (and thus killed) in this way.

Selection Test B, p. 37

Critical Reading

1. ANS: D	DIF: Average	OBJ: Comprehension
2. ANS: A	DIF: Average	OBJ: Interpretation
3. ANS: C	DIF: Average	OBJ: Reading
4. ANS: B	DIF: Average	OBJ: Literary Analysis
5. ANS: D	DIF: Challenging	OBJ: Interpretation
6. ANS: B	DIF: Challenging	OBJ: Literary Analysis
7. ANS: A	DIF: Average	OBJ: Comprehension
8. ANS: D	DIF: Average	OBJ: Reading

Vocabulary and Grammar

9. ANS: A	DIF: Challenging	OBJ: Vocabulary
10. ANS: D	DIF: Average	OBJ: Vocabulary
11. ANS: C	DIF: Average	OBJ: Vocabulary
12. ANS: B	DIF: Challenging	OBJ: Grammar

Essay

13. Students' essays should identify two ways in which the animal characters in the stories are different. For example, in Thurber's fable, the animals speak. They also have human qualities that create problems for them: ambition, boastfulness, willingness to go to war. In Tolstoy's folk tale, the animals do not speak, and they reveal "good" human qualities such as kindness and mercy toward each other. Students may point out that Thurber takes a humorous approach, while Tolstoy is more serious. While both writers teach moral lessons, Thurber encourages readers to laugh at his animals and the human weaknesses they illustrate.

Difficulty: *Average*

Objective: *Essay*

14. Students' essays should discuss the values of kindness, thoughtfulness, and mercy in "The Ant and the Dove." They might explain that these values are stressed as important to survival. A random act of kindness has great consequences for the dove when the ant repays the dove by biting the hunter. Tolstoy, the storyteller, is teaching that people should be kind and helpful to one another, for one never knows when a kindness will be returned.

Difficulty: *Challenging*

Objective: *Essay*

15. Students should explain that the animals were shaped by the community as they jumped into the battle

between the tiger and the lion. Most of them acted with-out thinking about their actions or even knowing why they were fighting. Most students will say the animals acted unwisely in allowing themselves to be shaped in this way.

"The Lion and the Bulls" by Aesop
"A Crippled Boy" by My-Van Tran

Vocabulary Warm-up Exercises, p. 40

A. 1. extremely
   2. reports
   3. unusual
   4. attention
   5. attempted
   6. interrupted
   7. miserable
   8. success

B. Sample Answers
   1. Joey provided his family with company by seeing them often.
   2. The official had one of the most important jobs in the organization.
   3. Lauren withdrew from the race by choosing not to run.
   4. Anthony tried to lure the bird into his hand by offer-ing it food.
   5. A palace is a place where a ruler lives.
   6. Kerry chose to demonstrate her skill as a writer by using perfect grammar.
   7. Marco remained at his friend's house and stayed for dinner.

Reading Warm-up A, p. 41

Sample Answers
   1. People have been interested in; When you give attention to something, you think a lot about it.
   2. (accounts); I no longer believe the weather reports because they are often wrong.
   3. (rare); I think that having blue hair is unusual.
   4. very much; I can play basketball extremely well.
   5. very unhappy; Someone who is miserable is very unhappy.
   6. (she must try again); I attempted to be on time for class today.
   7. the male lion will get to eat first; When I graduated from high school, I knew my education had been a success.
   8. (the lions' natural way of life); I interrupted my friend's story yesterday.

Reading Warm-up B, p. 42

Sample Answers
   1. king's/ large and grand building; I would love to live in a palace, but I would not want to be a ruler.

   2. (to show how well she could cook); To demonstrate is to show or explain something to someone else.
   3. drawn in; The smell of popcorn started to lure me into the movie theater.
   4. stayed there for a while; If you have remained some-where, you have stayed there for an amount of time.
   5. (this man held one of the most important positions in the king's government); The official at the company made important decisions.
   6. filled with shyness; The frightened turtle withdrew into his shell.
   7. giving me this delicious treat; To have provided some-thing means that you have given another person a much-needed gift or service.
   8. (They meant a lot to her.); When I was little, I treasured my favorite teddy bear.

Writing About the Big Question, p. 43

A. 1. isolated
   2. family
   3. values
   4. common

B. Sample Answers
   1. Once, when I moved to a new school, I felt very alone. Once, when I had a fight with my best friend, I didn't talk to anyone else and felt alone.
   2. When I moved to the new school, I felt very **isolated**, with no **connection** with anyone else. I would see **groups** of students hanging out, and I wanted to be **involved** with them, but I didn't know how.

C. Sample Answer
   One day, someone asked me for help with a homework assignment *because* he had missed the class. It was easy for me to help him, and that became my first **connection** with my new school. After that, I discovered I had a lot in **common** with some other students, and I became part of the **community** in my school. I don't feel **isolated** any more.

"The Lion and the Bulls" by Aesop
"A Crippled Boy" by My-Van Tran

Reading: Reread to Analyze Cause-and-Effect Relationships, p. 44

Sample Answers
   2. The bulls form a ring.
   4. The lion spreads evil reports.
   5. The bulls avoid one another.
Effect B. The lion kills the bulls one by one.

Literary Analysis: Fables and Folk Tales, p. 45

Sample Answers
   1. The main characters are a lion and three bulls.

2. None of the characters is admirable.

3. The lion is clever, but he spreads false rumors; the three bulls believe the rumors and bring about their own ruin.

4. If people stand together, they can defeat their enemies.

5. The main characters are a crippled boy named Theo and the King.

6. Theo is admirable.

7. He practices throwing pebbles until he is very good at it.

8. Perfecting a skill by practicing it can lead to success.

Vocabulary Builder, p. 46

Sample Answers

A. 1. People dislike hearing <u>slauderous</u> reworks about their friends.

2. In schools of the future, a robot may be <u>provided</u> to help students with their home work.

3. To <u>demonstrate</u> the law of gravity, Tom dropped a rock from the table to the floor.

4. Possible response: The <u>crippled</u> rabbit limped away slowly.

5. Possible response: The <u>official</u> Web site for the store says, "Our prices can't be beat!"

6. Possible response: We tried to <u>lure</u> my cat to sit on my lap by dangling a toy.

B. 1. Possible response: angry, because it is full of lies

2. Possible response: laugh, because it would be very funny

3. Possible response: reluctant to do it, because it would take a lot of work

Enrichment: Devising a Strategy, p. 47

Students' lists should include what a student might be expected to do in a typical day, including homework assignments in various subjects, as well as a few optional activities. Priorities should reflect the relative importance of completing required schoolwork.

"The Tiger Who Would Be King"
by James Thurber
"The Ant and the Dove" by Leo Tolstoy
"The Lion and the Bulls" by Aesop
"A Crippled Boy" by My-Van Tran

Integrated Language Skills: Grammar, p. 48

A. 1. independent

2. subordinate

3. independent

4. subordinate

B. Sample Answers

1. After we finished eating, we watched TV.

2. By the time we saw the bear, she was very close.

3. Although we got away that time, we learned our lesson.

"The Lion and the Bulls" by Aesop
"A Crippled Boy" by My-Van Tran

Open-Book Test, p. 51

Short Answer

1. Cause: lion lies to the bulls; Effects: bulls split up, and lion eats the bulls.

   The bulls cause their own downfall by distrusting and splitting apart from each other.

   Difficulty: *Average*   **Objective:** *Reading*

2. *Slanderous* means "including untrue and damaging statements." Students should be angry or upset if slanderous comments were made about them.

   Difficulty: *Easy*   **Objective:** *Vocabulary*

3. The bulls were distrustful. Because they did not trust each other, they believed the lion's lies and avoided each other.

   Difficulty: *Average*   **Objective:** *Interpretation*

4. The storyteller is teaching a lesson. The lesson appears at the end of the story.

   Difficulty: *Easy*   **Objective:** *Literary Analysis*

5. The mandarins demonstrate, or show clearly, that they like to talk and will not stop unless something makes them stop.

   Difficulty: *Average*   **Objective:** *Vocabulary*

6. The short-term effect is that the mandarins stop speaking. The long-term effect is that the King is so pleased, he lets Theo remain at the palace.

   Difficulty: *Easy*   **Objective:** *Reading*

7. Theo's disability leaves him lonely and alone. That is a negative result. The positive result is that because he could not play, he practiced aiming stones at targets and got a job working for the King.

   Difficulty: *Challenging*   **Objective:** *Reading*

8. The curtain hides Theo from the mandarins. Without the curtain, the King's plan to stop the mandarins from speaking would fail because they would not be surprised.

   Difficulty: *Average*   **Objective:** *Interpretation*

9. The lion and the King both have a goal. Both use trickery (telling lies and hiding a stone thrower) to get what they want.

   Difficulty: *Challenging*   **Objective:** *Interpretation*

10. The lesson is that hard work and practice will be rewarded. In the end, the boy is happily living in the palace. He is not alone and does not have to beg for food because he made the most of what he had.

    Difficulty: *Average*   **Objective:** *Literary Analysis*

Essay

11. Students should compare the characters: Both are clever, both use tricks to get what they want, both succeed in the end. Students will most likely choose the King as more admirable even though he tricks the mandarins.

    Difficulty: *Easy*   **Objective:** *Essay*

12. Students should explain the lessons from both stories, which should be something like "We're stronger together" and "Practice makes perfect," and tell which one they find more applicable in today's world.

Difficulty: *Average* **Objective:** *Essay*

13. Students should say that the bulls, by not trusting one another and by listening to the lion's lies, brought about their own deaths. They turned on each other and thus were brought down separately. Had they chosen to talk to each other about the lion's words, they might have remained friends and stood together to defeat him.

Difficulty: *Challenging* **Objective:** *Essay*

14. Students may say that Theo is shaped more by community because he depends on people to feed him and bring him stones. The King is part of Theo's community, and when he takes Theo to the palace, he permanently shapes his life. Other students may say Theo's life is shaped more by other factors: his disability and his own skill and patience at throwing pebbles. They may see the King as removed from the community and as more of a powerful individual force on Theo's life.

Difficulty: *Average* **Objective:** *Essay*

Oral Response

15. Oral responses should be clear, well organized, and well supported by appropriate examples from the selections.

Difficulty: *Average* **Objective:** *Oral Interpretation*

Selection Test A, p. 54

Critical Reading

1. ANS: D	DIF: Easy	OBJ: Reading
2. ANS: A	DIF: Easy	OBJ: Interpretation
3. ANS: B	DIF: Easy	OBJ: Literary Analysis
4. ANS: C	DIF: Easy	OBJ: Comprehension
5. ANS: B	DIF: Easy	OBJ: Reading
6. ANS: C	DIF: Easy	OBJ: Literary Analysis

Vocabulary and Grammar

7. ANS: D	DIF: Easy	OBJ: Vocabulary
8. ANS: D	DIF: Easy	OBJ: Vocabulary
9. ANS: C	DIF: Easy	OBJ: Vocabulary
10. ANS: B	DIF: Easy	OBJ: Grammar

Essay

11. Students' essays should choose either tale and identify its purpose. Students might say, for example, that the purpose of "The Lion and the Bulls" is primarily to teach a lesson. None of the characters is heroic. The situation is not entertaining. The storyteller may have had the moral in mind first and then made up a story to teach it. "A Crippled Boy" both entertains and teaches. Theo is a resourceful hero who overcomes his disability and achieves success.

Difficulty: *Easy*

Objective: *Essay*

12. Students may say Theo is shaped more by community because he depends on people to feed him and then to bring him rocks. The King is part of Theo's community, and when he takes Theo to the palace, he permanently shapes his life. Other students may say Theo's life is shaped more by the other factors: Without his disability, he would not have been alone as much. He would not have learned to throw rocks, and the king would not have noticed him.

Selection Test B, p. 56

Critical Reading

1. ANS: D	DIF: Average	OBJ: Reading
2. ANS: A	DIF: Average	OBJ: Comprehension
3. ANS: C	DIF: Challenging	OBJ: Interpretation
4. ANS: B	DIF: Average	OBJ: Literary Analysis
5. ANS: A	DIF: Average	OBJ: Reading
6. ANS: B	DIF: Average	OBJ: Interpretation
7. ANS: D	DIF: Average	OBJ: Comprehension
8. ANS: B	DIF: Challenging	OBJ: Literary Analysis

Vocabulary and Grammar

9. ANS: C	DIF: Average	OBJ: Vocabulary
10. ANS: B	DIF: Average	OBJ: Vocabulary
11. ANS: C	DIF: Challenging	OBJ: Vocabulary
12. ANS: A	DIF: Average	OBJ: Grammar

Essay

13. Students' essays should identify how the bulls and Theo cause and deserve the fates they receive. In "The Lion and the Bulls," the bulls foolishly believe the lion's evil reports. They begin to avoid one another, so the lion is able to kill and eat them one by one. The bulls' distrust and stupidity are the causes for their downfall. In "The Crippled Boy," Theo practices and develops his pebble-throwing skill instead of feeling sorry for himself. Becoming an expert helps Theo overcome his loneliness and attracts the attention of the King. Theo's skill and loyalty please the King and cause him to value Theo's presence and service. Theo's well-deserved fate is to live happily at the palace, where he no longer has to worry about loneliness or begging for food.

Difficulty: *Average*

Objective: *Essay*

14. Students' essays may state other lessons in "The Lion and the Bulls": Divide and conquer; Never trust what an enemy says; or Always keep faith with your friends. The lesson in "A Crippled Boy" might be: Practice makes perfect; Never give up; or Make the most of your skills and abilities. Students should choose one lesson as more relevant and support their choice with reasons.

Difficulty: *Challenging*

Objective: *Essay*

15. Students may say Theo is shaped more by community because he depends on people to feed him and then to bring him rocks. The King is part of Theo's community, and when he takes Theo to the palace, he permanently shapes his life. Other students may say Theo's life is shaped more by other factors: his disability, and his own skill and patience at throwing rocks. They may see the King as removed from the community and as more of a powerful individual force on Theo's life.

"Arachne" by Olivia E. Coolidge

Vocabulary Warm-up Exercises, p. 59

A. 1. marvelous
2. descend
3. olive
4. goddess
5. presence
6. challenged
7. products
8. judged

B. **Sample Answers**
1. A boy who found out that he had been *deceived* would probably be angry because he was not told the truth.
2. If a cow is *amid* its herd, it is surrounded by many other cows.
3. I would not get in a car with a *reckless* driver because he or she would take too many chances while driving.
4. *Strands* of thread are weaker than woven cloth because they are thin and stand alone, not connected to one another.
5. I would like to look at something *gorgeous* because it would be very beautiful.
6. A runner in a race would not like to be *overtaken* because someone else would then be in front of him or her.
7. If it is your *fate* to grow old, you will, because that is your destiny.

Reading Warm-up A, p. 60

Sample Answers
1. They would come down to Earth to watch the activities of the mortals. I must *descend* a steep flight of stairs to reach the basement.
2. A goddess is a female god or deity. This passage is about the *goddess* Athene.
3. (contest, winner); I once *challenged* my sister to a bicycle race.
4. (many onlookers, all who were there); If you are in someone's *presence*, you are close to him or her.
5. The spring created a sense of wonder in all who . . . saw it. The mountain climbers had a *marvelous* view of the valley below.

6. (tree created small fruits called olives); An *olive* tree was a very important gift for the Athenians because they could use its fruits and oil for many things.
7. (olives, oil . . . for cooking, fuel for lamps) There are many different *products* made out of paper, like books and paper towels.
8. They decided that the olive tree was the better gift. I once *judged* a Halloween costume contest between my friends.

Reading Warm-up B, p. 61

Sample Answers
1. (very beautiful); I looked beautiful while wearing the *gorgeous* dress.
2. A spider makes these long, thin threads out of a special protein created by its body. A head of hair is made up of many *strands*.
3. (weaving these threads together in a pattern); I am *skillful* at drawing pictures.
4. This seemingly careless maneuver; Something that is *reckless* is often dangerous.
5. As the spider crawls within these strands; I walked *amid* the trees in the forest.
6. (The barely visible webs trick other insects, which then fly right into them.); To be *deceived* is to be tricked into believing something that is not true.
7. Then the spider will move quickly to catch the bug. I was *overtaken* by my brother on the race home from school.
8. After the insect is trapped, its *fate* is to be eaten by the spider.

Writing About the Big Question, p. 62

A. 1. generation
2. culture, community
3. support
4. values

B. **Sample Answers**
1. Once I refused to eat my dinner, and my mom made me cook for the family the next night. Once I blamed the dog for something I did, and my dad wouldn't let me watch TV for a week.
2. Cooking dinner for everyone helped me see the **connection** between the meal and our life as a **family.** I found I wanted everyone to be **involved** in the meal I had prepared, that there was **value** in taking time to eat together.

C. **Sample Answer**
The story of the ant and the grasshopper *taught me that* you must think about the future. Planning for the future is an especially important **value** in our **culture** because we live in a difficult, uncertain world. This story teaches a good lesson to each **generation.** Young people might tend to be like the grasshopper, and focus only on present happiness. As they grow older, they will learn that there is a **connection** between present sacrifice and future security.

"Arachne" by Olivia E. Coolidge

Reading: Ask Questions to Analyze Cause-and-Effect Relationships, p. 63

Sample Answers

4. Arachne says she is a better weaver than Athene.
5. What happened?
6. An old woman scolds her.
7. Arachne needs to be taught a lesson.
10. Arachne does not apologize.
11. What happened?

Literary Analysis: Myths, p. 64

Sample Answers

1. It tells how the goddess Athene punished Arachne.
2. None
3. It explains where spiders come from and why they weave webs.
4. It teaches that too much confidence and pride can lead to a person's downfall.
5. It demonstrates and explains weaving; it expresses the importance of respect for old people (and parents) and respect for the gods.

Vocabulary Builder, p. 65

Sample Answers

A. 1. Arachne lived in a *obscure* village, a place that was not well known.
2. Someone who is *mortal* must eventually die.
3. Arachne showed her *obstinacy* when she stubbornly refused to apologize to Athene.
4. Possible response: very proud and boastful.
5. Possible response: Arachne had made her very angry.
6. Possible response: work hard to achieve it.

B. 1. Possible response: His speed record seemed immortal, since it lasted for decades.
2. Possible response: The young woman was a mortal, and so she was inferior to the mythological gods.

Enrichment: The Craft of Weaving, p. 66

A. Sample Answers

1. spin: to make yarn by drawing out, twisting, and winding fibers
2. loom: a hand-operated or power-driven machine for weaving fabrics
3. embroidery: the art of creating decorative designs on cloth, using a needle and thread
4. shuttle: a boat-shaped piece of wood for passing thread from one side of the loom to the other
5. distaff: a long stick for holding wool or thread when one is spinning by hand
6. skein: a length of yarn or thread wound or twisted in a coil

B. Students' answers should include the name of the craft, the name of the tool, the purpose of the tool, and a fairly detailed drawing.

Open-Book Test, p. 67

Short Answer

1. No, it does not remain "not well known." Word of Arachne's skill spreads, and more and more people come to the village to watch her weave.
   Difficulty: *Average* **Objective:** *Vocabulary*
2. People admire her skill by saying "Surely Athene herself must have taught her."
   Difficulty: *Average* **Objective:** *Reading*
3. Arachne's boasting that she is better than Athene causes the old woman (who is really Athene) to visit.
   Difficulty: *Easy* **Objective:** *Reading*
4. Arachne's design is insulting to the gods, and Athene is angry.
   Difficulty: *Average* **Objective:** *Reading*
5. They valued weaving.
   Difficulty: *Easy* **Objective:** *Literary Analysis*
6. Characters: Arachne; Nature: spiders; Value: being humble
   Lesson: Do not think mortals are in any way equal to gods.
   Difficulty: *Average* **Objective:** *Literary Analysis*
7. We can learn not to brag (or to be humble) and to be respectful.
   Difficulty: *Challenging* **Objective:** *Literary Analysis*
8. Either Arachne's initial boast that she is a better weaver than the goddess or her weaving an insulting cloth in front of the goddess shows Arachne's foolishness.
   Difficulty: *Challenging* **Objective:** *Interpretation*
9. They are both proud and clever. They both weave insults into their cloths.
   Difficulty: *Average* **Objective:** *Interpretation*
10. She wants all people to remember her power whenever they see a spider.
    Difficulty: *Easy* **Objective:** *Interpretation*

Essay

11. Students should explain that Arachne could have avoided her fate several times. She could have been more humble about her skill and not compared herself to a goddess. She could have showed respect to the old woman and heeded her warning. She could have accepted that Athene was in fact more skilled instead of insulting her.
    Difficulty: *Easy* **Objective:** *Essay*
12. Students should explain each weaving. Arachne's showed the gods misbehaving and tricking mortals. Athene's showed the gods battling not only each other but also the fates of mortals who had tried to trick the gods. The weavings show that the Greeks recognized that the gods were not all good but also that it was futile to try to outwit them.
    Difficulty: *Average* **Objective:** *Essay*

13. Students should give an explanation of any lesson taught by the myth and provide an argument as to whether the lesson is still important today.
   Difficulty: *Challenging*   **Objective:** *Essay*

14. Students may say that Arachne's mortal community failed her. They praised her too much, and the praise led to her being too proud. Others may say the community was responsible only for the praise, not for Arachne's reaction to it.
   Difficulty: *Average*   **Objective:** *Essay*

Oral Response

15. Oral responses should be clear, well organized and well supported by appropriate examples from the selection.
   Difficulty: *Average*   **Objective:** *Oral Interpretation*

"Arachne" by Olivia E. Coolidge

Selection Test A, p. 70

Critical Reading

1. ANS: A	DIF: Easy	OBJ: Literary Analysis
2. ANS: C	DIF: Easy	OBJ: Literary Analysis
3. ANS: D	DIF: Easy	OBJ: Reading
4. ANS: B	DIF: Easy	OBJ: Interpretation
5. ANS: C	DIF: Easy	OBJ: Comprehension
6. ANS: B	DIF: Easy	OBJ: Comprehension
7. ANS: D	DIF: Easy	OBJ: Interpretation
8. ANS: A	DIF: Easy	OBJ: Reading
9. ANS: B	DIF: Easy	OBJ: Interpretation
10. ANS: C	DIF: Easy	OBJ: Reading
11. ANS: A	DIF: Easy	OBJ: Literary Analysis

Vocabulary and Grammar

12. ANS: C	DIF: Easy	OBJ: Vocabulary
13. ANS: B	DIF: Easy	OBJ: Vocabulary
14. ANS: D	DIF: Easy	OBJ: Vocabulary
15. ANS: B	DIF: Easy	OBJ: Grammar

Essay

16. Students should describe Arachne as beautiful, skilled, and conceited. They should identify Arachne's pride and stubbornness as the character traits that drive the events of the story and bring about her downfall. Athene punishes Arachne for her conceit by making her an ugly creature whose spinning is hidden away in corners.
   Difficulty: *Easy*
   Objective: *Essay*

17. Students' essays may identify the lesson as some variation of "Do not be too arrogant about your skills." They should explain that this is an important lesson to learn

even today; someone who has too much confidence is usually disliked and thought of as conceited.
   Difficulty: *Easy*
   Objective: *Essay*

18. Students may say that Arachne's mortal community was directly responsible for her downfall. They praised her too much, and the praise led to her being too proud. Others may say the community was only responsible for the praise, not for Arachne's reaction to it. She could have accepted the praise graciously instead of insulting the goddess.

Selection Test B, p. 73

Critical Reading

1. ANS: A	DIF: Average	OBJ: Literary Analysis
2. ANS: C	DIF: Average	OBJ: Literary Analysis
3. ANS: B	DIF: Challenging	OBJ: Reading
4. ANS: D	DIF: Average	OBJ: Reading
5. ANS: C	DIF: Average	OBJ: Reading
6. ANS: C	DIF: Average	OBJ: Comprehension
7. ANS: B	DIF: Average	OBJ: Comprehension
8. ANS: C	DIF: Challenging	OBJ: Comprehension
9. ANS: A	DIF: Challenging	OBJ: Interpretation
10. ANS: B	DIF: Average	OBJ: Interpretation
11. ANS: B	DIF: Average	OBJ: Reading
12. ANS: D	DIF: Average	OBJ: Interpretation
13. ANS: D	DIF: Average	OBJ: Interpretation
14. ANS: B	DIF: Challenging	OBJ: Literary Analysis
15. ANS: A	DIF: Average	OBJ: Literary Analysis

Vocabulary and Grammar

16. ANS: C	DIF: Average	OBJ: Vocabulary
17. ANS: B	DIF: Average	OBJ: Vocabulary
18. ANS: D	DIF: Challenging	OBJ: Vocabulary
19. ANS: A	DIF: Average	OBJ: Grammar

Essay

20. Students' essays should focus on the combination of realism and fantasy in "Arachne." For example, the story treats Arachne's history and achievements realistically in the first part of the story. Arachne is described as a young girl who looks quite ordinary; she is a tireless worker who spins wool into beautiful cloth. Her father is a skillful dyer of wool, but he is a humble person and they both live in an obscure village. The only fantastic element at the beginning of the story is the mention of nymphs visiting Arachne to admire her work. Arachne's comments to her visitors seem realistic, even though she dares to compare herself to Athene. The first fantastic event is the magical transformation of the old

woman into Athene. The contest between girl and goddess is portrayed realistically, but at the end of the story there is a second magical transformation when Athene changes Arachne into a spider.

Difficulty: *Average*

Objective: *Essay*

21. Students' essays should identify two or three events in "Arachne" that show the effects of Arachne's lack of respect and her discontent. For example, Arachne is so proud of her skill that she is displeased when people assume that Athene must have taught her. She is disrespectful to the visitors and to her father's skill. She is disrespectful to Athene in both her disguised form and as a goddess. In her competition with Athene, the insulting design she weaves continues to show her disrespect. Throughout the story, Arachne might have saved herself if she had been content with her fame as the best human weaver and had shown respect for the superior powers of Athene. Instead, she insists that she is equal to the goddess, and she is punished for it.

Difficulty: *Challenging*

Objective: *Essay*

22. Students may say that Arachne's mortal community failed her. They praised her too much, and the praise led to her being too proud. Others may say the community was only responsible for the praise, not for Arachne's reaction to it.

Prologue *from* The Whale Rider
by Witi Ihimaera

Vocabulary Warm-up Exercises, p. 77

A.
1. brilliant
2. downward
3. perfumes
4. blessing
5. swirling
6. dazzled
7. noble
8. reflected

B. Sample Answers

1. Large, green leaves had grown on all of the plants in the lush garden.
2. The two friends were similar because they had many interests in common.
3. The gigantic skyscraper looked huge next to the tiny cottage.
4. Sandra found the wondrous experience to be very exciting.
5. The depths of the ocean are difficult to navigate because they are so far down.
6. Thirty books were sufficient to supply the classroom.
7. Martin was hurling himself against the door because he wanted to open it forcefully.

Reading Warm-up A, p. 78

Sample Answers

1. She always enjoyed going down the hill to the valley. I looked *downward* and noticed my shoelaces were untied.
2. one of the most special and sacred events of the year; My family always says a *blessing* before we eat dinner.
3. (a good and true soul); I would like to be *noble*, because that means being the best person I can be.
4. the water spun in circles; Something that is *swirling* is moving in a circular pattern.
5. (the colors of the sky); I like to see myself *reflected* in the mirror because then I know what I look like.
6. (shine brightly); The lightning lit up the sky with its *brilliant* flash.
7. landscape around her; The *perfumes* of the forest included decaying leaves and pine needles.
8. filled with a sense of amazement; I was *dazzled* the first time I went up to the top of a skyscraper.

Reading Warm-up B, p. 79

Sample Answers

1. (Some adult whales can grow to be more than one hundred feet long. They can weigh as much as 220 tons. These extremely large . . .); I think my school is *gigantic.*
2. They spend most of their lives below the surface of the ocean. Many creatures live *underwater*, such as coral and giant squid.
3. (share, related); If two things are *similar*, they have many of the same traits in common.
4. If the whale does not breathe in (enough) air, it cannot stay in the depths of the ocean. My lunch was not *sufficient* and I was hungry later on in the day.
5. (the deep and remote areas of the sea); I would not like to see the *depths* of the ocean because I'm afraid of large fish.
6. life-filled, rich; Something that is *lush* is growing and alive.
7. (forcefully throw themselves against); My little brother would not stop *hurling* his ball at my bedroom door.
8. remarkable and impressive; The new museum has a lot of *wondrous* art.

Writing About the Big Question, p. 80

A.
1. involve
2. Participation
3. influence
4. family

B. Sample Answers

1. Every morning when I walk my dog, I rediscover the nature right around my home. When I camped near

the Grand Canyon, I spent time in a majestic environment totally different from what I was used to.

2. Camping near the Grand Canyon taught me a lot because I was an inexperienced member of a camping **group,** and I learned from the others how to meet our **common** needs. I also felt a strong **connection** to the sounds, sights, and smells of the natural world around me.

C. Sample Answer

If I could be an animal for one day, I would be a dolphin *because I would be able to* explore the ocean and still see the sky. I would feel the physical **connection** between the sea and the other animals that live there. I would also become part of a new **community,** as I would spend time with other dolphins and become **involved** in their day-to-day lives and sense their **values.** I imagine this experience would influence me to have a new understanding of the natural world.

Prologue from **The Whale Rider**
by Witi Ihimaera

Reading: Ask Questions to Analyze Cause-and-Effect Relationships, p. 81

Sample Answers

4. The Ancients come in their canoes and find the land.
5. What happened?
6. Land and sea sigh with gladness.
9. The man sees the land and travels toward it.
10. The man throws spears at the land as he greets it.
11. What happened?

Literary Analysis: Myths, p. 82

Sample Answers

1. It tells how the Ancients (gods) brought mankind to the Maori. A superhuman hero rides to the land on the back of a whale.
2. It tells how the Maori people began.
3. It explains the origins of some living creatures (coming from spears thrown by the hero). It also suggests that the Ancients sent the whale and the man.
4. None. OR It does not teach a lesson, but it explains that when there is a need, the gift of the mythical hero will save the people.
5. It expresses a closeness with nature between people and the land and sea; it also suggests that the beauties of nature are important, as are respect for the gods and gratitude for their gifts.

Vocabulary Builder, p. 83

Sample Answers

A. 1. The forest was filled with *clatter* as animals raced over the tree bark.
2. The fairy people were *reluctant* to welcome people because they were unwilling to give up their land.

3. The flying fish saw *splendor* in the whale rider's shining eyes.
4. His political career reached its *apex* when he was elected to the U.S. Senate.
5. Adele's *yearning* for her old home house was finally satisfied when her family moved back to the area.
6. Yesterday the music store *teemed* with autograph seekers because a popular local musician was making an appearance there.

B. 1. Possible response: If a house is noted for its *splendor,* I would expect to see large rooms and beautiful, expensive furniture.
2. Possible response: A *resplendent* sky would be one filled with stars or one with a very colorful sunset.

Enrichment: Myths and Science, p. 84

1. M
2. S
3. S
4. M
5. M
6. S
7. M
8. Students may say that 2, 3, and 6 describe things in nature (such as a colorful, changing sky) that can be observed.

"Arachne" by Olivia E. Coolidge
Prologue from **The Whale Rider**
by Witi Ihimaera

Integrated Language Skills: Grammar, p. 85

A. 1. CX
2. S
3. CX
4. CP
B. Students' paragraphs should include at least one simple, one compound, and one complex sentence.

Open- Book Test, p. 88

Short Answer

1. A myth often tells how the universe or a culture began. The beginning of the story talks about the old days and a yearning felt by the land and sea.
   Difficulty: *Average*   **Objective:** *Literary Analysis*
2. *Clatter* is a "loud rattling sound." The sound of fairy laughter was hidden because the forest was so noisy.
   Difficulty: *Average*   **Objective:** *Vocabulary*
3. The arrival of the Ancients causes the land and sea to sigh with gladness.
   Difficulty: *Easy*   **Objective:** *Reading*
4. Yes, they are gods. They are capable of providing blessings. When the man comes, he says he is a "gift of the Gods."
   Difficulty: *Average*   **Objective:** *Literary Analysis*

5. The Maori think whales are special. The whale is described as "awesome" and "that noble beast." It is marked with a sacred sign.

   Difficulty: *Easy*   **Objective:** *Interpretation*

6. GO: land and sea, "felt a great emptiness"; land and sea, "sighed with gladness"; spear "leaped with gladness"

   The personification makes the connection between the man and the world more personal.

   Difficulty: *Average*   **Objective:** *Reading*

7. The man was happy. He cried out "With great gladness and thanksgiving."

   Difficulty: *Easy*   **Objective:** *Interpretation*

8. The last spear flies through time to land in the future to wait until it is most needed. It shows that the Maori believe help will always come when it is needed.

   Difficulty: *Challenging*   **Objective:** *Literary Analysis*

9. The last wooden spear would not fly, so the man said a prayer over it. The effect of his prayer was that the spear leapt from him and flew into the future.

   Difficulty: *Challenging*   **Objective:** *Reading*

10. He seems to understand that people will be troubled and will need help in the future, so he throws his last spear through time to wait until "it is most needed."

    Difficulty: *Challenging*   **Objective:** *Interpretation*

Essay

11. Students should use details about the Ancients (gods), the whale rider (hero), beginnings of the culture, and things in nature (spears turning into birds and eels).

    Difficulty: *Easy*   **Objective:** *Essay*

12. Students should use examples of descriptive language to explain the Maori's reverence for nature.

    Difficulty: *Average*   **Objective:** *Essay*

13. Students may say the arrival of man was a good thing because man brought with him gifts from the gods that added to the land and sea. His arrival made the land and sea happy. Others may say the arrival, in the long run, was a bad thing. Man has disrespected and harmed the land and sea.

    Difficulty: *Challenging*   **Objective:** *Essay*

14. Students may say myths like *The Whale Rider* are important because they pass down cultural ideas and beliefs. In this way, they *do* shape the community by giving everyone shared information. Students should express an opinion about the importance of the myth and use details from the selection for support.

    Difficulty: *Average*   **Objective:** *Essay*

Oral Response

15. Oral responses should be clear, well organized, and well supported by appropriate examples from the selection.

    Difficulty: *Average*   **Objective:** *Oral Interpretation*

Selection Test A, p. 91

Critical Reading

	ANS:	DIF:	OBJ:
1.	A	Easy	Literary Analysis
2.	C	Easy	Literary Analysis
3.	C	Easy	Comprehension
4.	A	Easy	Comprehension
5.	D	Easy	Interpretation
6.	D	Easy	Interpretation
7.	C	Easy	Reading
8.	C	Easy	Reading
9.	B	Easy	Reading
10.	D	Easy	Interpretation

Vocabulary and Grammar

	ANS:	DIF:	OBJ:
11.	A	Easy	Vocabulary
12.	B	Easy	Vocabulary
13.	B	Easy	Vocabulary
14.	B	Easy	Grammar

Essay

15. Students' essays should note three elements in the myth that would make them feel proud to be Maori. They might mention, for example, the close connection between nature and people, the idea that everything in nature is waiting for the first human to appear, the description of the first man as a gift or a blessing from the gods, the description of the first human as brave and heroic, and the idea that the first man cared about the future of his people. They might dislike the absence of any females in the story; they might say that they do not like the man's dependence on the whale. Some students might say that the whale seems more heroic and majestic than the man even though the man has power over the whale.

    Difficulty: *Easy*

    Objective: *Essay*

16. Students' essays should note the details about the spear that flies into the future to wait until it will be needed by a future generation. Students should be able to guess that the book will be set in that future time, perhaps the present, and that it will be about a time of trouble when the whale and the spear will save the people. They may guess that the person who saves the people will be a descendant of the whale rider, and that this person will have the whale rider's unique characteristics.

    Difficulty: *Easy*

    Objective: *Essay*

17. Students may say myths like *The Whale Rider* can shape the community by giving everyone shared information

about cultural ideas and beliefs. This myth tells a story about the beginning of the culture and gives the community common knowledge. Students should express an opinion about the importance of the myth and use details from the selection for support.

Selection Test B, p. 94

Critical Reading

1. ANS: A	DIF: Average	OBJ: Literary Analysis
2. ANS: C	DIF: Average	OBJ: Literary Analysis
3. ANS: C	DIF: Average	OBJ: Comprehension
4. ANS: B	DIF: Challenging	OBJ: Reading
5. ANS: B	DIF: Average	OBJ: Comprehension
6. ANS: A	DIF: Average	OBJ: Comprehension
7. ANS: D	DIF: Challenging	OBJ: Interpretation
8. ANS: D	DIF: Average	OBJ: Interpretation
9. ANS: D	DIF: Average	OBJ: Reading
10. ANS: C	DIF: Average	OBJ: Reading
11. ANS: B	DIF: Average	OBJ: Reading
12. ANS: D	DIF: Average	OBJ: Interpretation
13. ANS: B	DIF: Challenging	OBJ: Literary Analysis
14. ANS: A	DIF: Average	OBJ: Literary Analysis

Vocabulary and Grammar

15. ANS: C	DIF: Average	OBJ: Vocabulary
16. ANS: C	DIF: Average	OBJ: Vocabulary
17. ANS: D	DIF: Average	OBJ: Vocabulary
18. ANS: A	DIF: Average	OBJ: Grammar

Essay

19. Students' essays should identify three elements, characteristics, or values of Maori culture. Students may write about a connection to nature, respect for nature, respect for the gods, and an appreciation of beauty and strength. Each element should be supported by examples from the text.
Difficulty: *Average*
Objective: *Essay*

20. Students' summaries should include three events that demonstrate cause-and-effect relationships. For example, they might write that the land and sea feel empty because they yearn for the gift of mankind. The Ancients find the land. As a result, the Ancients send the gift, or blessing. A great whale is seen soaring and diving. It has been sent because it will bear the gift of man riding on its back. The man cries out to the land as he throws spears that become living creatures. He cries out because he feels glad and thankful. Because one spear will not fly from his hand, he prays over it. Because of his prayer,

the spear soars into the future where it will wait until it is needed.
Difficulty: *Average*
Objective: *Essay*

21. Students may say myths like *The Whale Rider* are important because they pass down cultural ideas and beliefs. In this way, they do shape the community by giving everyone shared information. Students should express an opinion about the importance of the myth and use details from the selection for support.

"Mowgli's Brothers" by Rudyard Kipling
from **James and the Giant Peach**
by Roald Dahl

Vocabulary Warm-up Exercises, p. 98

A. 1. peculiar
2. knelt
3. pebbles
4. splendid
5. comfortably
6. horror
7. newly
8. rejoicing

B. Sample Answers
1. T; You can <u>identify</u> something if you recognize it.
2. F; If the law <u>forbids</u> you from doing something, it is illegal and you shouldn't do it.
3. T; <u>Cunning</u> people are crafty and can be tricky.
4. F; A beautiful building is a pleasant sight to <u>behold</u>.
5. F; To <u>withdraw</u> from a situation is to remove oneself from it.
6. F; If someone does something <u>assuredly</u>, he or she does it with great confidence.
7. F; Something that is <u>extremely</u> pleasurable is a lot of fun to do.
8. T; A <u>magnificent</u> house would be very impressive and almost certainly large.

Reading Warm-up A, p. 99

Sample Answers
1. <u>bent knees</u>; I *knelt* on the sidewalk to pick up the toy I had dropped.
2. (His bent knees were gently cupped by the soft ground); I *comfortably* read books in bed to fall asleep.
3. <u>fear and shock</u>; A haunted house is supposed to be full of *horror*.
4. (sensation of the beetle walking on his face); Something is *peculiar* when it is odd or strange.
5. <u>the beetle</u>; <u>his find</u>; <u>the insect's body</u>; The student was *rejoicing* in his first A grade on a test.

6. (beautifully); I think the holiday lights on my block are *splendid*.

7. (the group of small stones); There were many *pebbles* at the bottom of the river.

8. he had just learned about what a beetle looked like up close; I was happy to play with my *newly* found friends.

Reading Warm-up B, p. 100

Sample Answers

1. (impressive and beautiful); The Empire State Building is *magnificent* because it is one of the tallest buildings in the world.

2. by examining their special markings; To *identify* something is to recognize it based on the way it looks or behaves.

3. (They cleverly hide in the jungle until they discover their prey.) My *cunning* housecat is very good at hunting and capturing mice.

4. Their sharp sense of smell; To do something *assuredly* is to do it with confidence and certainty.

5. As more jungle is taken up by human use, tigers remove themselves ever farther in search of safety. Animals *withdraw* when they sense danger.

6. (killing tigers for sport); I think this is a good law because it saves the lives of many tigers.

7. (Because there are so few tigers living today); I am *extremely* happy when I get to go on vacation.

8. to observe a tiger's behavior in its natural habitat; I think a tiger would be an amazing sight to *behold* because this animal is so strong and powerful.

Writing About the Big Question, p. 101

A. 1. culture
   2. common
   3. history
   4. group or community

B. Sample Answers

1. When my family traveled to Alaska, I felt I was in a totally different world. When I was involved in making a movie, I entered a really unusual world.

2. When I worked on a movie last summer, I discovered that I had entered a whole new **community,** with its own **culture** and **values.** The work **involved** repetition to an amazing degree, and the high point of our day was always the catered lunch, during which we would sit around like a huge **family** eating rubbery spaghetti.

C. Sample Answer

If I could spend time in any place in the universe, I would like to go to the space station *because* I would love to see Earth from such a distant perspective. I would worry a little about being **isolated.** However, I imagine that the astronauts form a little **family** of their own, as they **support** each other and work together for the **common** good. Next to seeing Earth from that perspective, I think

the best part about **participation** in space-station life would be weightlessness.

"Mowgli's Brothers" by Rudyard Kipling
from James and the Giant Peach
by Roald Dahl

Literary Analysis: Elements of Fantasy, p. 102

Sample Answers

1. jackal who tells tales
   a wolf who speaks

2. a jackal who rummages in village trash heaps
   a jackal who chews on bones

3. a centipede who speaks
   a centipede who sleeps in a hammock

4. a boy who speaks
   a Glow-worm described as a lady firefly without wings

Vocabulary Builder, p. 103

A. 1. Sample answer: The *colossal* storm clouds darkened the entire sky.

2. Sample answer: The mother bear spent most of her time *fostering* her cubs.

3. The sentence makes sense because a disagreement might end that way.

4. Sample answer: If you read the book *intently*, you will not miss any important details.

5. The sentence makes sense because leopards do eye their prey and prepare to pounce.

6. Sample answer: The movie was long, *monotonous*, and boring.

B. 1. intently
   2. colossal
   3. dispute
   4. quarry

Open-Book Test, p. 105

Short Answer

1. The wolves dislike and fear humans. Father Wolf compares man to beetles and frogs. The wolves are forbidden to kill man because they fear what will happen in return.
   Difficulty: *Challenging* **Objective:** *Interpretation*

2. He refuses because he will not take orders from the tiger. He says the wolves are a Free People who answer only to the pack leader.
   Difficulty: *Average* **Objective:** *Interpretation*

3. She is not afraid of him. She calls him the Lame One and threatens him when he comes to her den.
   Difficulty: *Easy* **Objective:** *Interpretation*

4. Students may say that James behaves realistically. He is scared at first like a real boy would be. His face is "white with horror." On the other hand, they may say

that he accepts the bugs too easily. For example, he is soon helping the Centipede with his boots.

Difficulty: *Average*   **Objective:** *Literary Analysis*

5. They were looking at him with great attention because they were waiting to see what his reaction would be.

Difficulty: *Average*   **Objective:** *Vocabulary*

6. Both: lots of legs, insects; Real: very small, doesn't talk; Story: huge, talks, makes jokes

James likes the Centipede because he is a rascal and is funny.

Difficulty: *Average*   **Objective:** *Literary Analysis*

7. Both have non human creatures who speak.

Difficulty: *Easy*   **Objective:** *Literary Analysis*

8. Students should list James as a realistic element. He is a regular human boy in a fantastic place. The jungle is a realistic setting in "Mowgli's Brothers." Man and all the animals do live there.

Difficulty: *Average*   **Objective:** *Literary Analysis*

9. The setting in *James and the Giant Peach* is all fantasy. They are inside a giant peach.

Difficulty: *Easy*   **Objective:** *Literary Analysis*

10. The realistic characters are all human: baby Mowgli, the men who hunt in the jungle, and James.

Difficulty: *Challenging*   **Objective:** *Literary Analysis*

Essay

11. Students should use details from both stories to explain a fantastic element.

Difficulty: *Easy*   **Objective:** *Essay*

12. Students should note that both characters are human boys. Mowgli is very young but fearless. James is older and more cautious. Students may say that both boys are realistic with fantastic elements: Mowgli settles right in with the wolves, and James settles in with the giant bugs with only a brief hesitation.

Difficulty: *Average*   **Objective:** *Essay*

13. Students should use details from the story to describe each character. They should point out that Baloo sees only what is in front of him—a harmless baby. He sees no harm in letting him stay with the pack. Bagheera sees what the man cub will grow into—a man who can be useful in getting rid of Shere Khan.

Difficulty: *Challenging*   **Objective:** *Essay*

14. Students should choose to discuss how either James or Mowgli will be shaped by his new community. They should say whether the changes will be positive or negative and support their answers with details from the selection.

Difficulty: *Average*   **Objective:** *Essay*

Oral Response

15. Oral responses should be clear, well organized, and well supported by appropriate examples from the selections.

Difficulty: *Average*   **Objective:** *Oral Interpretation*

Selection Test A, p. 108

Critical Reading

1. ANS: B	DIF: Easy	OBJ: Comprehension
2. ANS: C	DIF: Easy	OBJ: Literary Analysis
3. ANS: D	DIF: Easy	OBJ: Comprehension
4. ANS: A	DIF: Easy	OBJ: Interpretation
5. ANS: A	DIF: Easy	OBJ: Interpretation
6. ANS: B	DIF: Easy	OBJ: Comprehension
7. ANS: B	DIF: Easy	OBJ: Literary Analysis
8. ANS: D	DIF: Easy	OBJ: Interpretation
9. ANS: C	DIF: Easy	OBJ: Literary Analysis
10. ANS: D	DIF: Easy	OBJ: Comprehension
11. ANS: C	DIF: Easy	OBJ: Literary Analysis
12. ANS: C	DIF: Easy	OBJ: Interpretation

Vocabulary

13. ANS: B	DIF: Easy	OBJ: Vocabulary
14. ANS: A	DIF: Easy	OBJ: Vocabulary

Essay

15. Students should choose one creature from each story and identify at least one way in which the creature is realistic and one way in which the creature is fantastic. For example, students may say that Father Wolf in "Mowgli's Brothers" is similar to a real wolf because he tries to protect his family, and that he is different from a real wolf because he speaks. They may say that the Glow-worm in *James and the Giant Peach* is similar to a real glow-worm because her tail lights up, and different from a real Glow-worm because she is as big as James.

Difficulty: *Easy*

Objective: *Essay*

16. Students should discuss how either James or Mowgli will be shaped by his new community. They should say whether the changes will be good or bad and support their answers with details from the selection.

Selection Test B, p. 111

Critical Reading

1. ANS: B	DIF: Average	OBJ: Comprehension
2. ANS: C	DIF: Challenging	OBJ: Literary Analysis
3. ANS: B	DIF: Challenging	OBJ: Interpretation
4. ANS: A	DIF: Average	OBJ: Interpretation
5. ANS: D	DIF: Challenging	OBJ: Interpretation
6. ANS: C	DIF: Average	OBJ: Literary Analysis
7. ANS: D	DIF: Average	OBJ: Comprehension
8. ANS: A	DIF: Average	OBJ: Literary Analysis
9. ANS: B	DIF: Average	OBJ: Comprehension
10. ANS: D	DIF: Average	OBJ: Literary Analysis
11. ANS: A	DIF: Challenging	OBJ: Interpretation

12. ANS: C	DIF: Average	OBJ: Comprehension
13. ANS: A	DIF: Challenging	OBJ: Literary Analysis
14. ANS: B	DIF: Average	OBJ: Literary Analysis
15. ANS: C	DIF: Average	OBJ: Literary Analysis
16. ANS: D	DIF: Average	OBJ: Interpretation

Vocabulary

17. ANS: A	DIF: Challenging	OBJ: Vocabulary
18. ANS: B	DIF: Average	OBJ: Vocabulary
19. ANS: D	DIF: Average	OBJ: Vocabulary

Essay

20. Students should identify two fantastic and two realistic elements from each story. For example, they may identify the animals' speech as fantastic in both stories and identify some of the animals' traits as realistic in each story. Students should also express an opinion as to why the author included the realistic elements he did. For example, they may say that the authors have their animals behave in realistic ways in order to help readers relate to the story.

Difficulty: *Average*

Objective: *Essay*

21. Students should compare and contrast the characters of James and Mowgli. They might point out that the curiosity of each character leads him into an unusual situation, but that James seems more aware of his surroundings than Mowgli does. Some students may conclude that James's behavior is more realistic because he responds to his situation in a way that most young boys would. Other students may conclude that Mowgli's toddler behavior is more realistic, as he wanders away from his parents, wrestles with the wolf pups, and plays with rocks in the moonlight.

Difficulty: *Average*

Objective: *Essay*

22. Students should choose to discuss how either James or Mowgli will be shaped by his new community. They should say whether the changes will be positive or negative and support their answers with details from the selection.

Writing Workshop

Multimedia Report: Integrating Grammar Skills, p. 115

A. 1. sentence; 2. fragment; 3. fragment; 4. sentence; 5. fragment

B. Sample Answers

1. Unless we invite everyone, someone will feel left out.
2. The biggest problem was where to have the celebration.

3. In order to use the clubhouse at my apartment complex, we promised to clean up.
4. If you don't have an idea for a gift, ask Celi's mom.
5. Maya and Sandra know exactly how to decorate for a party.

Benchmark Test 11, p. 116

MULTIPLE CHOICE

1. ANS: A
2. ANS: D
3. ANS: B
4. ANS: A
5. ANS: C
6. ANS: C
7. ANS: D
8. ANS: C
9. ANS: A
10. ANS: D
11. ANS: D
12. ANS: C
13. ANS: B
14. ANS: A
15. ANS: B
16. ANS: B
17. ANS: D
18. ANS: D
19. ANS: A
20. ANS: D
21. ANS: A
22. ANS: B
23. ANS: D
24. ANS: A
25. ANS: C
26. ANS: C
27. ANS: A
28. ANS: B
29. ANS: C
30. ANS: D
31. ANS: C
32. ANS: A
33. ANS: A

ESSAY

34. Students' essays should clearly identify the situation and people involved. They should tell what happened, indicate their feelings about the experience, and make clear the lesson they learned.

35. Students should clearly indicate the topic of their project. They should list materials in a variety of media that they hope to include in the project, including text, graphics such as maps and charts, art or photo illustrations, and perhaps music, videos, and slides. Students should also indicate sources of information they would consult, including print materials, online sources, and perhaps organizations or museums they might contact.

"Why the Tortoise's Shell Is Not Smooth"
by Chinua Achebe

Vocabulary Warm-up Exercises, p. 124

A. 1. custom
2. compound
3. preparations
4. invitation
5. grumbled
6. arrived
7. hosts
8. ungrateful

B. Sample Answers

1. The plumage on the bird helps keep it warm.
2. Ron presented the award to me so I could take a look at it.
3. A tortoise, unlike a lizard, has a shell.
4. A yam isn't something that you wear, it's something that you eat.
5. It was a real feast, so no one walked away hungry.
6. If you don't like the color of the dress, dip it in dye to change its color.
7. Lee is known for her cunning; she's extremely clever.

Reading Warm-up A, p. 125

Sample Answers

1. the way people do things; My family has a custom of having a 4th of July picnic.
2. (Driving on the left side just seemed too hard.); Ungrateful means "not thankful for something."
3. to visit someone's home; I haven't seen the invitation to the birthday party.
4. (a pair of slippers); Hosts are people who have guests over.
5. (Mali, a country in West Africa); Arrived means "reached a place."
6. buildings; The compound contains about twenty buildings.
7. (everyone washed his or her hands); Preparations are things people do to get ready for something.
8. I realize that in different places, things are done in different ways; Grumbled means "complained."

Reading Warm-up B, p. 126

Sample Answers

1. feathers; Sparrows and seagulls have plumage.

2. (blue "eyes," bright dots of color); Dye is a liquid used to give color to something.
3. (orange); A yam is a sweet potato-like vegetable.
4. better to eat another red-back; Famine means "a shortage of food."
5. in order to stay alive around the females; Cunning means "cleverness."
6. (turtle); You might see a tortoise in a pet store or in a zoo.
7. bigger fishes; A feast is a huge meal.
8. (the butterfly fish's markings); The trophy was presented to the team in front of the fans.

Writing About the Big Question, p. 127

A. 1. isolate
2. support
3. community
4. connection

B. Sample Answers

1. When I was about five, my older brother told me that my birthday was being cancelled that year. In order to surprise me, my best friend told me that she had broken my guitar, when she actually was buying me a new one.
2. My big brother had a **history** of tricking me, but I was very young, so I still believed him when he said my birthday was cancelled. Fortunately, when the day came, the rest of my **family** celebrated my birthday, and my parents gave me extra **support** by scolding my brother for tricking me.

C. Sample Answer

I played a trick on my mom *when I* put salt in the sugar canister as she was getting ready to bake her pumpkin pie. I was under the **influence** of my trickster brother. The joke was on us, however, because my mom caught on to the salt substitution before she made the pie, which turned out great. So she **involved** the whole **family,** except my brother and me, in a trick of her own. She made us take our slices of pie first, and we squirmed and tried to get out of it without admitting what we'd done. I learned that it's better to be in a large **group** when you are playing a trick than to be **isolated**.

"Why the Tortoise's Shell Is Not Smooth"
by Chinua Achebe

Reading: Preview the Text to Set a Purpose for Reading, p. 128

Sample Answers

1. The title tells me this story could be a folk tale because it explains something in nature. There is at least one animal character, a tortoise.
2. Chinua Achebe is an African writer who was born in Nigeria.

3. The art gives me clues about what the story is about. Knowing what the story is about helps me set a purpose for reading.
4. The story seems to be an entertaining folk tale that teaches a lesson.
5. My purpose will be to read for enjoyment and to gain understanding of this type of folk tale.

Literary Analysis: Personification, p. 129

Sample Answers

1. Animal: hungry, cannot fly, has a shell; human: sneaky, tricky, ungrateful, mischievous
2. Animal: have feathers, can fly; human: happy, easily fooled, generous
3. Animal: has feathers, can fly, clever; human: gets angry, gets even, tells lies

Vocabulary Builder, p. 130

Sample Answers

A. 1. People in a famine would become very hungry, and without food they might die.
2. A president might need to be a skilled orator because he gives lots of important speeches.
3. I would write an eloquent article about why it is important to adopt animals from shelters.
4. Possible response: It helps to be cunning in a competition because you can think quickly and outwit your opponent.
5. Possible response: A single house could have rooms and other structures added onto it, turning it into a compound.
6. Possible response: Thanksgiving dinner is my favorite family custom, because it's fun, and you can look forward to the rest of the holiday season.

B. 1. B; 2. C; 3. D

C. 1. customary
2. imaginary
3. honorary

Enrichment: Telling a Story, p. 131

Students should present a brief story that explains something in nature, using references to current culture and customs.

Open-Book Test, p. 132

Short Answer

1. You might set a purpose to find out why the tortoise's shell is not smooth.
   Difficulty: *Easy* **Objective:** *Reading*
2. Sample: It tells me that the story is a folk tale that has animal characters.
   Difficulty: *Average* **Objective:** *Reading*

3. Tortoise is described as "full of cunning" and able to make a plan.
   Difficulty: *Average* **Objective:** *Literary Analysis*
4. Tortoise is very cunning and has a "sweet tongue." He convinces the birds he has changed. The birds are easily fooled.
   Difficulty: *Challenging* **Objective:** *Interpretation*
5. *Eloquent* means "persuasive and expressive." Tortoise is representing the birds, so his persuasive and expressive speech makes a good impression on the birds' hosts.
   Difficulty: *Challenging* **Objective:** *Vocabulary*
6. An orator speaks well in public. Tortoise uses his speaking ability to talk the birds into letting him go to the feast and letting him speak for them.
   Difficulty: *Average* **Objective:** *Vocabulary*
7. He shows selfishness. He eats the best part of the food.
   Difficulty: *Average* **Objective:** *Literary Analysis*
8. They are angry. Some of them are too angry to eat.
   Difficulty: *Easy* **Objective:** *Literary Analysis*
9. Lessons could include: be careful whom you trust; a trickster could get tricked in return; treat others as you want to be treated. Students should support their answers with details from the story.
   Difficulty: *Average* **Objective:** *Interpretation*
10. Characteristic: trickiness, anger
    Students should explain why they do or do not agree with Parrot's actions.
    Difficulty: *Average* **Objective:** *Literary Analysis*

Essay

11. Students should explain that Tortoise's words let him go to the feast, be the spokesman for the birds, trick the birds, eat all the food, and (he thinks) prepare his landing spot. They should explain that Parrot changes Tortoise's words to teach him a lesson.
    Difficulty: *Easy* **Objective:** *Essay*
12. Students should explain that the birds could have avoided their problems from the very beginning. They could have trusted their initial reaction and left Tortoise at home. They could have spoken up for themselves at the feast. They could have questioned his new name. They could have spoken up when he took all the food.
    Difficulty: *Average* **Objective:** *Essay*
13. Students should explain that Tortoise is put back together in bits and pieces by the medicine man. The story is a folk tale meant to teach a lesson: tricking people does not end well for the trickster. It is also meant to explain something in nature: the tortoise's bumpy shell. Having Tortoise die at the end would not explain the bumpy shell, and it would seem to be a very harsh lesson to teach.
    Difficulty: *Challenging* **Objective:** *Essay*

14. Students should offer an opinion about the fairness of what happens to Tortoise. They should make a reasonable case using the story for support for their position.
  Difficulty: *Average* **Objective:** *Essay*

Oral Response

15. Oral responses should be clear, well organized, and well supported by appropriate examples from the selection.
  Difficulty: *Average* **Objective:** *Oral Interpretation*

"Why the Tortoise's Shell Is Not Smooth"
by Chinua Achebe

Selection Test A, p. 135

Critical Reading

1.	ANS: B	DIF: Easy	OBJ: Reading Skill
2.	ANS: A	DIF: Easy	OBJ: Reading Skill
3.	ANS: D	DIF: Easy	OBJ: Comprehension
4.	ANS: C	DIF: Easy	OBJ: Literary Analysis
5.	ANS: A	DIF: Easy	OBJ: Interpretation
6.	ANS: A	DIF: Easy	OBJ: Literary Analysis
7.	ANS: D	DIF: Easy	OBJ: Comprehension
8.	ANS: C	DIF: Easy	OBJ: Interpretation
9.	ANS: B	DIF: Easy	OBJ: Literary Analysis
10.	ANS: A	DIF: Easy	OBJ: Interpretation

Vocabulary and Grammar

11.	ANS: A	DIF: Easy	OBJ: Vocabulary
12.	ANS: C	DIF: Easy	OBJ: Vocabulary
13.	ANS: D	DIF: Easy	OBJ: Vocabulary
14.	ANS: B	DIF: Easy	OBJ: Grammar

Essay

15. Students' essays should identify at least two human qualities in Tortoise and two in the birds. They might say, for example, that Tortoise is clever and selfish while the birds are easy to trick and become angry. Students should explain that the structure of the story would be different with human characters (no shell to explain) but may point out that the same lesson could be taught.
  Difficulty: *Easy*
  Objective: *Essay*

16. Most students will say that they would not have believed Tortoise because he has a bad reputation and had been a trouble-maker in the past. Students might say they would have suggested to Tortoise that he come up with a more normal-sounding name; otherwise, they would not allow him to go to the feast. If Tortoise had taken another name, everyone would have eaten well at the feast. The birds would have let Tortoise use their feathers to get back to the ground. The story would have

ended happily. Tortoise's shell would be smooth, but the story would not teach the same lesson.
  Difficulty: *Easy*
  Objective: *Essay*

17. Students should offer an opinion about the fairness of what happens to Tortoise. They should make a reasonable case using the story for support for either position.

Selection Test B, p. 138

Critical Reading

1.	ANS: D	DIF: Average	OBJ: Reading Skill
2.	ANS: B	DIF: Average	OBJ: Reading Skill
3.	ANS: C	DIF: Average	OBJ: Reading Skill
4.	ANS: B	DIF: Challenging	OBJ: Reading Skill
5.	ANS: B	DIF: Average	OBJ: Literary Analysis
6.	ANS: D	DIF: Challenging	OBJ: Comprehension
7.	ANS: A	DIF: Average	OBJ: Interpretation
8.	ANS: A	DIF: Average	OBJ: Literary Analysis
9.	ANS: D	DIF: Average	OBJ: Comprehension
10.	ANS: C	DIF: Challenging	OBJ: Literary Analysis
11.	ANS: C	DIF: Average	OBJ: Interpretation
12.	ANS: D	DIF: Average	OBJ: Literary Analysis
13.	ANS: A	DIF: Average	OBJ: Interpretation
14.	ANS: C	DIF: Challenging	OBJ: Comprehension
15.	ANS: B	DIF: Average	OBJ: Comprehension

Vocabulary and Grammar

16.	ANS: C	DIF: Average	OBJ: Vocabulary
17.	ANS: A	DIF: Average	OBJ: Vocabulary
18.	ANS: C	DIF: Challenging	OBJ: Vocabulary
19.	ANS: D	DIF: Average	OBJ: Grammar

Essay

20. Students' essays should describe the kind of human that each animal personifies: Tortoise is clever and greedy; the birds are trusting and foolish; Parrot is angry and vengeful; Tortoise's wife is easily tricked. Students may choose any of the characters as most human, although most will say Tortoise seems most fully developed. Students may say that they think the birds and Tortoise's wife are too foolish and trusting to be realistic humans. Parrot's anger and desire for revenge may seem very human to students. Students should support their answers with details from the story.
  Difficulty: *Average*
  Objective: *Essay*

21. Students should clearly explain why it is important that traditional tales be preserved. Students may say that tales such as "Why the Tortoise's Shell Is Not Smooth" should be preserved because they continue to entertain, continue to teach valuable lessons about life, and help

us learn about and appreciate ancient and traditional cultures. Where appropriate, students should offer examples from the story to support or illustrate their reasons. For example, the description of the feast in the sky introduces students to traditional foods (such as kola nuts and yam pottage) as well as how such a feast would be given (with the hosts tasting each dish before it is presented).

Difficulty: *Challenging*

Objective: *Essay*

22. Students should offer an opinion about the fairness of what happens to Tortoise. They should make a reasonable case using the story for support for either position.

"He Lion, Bruh Bear, and Bruh Rabbit"
by Virginia Hamilton

Vocabulary Warm-up Exercises, p. 142

A. 1. fellow
2. dangerous
3. awhile
4. thunder
5. lair
6. drags
7. whatever
8. distance

B. Sample Answers
1. F; A riddle that has been <u>figured</u> out has been solved.
2. T; People who <u>mumble</u> speak softly and are hard to understand.
3. T; <u>Ninety</u> is ten smaller than one hundred.
4. F; A <u>hare</u> has long legs and a short tail.
5. F; A <u>scrawny</u> animal is small and skinny.
6. F; If you do something <u>anyhow</u>, you want to do it under any situation.
7. T; A <u>thicket</u> is dense with plants.
8. T; Days filled with <u>sunshine</u> are warm and bright.

Reading Warm-up A, p. 143

Sample Answers
1. <u>anything that they can</u>; I try to read *whatever* I can.
2. (as they enter a man's tent, searching for food); A *fellow* is a man or a boy.
3. (Most bears are not actually likely to harm people.); Crossing a busy street without looking both ways is *dangerous*.
4. <u>booming roar/shout/loud</u>; The sound of the *thunder* during the storm frightened me.
5. <u>for these short periods of time</u>; I would like to go jogging for *awhile*.
6. (home); A *lair* is the home of a wild animal.

7. (a group of logs); My cousin always *drags* his backpack on the ground.
8. (nine miles); The *distance* between my house and the high school is about one mile.

Reading Warm-up B, p. 144
Sample Answers
1. <u>the light from the sun</u>; My favorite summer activities are swimming and picnicking on the beach in the bright *sunshine*.
2. (only ten shy of a hundred); I received *ninety* points out of a hundred on my last quiz.
3. <u>The dense growth of plants and bushes</u>; A *thicket* is a place where bushes, plants, and trees grow closely together.
4. <u>how to get into the garden</u>; I *figured* out that studying helps me do better on tests.
5. (jumped over the fence/started to eat the lettuce); A *hare* is a large, wild rabbit with strong back legs.
6. <u>smaller and so thin</u>; My little brother is *scrawny*.
7. <u>Strangely, they were not frightened by the noise.</u> Though I didn't plan to see the movie, I was happy to watch it *anyhow*.
8. (said softly, under her breath); To *mumble* is to speak quietly without sounding clear.

Writing About the Big Question, p. 145

A. 1. influence
2. family
3. community
4. influence

B. Sample Answers
1. I asked my older sister for advice about how to tell my parents I wanted a new bike. I asked my music teacher about whether I would like being in the school show.
2. I was thinking about auditioning for the school musical, but I was new to the **community** and didn't know the **group** of students who worked on the musicals. So I asked my singing teacher for advice because she had a **connection** to many of those students and would know if I would enjoy being **involved** with them.

C. Sample Answer

If I had to classify myself as a leader or a follower, I would say that I am a leader *because* I enjoy directing a **group** of people as they work toward a **common** goal. **Participation** in a group is fun for me. I am good at figuring out how to **influence** people to **support** my way of doing things. I can also see when someone else has a better idea, and that kind of give-and-take helps create a spirit of **community.**

"He Lion, Bruh Bear, and Bruh Rabbit"
by Virginia Hamilton

Reading: Preview the Text to Set a Purpose for Reading, p. 146

Sample Answers

1. The title reveals that there are three animal characters. Their names are funny, so it might be a funny story.
2. Virginia Hamilton. She is an African American writer who has written other folk tales.
3. The art gives me clues about what the story is about. Knowing what the story is about helps me set a purpose for reading.
4. The text has a lot of dialogue, and it is written the way people talk. It seems to be a funny folk tale.
5. My purpose will be to read for enjoyment and to learn about this type of folk tale.

Literary Analysis: Personification, p. 147

Sample Answers

1. Animal: fierce, dangerous, wild; human: conceited, boastful, mean
2. Animal: has been around the forest, afraid of loud noises; human: helpful, sensible, polite
3. Animal: runs and hides, has been to many places, careful of man; human: clever, brave, quick-witted

Vocabulary Builder, p. 148

A. Sample Answers

1. You look so nice today!
2. You might find a bear in a lair.
3. Possible response: Someone who is peaceable would try to get people to agree.
4. Possible response: A thicket is a good hiding place because it is filled with branches and leaves.
5. Possible response: A scrawny person could change his appearance by trying to gain weight.
6. Possible response: People's memories of olden times are often hazy and nostalgic.

B. Sample Answers

1. If the lair was big, I'd get away from it quickly.
2. I would not be cordial at all because a bear is a wild animal. I would bang on something to scare the bear away.

C. 1. redden
2. weaken
3. frighten

Enrichment: Telling a Story, p. 149

Students' oral presentations should be engaging and well-practiced.

"Why the Tortoise's Shell Is Not Smooth"
by Chinua Achebe
"He Lion, Bruh Bear, and Bruh Rabbit"
by Virginia Hamilton

Integrated Language Skills: Grammar, p. 150

A. 1. Bears, rabbits, wild pigs, and foxes are all creatures of the forest.
2. They came out of the woods, crept closer to the farm-house, and scared away the cat.
3. We drove to the park, the river, my school, and the store before we came home.

B. Students should write three sentences that correctly use items or phrases in a series.

Open-Book Test, p. 153

Short Answer

1. Setting a purpose helps the reader focus on the reading. Students should set a purpose of reading for enjoyment or reading to gain understanding.
   Difficulty: *Average* **Objective:** *Reading*
2. Bruh Bear: big, slow, quiet; Bruh Rabbit: small, quick, clever; both: not scared of he Lion
   Bruh Rabbit is more helpful because he has seen Man. Bruh Bear has not.
   Difficulty: *Average* **Objective:** *Interpretation*
3. *Cordial* means "warm and friendly." They are acting this way because they want something from he Lion.
   Difficulty: *Average* **Objective:** *Vocabulary*
4. He Lion is proud or vain. He walks around saying "Me and myself" all day and doesn't care that he is scaring the animals.
   Difficulty: *Average* **Objective:** *Literary Analysis*
5. Bruh Rabbit is clever. He solves the problem of he Lion scaring everyone by showing him Man, who is more powerful than he Lion.
   Difficulty: *Average* **Objective:** *Literary Analysis*
6. Intelligence and modesty are valued. Bruh Rabbit is smart, and he is the hero of the story. He Lion gets himself in trouble by believing he is more important than everyone else.
   Difficulty: *Challenging* **Objective:** *Literary Analysis*
7. Bruh Rabbit has seen Man and his gun. He knows what will happen with the gun, so he drags Bruh Bear out of the way.
   Difficulty: *Easy* **Objective:** *Interpretation*
8. Bruh Rabbit thinks he Lion will expect Man to be small or weak like Will Be and Once Was. He wants he Lion to be louder than ever because he knows Man will shoot at him then.
   Difficulty: *Challenging* **Objective:** *Interpretation*

9. A thicket is a dense growth of small trees. They hide from Man in the thicket.
   Difficulty: *Easy*   **Objective:** *Vocabulary*
10. Yes, he Lion has animal qualities. He roars and scares the other animals.
    Difficulty: *Easy*   **Objective:** *Literary Analysis*

Essay

11. Students should choose a character and use details from the story to explain why that character seems most human.
    Difficulty: *Easy*   **Objective:** *Essay*
12. Students should select a character that they admire, tell why they admire the character, describe the personality traits of the character, and say what they can learn from the character.
    Difficulty: *Average*   **Objective:** *Essay*
13. Students should take a position about whether the story teaches it is better to be smart (like Bruh Rabbit) or strong and powerful (like he Lion or Man). They should support their answer with evidence from the story. They should state whether they agree or disagree with the lesson and give reasons.
    Difficulty: *Challenging*   **Objective:** *Essay*
14. Students should explain that he Lion is forced to tone down his roaring and recognize that Man shares some of the power. The change is a good one for the little animals who are now not so scared. Some students may say the change is good for he Lion too, because it helps him be a better part of the community. Others may say the change is not good for he Lion because it makes him seem defeated.
    Difficulty: *Average*   **Objective:** *Essay*

Oral Response

15. Oral responses should be clear, well organized, and well supported by appropriate examples from the selection.
    Difficulty: *Average*   **Objective:** *Oral Interpretation*

Selection Test A, p. 156

Critical Reading

1. ANS: A	DIF: Easy	OBJ: Reading Skill
2. ANS: C	DIF: Easy	OBJ: Literary Analysis
3. ANS: C	DIF: Easy	OBJ: Comprehension
4. ANS: B	DIF: Easy	OBJ: Literary Analysis
5. ANS: D	DIF: Easy	OBJ: Reading Skill
6. ANS: A	DIF: Easy	OBJ: Literary Analysis
7. ANS: C	DIF: Easy	OBJ: Comprehension
8. ANS: C	DIF: Easy	OBJ: Interpretation
9. ANS: D	DIF: Easy	OBJ: Comprehension
10. ANS: C	DIF: Easy	OBJ: Interpretation

Vocabulary and Grammar

11. ANS: A	DIF: Easy	OBJ: Vocabulary
12. ANS: B	DIF: Easy	OBJ: Vocabulary
13. ANS: C	DIF: Easy	OBJ: Vocabulary
14. ANS: A	DIF: Easy	OBJ: Grammar

Essay

15. Students should identify the animal character that seems most human to them and clearly explain why they chose that animal. Essays should include at least two examples of human qualities displayed by the chosen character.
    Difficulty: *Easy*
    Objective: *Essay*
16. Students should realize that the folk tale teaches that it is better to be smart, like Bruh Rabbit, than to be strong, like he Lion. Students may agree or disagree with the lesson in the story. They should support either opinion with a plausible reason or example.
    Difficulty: *Easy*
    Objective: *Essay*
17. Students should explain that he Lion is forced to tone down his roaring and recognize that Man shares some of the power. The change is a good one for the little animals who are not so scared. Some students may say the change is good for he Lion too, because it helps him be a better part of the community. Others may say the change is not good for he Lion because it makes him seem defeated.

Selection Test B, p. 159

Critical Reading

1. ANS: A	DIF: Average	OBJ: Reading Skill
2. ANS: D	DIF: Challenging	OBJ: Literary Analysis
3. ANS: B	DIF: Average	OBJ: Literary Analysis
4. ANS: C	DIF: Average	OBJ: Comprehension
5. ANS: A	DIF: Challenging	OBJ: Comprehension
6. ANS: A	DIF: Challenging	OBJ: Interpretation
7. ANS: B	DIF: Average	OBJ: Literary Analysis
8. ANS: A	DIF: Average	OBJ: Literary Analysis
9. ANS: B	DIF: Average	OBJ: Interpretation
10. ANS: C	DIF: Average	OBJ: Comprehension
11. ANS: A	DIF: Average	OBJ: Interpretation
12. ANS: C	DIF: Average	OBJ: Interpretation
13. ANS: B	DIF: Average	OBJ: Interpretation
14. ANS: D	DIF: Average	OBJ: Literary Analysis

Vocabulary and Grammar

15. ANS: C	DIF: Average	OBJ: Vocabulary
16. ANS: B	DIF: Average	OBJ: Vocabulary

17. **ANS:** B   **DIF:** Challenging   **OBJ:** Vocabulary
18. **ANS:** D   **DIF:** Average   **OBJ:** Grammar

Essay

19. Students' essays should describe the kind of human that each animal personifies. For example, he Lion represents the proud person who is not too bright. Bruh Bear personifies a big, strong person who is not as brave as he appears. Bruh Rabbit is the clever person who can outsmart more powerful people. Most students will agree that it is a good idea to teach human lessons with animal characters. Students may say that if human characters were used to teach the same lesson, the story might not be as amusing. Teaching the lesson indirectly through animal characters is more interesting as well as more effective.

    Difficulty: *Average*

    Objective: *Essay*

20. Students should explain that the tale's message—it is not a good idea to be vain and conceited—is successfully taught through the humor in the story. The animals are entertaining and humorous because they seem human. The lesson is successfully put across through humor. Even he Lion's encounter with Man, which could be scary, is told lightly.

    Difficulty: *Average*

    Objective: *Essay*

21. Students' essays should identify at least three ways of previewing the text; for example, looking at the title, looking at the beginnings of paragraphs, and looking at the pictures. They might say that, as a result of their preview, they expected that the text would be a humorous folk tale with animal characters. They might say that they were surprised by the pronunciation, grammar, spelling, and word choice in the story, and that it took them a while to get used to these elements of the tale. They should state in their essay that their purpose for reading was to enjoy a folk tale. Most students will state that the story more than met their expectations because it is a humorous story that teaches an important lesson.

    Difficulty: *Challenging*

    Objective: *Essay*

22. Students should explain that he Lion is forced to tone down his roaring and recognize that Man shares some of the power. The change is a good one for the little animals who are not so scared. Some students may say the change is good for he Lion too, because it helps him be a better part of the community. Others may say the change is not good for he Lion because it makes him seem defeated.

"The Three Wishes" by Ricardo E. Alegría

Vocabulary Warm-up Exercises, p. 163

A. 1. kindness
2. scarcely

3. comfort
4. knowledge
5. scolded
6. forgiveness
7. reward
8. granted

B. Sample Answers

1. F; Sharing what you have is an example of generosity, not *greed*.
2. T; It would be very surprising since only adults are allowed to run.
3. T; That is exactly what *nevertheless* means.
4. F; A spoonful is a very small *portion* of ice cream, unless you are an ant.
5. F; Since *poverty* means "the state of being poor," it does not include people with a lot of money.
6. T; You can only show *repentance* if you've done something wrong.
7. F; Even good friends have quarreled, or disagreed, from time to time.
8. T; Asking for something back once you've given it away is rude.

Reading Warm-up A, p. 164

Sample Answers

1. barely; It was raining so lightly that I *scarcely* felt it.
2. (for doing well in school); A *reward* is something a person gets for doing something well.
3. He could see I was upset. *Comfort* means "to make someone feel better."
4. (a tone); *Forgiveness* means "pardon for doing something wrong."
5. (I couldn't even do my homework); I *scolded* the dog when he chewed up my shirt.
6. that I had ruined Mel's model; *Knowledge* is understanding or information.
7. (gave); We were *granted* five hours to finish the job.
8. thanked me; *Kindness* means "niceness or caring."

Reading Warm-up B, p. 165

Sample Answers

1. with little food to eat or nowhere to live; Sadly, many people throughout the world live in *poverty*.
2. (three wishes); *Give* or *grant* are synonyms for *bestow*.
3. (the desire for too much wealth); *Greed* causes people to do terrible things, like cheating others to gain wealth for themselves.
4. over how to use the wishes; *Quarreled* means "argued."
5. In others, characters have argued over who gets the bigger *share* of any riches that result.
6. "waste" a wish; A *mere* French fry won't satisfy my hunger.

7. the character who did it; Jack was filled with *repentance* after stealing the chocolate bar.

8. (keep reading and learn the details); I enjoyed the project; *nevertheless*, I was quite happy it was over.

Writing About the Big Question, p. 166

A. 1. support

2. generation

3. participation

4. connection

B. Sample Answers

1. When I was little, I wished very hard for an action figure that all the other kids wanted. I wished that I would get on the basketball team last year.

2. My wish to get on the basketball team came true, and my family was very proud of me. I loved being part of a cool **group** of people with a **common** goal. Most important, my family attended every game, even after I hurt my arm and couldn't play, to **support** the team.

C. Sample Answer

If I could make sure that everyone knew one particular old story, it would be the story of King Midas *because* of the way his wish taught him a lesson about **values**. Midas wished that everything he touched would turn to gold. At first, he was happy because his wish made him very rich. But pretty soon he lost his **connection** to the real world and began to **isolate** himself in a world of gold. Even his food and water turned to gold. Finally, the person he loved most, his young daughter, turned to gold when she hugged him. Midas realized that **family** and **community** are much more important for happiness than wealth.

"The Three Wishes" by Ricardo E. Alegría

Reading: Adjust Your Reading Rate, p. 167

Slowly: Students should choose two passages to be read slowly, such as paragraphs 2 and 7, which include some difficult sentence construction and detail.

Moderately: Students should choose two passages to be read moderately, such as the opening and concluding paragraphs.

Quickly: Students should choose two passages to be read quickly, such as the dialogue between the old man and the woman or between the old man and the woodsman.

Literary Analysis: Universal Theme, p. 168

Sample Answers

1. the husband

2. husband vs. wife; desire for wealth vs. love and respect for each other

3. The husband yells at his wife in anger and uses the second wish to punish his wife. When he realizes what he has done, he is sorry.

4. The couple realize how happy they have always been together even without money.

5. Money can't buy happiness.

Vocabulary Builder, p. 169

Sample Answers

A. 1. hugged; My mother hugged me when I came back from summer camp.

2. extreme desire for possessions; Her extreme desire for possessions made her lose sight of more valuable, nonmaterial things.

3. need to own more than others; The executive's great need to own more than others made him spend money very quickly.

4. hardly; We had hardly enough money to buy lunch for the whole group.

5. sorrow for wrongdoing; His sorrow for his cruel action made us forgive him.

B. 1. I felt <u>repentant</u> because I had done something to hurt my friend.

2. The team grumbled when the referee gave their star player a <u>penalty</u>.

3. The prisoner was given a shorter sentence because he expressed <u>penitence</u> for his crime.

Enrichment: Creating a Wish Poster, p. 170

A. Students' wishes should include at least one wish with universal value.

B. Students' poster designs should clearly express a wish that, from the student's point of view, might make the world a better place.

Open-Book Test, p. 171

Short Answer

1. The first two wishes are accidents. The wife wishes her husband were home. The husband speaks out of anger and wishes his wife had donkey ears.

   Difficulty: *Average* **Objective:** *Interpretation*

2. Think before you speak. They wasted two wishes instantly.

   Difficulty: *Challenging* **Objective:** *Literary Analysis*

3. He might have embraced, or hugged, her when he comforted her after giving her donkey ears.

   Difficulty: *Average* **Objective:** *Vocabulary*

4. The husband worded the wish very carefully. If he had just asked for the donkey ears to be gone, they might not have been happy again.

   Difficulty: *Challenging* **Objective:** *Interpretation*

5. The third wish demonstrates that the husband loves his wife and that he values her and their happiness more than he values riches. It also shows that he has learned to think before he speaks.

   Difficulty: *Average* **Objective:** *Interpretation*

6. Greed is a selfish desire for more than one's share. He might have wished for money or riches.

   Difficulty: *Easy* **Objective:** *Vocabulary*

7. I found the last paragraph of "The Three Wishes" to be challenging because the sentences are very long and it uses new vocabulary. I needed to reread this paragraph a few times to make sure I didn't miss important information. Reading slowly and checking definitions of new words helped me to better understand the story's ending.

   Difficulty: *Average* **Objective:** *Reading*

8. Statements of the universal theme include: Love, not money, brings happiness. There can be happiness in poverty and unhappiness in riches. Money cannot buy you love.

   Difficulty: *Easy* **Objective:** *Vocabulary*

9. Children are highly valued in the Puerto Rican culture. The old man grants them a child, calling it "the greatest happiness a married couple could know."

   Difficulty: *Average* **Objective:** *Reading*

10. Wish 1: angry at wife; Wish 2: regret; Wish 3: happiness
    He understands that they were happy the way they were right before he makes the third wish.

    Difficulty: *Average* **Objective:** *Literary Analysis*

Essay

11. Students should say the woodsman seems most affected. He changes the most, going from happy to angry to regretful and back to happy. He also learns the lesson: Love is more important than riches.

    Difficulty: *Easy* **Objective:** *Essay*

12. Students should make a connection between their lives and the folk tale's universal theme (love is more important than money) using details from the story as well as from their own lives.

    Difficulty: *Average* **Objective:** *Essay*

13. Students should write a story about the couple's son as he is faced with three wishes. Students can decide whether the boy has learned his parents' lesson already or has to learn it for himself.

    Difficulty: *Challenging* **Objective:** *Essay*

14. Students should compare their own community's view of love and money to that shown in "The Three Wishes." They may say that the community of their peers values money more than love or that society in general values money a great deal. They should voice an opinion about their community's ideas.

    Difficulty: *Average* **Objective:** *Essay*

Oral Response

15. Oral responses should be clear, well organized, and well supported by appropriate examples from the selection.

    Difficulty: *Average* **Objective:** *Oral Interpretation*

"The Three Wishes" by Ricardo E. Alegría

Selection Test A, p. 174

Critical Reading

1. ANS: A	DIF: Easy	OBJ: Reading Skill
2. ANS: D	DIF: Easy	OBJ: Comprehension
3. ANS: B	DIF: Easy	OBJ: Comprehension
4. ANS: C	DIF: Easy	OBJ: Interpretation
5. ANS: B	DIF: Easy	OBJ: Comprehension
6. ANS: B	DIF: Easy	OBJ: Literary Analysis

Vocabulary and Grammar

7. ANS: C	DIF: Easy	OBJ: Vocabulary
8. ANS: B	DIF: Easy	OBJ: Vocabulary
9. ANS: A	DIF: Easy	OBJ: Vocabulary
10. ANS: D	DIF: Easy	OBJ: Grammar

Essay

11. Students' essays should describe the couple before, during, and after they get the three wishes. They should mention the couple's happiness—even though they are poor—before they get the wishes. Students should briefly describe what happens in the story: The wife accidentally wastes a wish. The husband gets angry and wishes donkey ears on her. When he realizes he has hurt her, he wishes that they could be as happy and loving as they were before they got the wishes. The essays should point out that happiness and love are more important to the couple than the wealth they might have been able to gain from the third wish.

    Difficulty: *Easy*

    Objective: *Essay*

12. Students should define their community, tell what they see as their community's view on love and money, and compare their own community's view of love and money to that shown in "The Three Wishes." They may say that the community of their peers values money more than love or that society in general values money a great deal. They should voice an opinion about their community's ideas.

Selection Test B, p. 176

Critical Reading

1. ANS: A	DIF: Average	OBJ: Reading Skill
2. ANS: B	DIF: Average	OBJ: Comprehension
3. ANS: D	DIF: Average	OBJ: Interpretation
4. ANS: C	DIF: Average	OBJ: Interpretation
5. ANS: A	DIF: Average	OBJ: Comprehension
6. ANS: D	DIF: Challenging	OBJ: Literary Analysis
7. ANS: B	DIF: Average	OBJ: Literary Analysis
8. ANS: C	DIF: Challenging	OBJ: Reading Skill

Vocabulary and Grammar

Essay

13. Students' essays should briefly tell the events of the story and identify the universal theme: Happiness is more important than money. As a result of the test, the couple realize that the love they have for each other is more important than any amount of money. The husband, the major character in the story, is the person who changes. Momentary greed makes him angry and unhappy; when he realizes the mistake he has made, he is sorry and wishes again for the happiness they had.

    Difficulty: *Average*

    Objective: *Essay*

14. Students' essays should identify three elements in the story that relate in some way to their own life experience. Responses should be clearly connected to the text and supported with examples from real life.

    Difficulty: *Challenging*

    Objective: *Essay*

15. Students should compare their own community's view of love and money to that shown in "The Three Wishes." They may say that the community of their peers values money more than love or that society in general values money a great deal. They should voice an opinion about their community's ideas.

"The Stone" by Lloyd Alexander

Vocabulary Warm-up Exercises, p. 179

A.
1. squinted
2. astonishment
3. wits
4. clutched
5. claim
6. glee
7. flung
8. pouch

B. Sample Answers
1. Kathy decided to <u>heed</u> her teacher's warning and do exactly as she was told.
2. The boat was in the <u>midst</u> of the ocean, miles away from land.
3. The <u>feeble</u> old man was too weak to run in the race.
4. The boy <u>reluctantly</u> went to the principal's office.
5. Fred wanted to get <u>revenge</u> on Jose for stealing his hat.
6. The <u>ungrateful</u> girl refused to thank her parents for the present.

7. Doing different things every day filled Jill with <u>amazement</u>.

Reading Warm-up A, p. 180

Sample Answers
1. <u>excitement and delight</u>; Going to my favorite restaurant fills me with *glee*.
2. (narrowing his eyes to get a better look at its details); I *squinted* as the sun shone brightly in my face.
3. (as his own/to buy it); When you *claim* something, you take it or make it yours.
4. <u>holding it tightly in his fist</u>; I *clutched* the handlebars of my bicycle as I rode away.
5. <u>small, leather</u>; The gold miner's *pouch* was filled with gold dust.
6. <u>shocked and amazed</u>; To feel *astonishment* is to feel greatly surprised.
7. (think quickly and clearly) I had to use my *wits* to answer the pop quiz questions correctly.
8. (with all his might); My brother *flung* his hat up in the air.

Reading Warm-up B, p. 181

Sample Answers
1. <u>They hide within everyday places such as farmhouses and cellars</u>; The book I was looking for was in the *midst* of the shelves of the library.
2. (sharp thinking abilities); *Cleverness* is the state of being smart and mentally sharp.
3. <u>weak</u>; The elderly cat was *feeble* and had trouble moving.
4. <u>if they feel that they have been wronged</u>; The angry man wanted to get *revenge* on the person who dented his car.
5. (are unwilling to part with their treasure); I *reluctantly* got out of bed this morning.
6. <u>thankful</u>; To be *ungrateful* means "to not express thanks or be glad about something."
7. <u>pay close attention to</u>; A person should *heed* the warning of a fire alarm.
8. (wonder and surprise); The beauty of the song filled me with *amazement*.

Writing About the Big Question, p. 182

A.
1. community
2. isolate
3. influence
4. connection

B. Sample Answers
1. Last year, I got a lead in the school musical, and my best friend was up for the same part. A few months ago, I wrote a story about my little sister, and it embarrassed her when the school literary magazine published it.

2. When I got the lead in the musical, my friend tried to **support** me and not show her own disappointment. But we had a lot in **common** and were almost like **family,** so I knew pretty much how she felt.

C. Sample Answer

If I could make one wish come true for my life, I would want to be a famous writer *because* I would want to share my thoughts and feelings with thousands of people. But I realize that fame has a high cost in our **culture.** It can **isolate** you and weaken your **connection** to everyday, real life. Fame can warp your **values,** and it certainly can **influence** the way other people view you. So maybe I would like to be a great writer, but not a famous one.

"The Stone" by Lloyd Alexander

Reading: Adusting Your Reading Rate, p. 183

Sample Answers

Slowly: Students should choose two passages to be read slowly, such as complex descriptive passages like the one in which Maibon first views the dwarf.

Moderately: Students should choose two passages to be read moderately, such as those with simple exposition like the opening paragraph.

Quickly: Students should choose two passages to be read quickly, such as any of the passages that contain dialogue.

Literary Analysis: Universal Theme, p. 184

Sample Answers

1. Maibon, a cottager
2. Maibon vs. his wife; Maibon's desire never to grow old vs. his family's needs; Maibon vs. Doli, the dwarf
3. The magic stone gives Maibon what he wished for: he stops aging, but so do everything and everyone else.
4. Maibon is unhappy when he sees the effects of his wish. He gets rid of the stone, grows old, and is happy.
5. Change is a natural part of being alive.

Vocabulary Builder, p. 185

Sample Answers

A. 1. severe problem; Famine is a severe problem in many parts of the world.
   2. very weak; His long illness has reduced his energy and made him very weak
   3. planted; Just after the seeds were planted, we had a good rainfall.
   4. disappeared; The dinosaurs disappeared from the earth millions of years ago.
   5. great joy; The wedding of the two old friends was celebrated with great joy.
   6. regret; We often regret getting our wishes, because they bring unforeseen problems.

B. 1. A good way to make a rumor vanish is not to share it with anyone.
   2. Mist becomes evanescent as the day goes on because the warm sun makes it evaporate.

3. I feel angry and frustrated when I work hard in vain.

Enrichment: Be Careful What You Wish For, p. 186

Answers will vary but should include a physical description of the magic item, an explanation of its desired power, and an explanation of its unintended consequences.

"The Three Wishes" by Ricardo E. Alegría
"The Stone" by Lloyd Alexander

Integrated Language Skills: Grammar, p. 187

A. 1. We discussed three figures of speech: simile, metaphor, and personification.
   2. Warning: No skateboarding here after 4:00 P.M.
   3. My sister and I share a bedroom; sometimes that room seems very small.
   4. The train stops in Dallas, Texas; St. Louis, Missouri; and Chicago, Illinois.

B. Answers will vary but should include correct usage of semicolons or colons in three sentences.

Open-Book Test, p. 190

Short Answer

1. Students should make a reasonable connection to their own lives.
   Difficulty: *Average*   **Objective:** *Reading*
2. Students should relate Maibon's desire to stay young with society's obsession with looking young and beautiful, as seen in magazines, on television, and so on.
   Difficulty: *Challenging*   **Objective:** *Reading*
3. Modrona tells him he is "borrowing trouble" and should be focused on what's in front of him. She is practical and sensible.
   Difficulty: *Average*   **Objective:** *Interpretation*
4. Students may say that Maibon is foolish and/or selfish. He insists on receiving the stone despite the warnings of the dwarf and the needs of his family.
   Difficulty: *Average*   **Objective:** *Interpretation*
5. He thinks humans are greedy and "muddled." The dwarf says that all humans do is "Grab, grab, grab" and ask for impractical things.
   Difficulty: *Easy*   **Objective:** *Interpretation*
6. Doli tries to warn Maibon about what will happen with the stone. He begins, "There's a difficulty." But Maibon cuts him off impatiently and demands the stone without learning about the difficulty.
   Difficulty: *Challenging*   **Objective:** *Interpretation*
7. Beginning: "There's no fate worse in all the world."
   Middle: "very reluctantly, threw the stone out"
   End: "Whatever may happen, let it happen."
   He is happy to be old. He is "proud of his white hair and long beard."
   Difficulty: *Average*   **Objective:** *Literary Analysis*

Unit 6 Resources: Themes in Folk Literature

8. The universal theme is that change is a part of life and, without it, we would not be happy. When everything around Maibon stopped aging, everyone was miserable.

   Difficulty: *Easy* **Objective:** *Literary Analysis*

9. Everything around Maibon stops changing—the crops won't grow, the eggs won't hatch, and the apples won't ripen. It is easy to see that change is needed when seeing that the farm is not productive.

   Difficulty: *Challenging* **Objective:** *Literary Analysis*

10. *Jubilation* means "great joy." He shows his great joy by hugging his wife and children and laughing with glee at the baby's first tooth.

    Difficulty: *Average* **Objective:** *Vocabulary*

Essay

11. Students should make a reasonable choice for Modrona—the cook pot brimming with food, the sharp ax, or even gold. Modrona is a very practical mother. She is concerned about food and clothes for her family.

    Difficulty: *Easy* **Objective:** *Essay*

12. Students should use details from the story to explain that Doli has a very low opinion of humans that turns out to be justified in the case of Maibon. They might point out that Maibon's actions at the end of the story might soften Doli's opinion a little.

    Difficulty: *Average* **Objective:** *Essay*

13. Student essays should indicate that the reading rate changes according to purpose in "The Stone." Although the students are basically reading for enjoyment, they should indicate that there are other purposes. At the beginning, they are reading to find out the basic storyline. So they probably start out at a moderate rate. When they come to the snappy dialogue, they can just enjoy the easy flow of conversation. As a result, the pace quickens. However, when they come to descriptive passages, they need to understand what Maibon is seeing so that they can fully comprehend his dilemma. This causes them to read more slowly.

14. Students can make a reasonable case for either position. Some may say Maibon would have avoided a lot of trouble if he had listened to his wife from the very beginning. Others may say he got to the right place on his own, eventually, and might not have ever been happy if he had just gone along with his wife at first.

    Difficulty: *Average* **Objective:** *Essay*

Oral Response

15. Oral responses should be clear, well organized, and well supported by appropriate examples from the selections.

    Difficulty: *Average* **Objective:** *Oral Interpretation*

Selection Test A, p. 193

Critical Reading

1. ANS: C	DIF: Easy	OBJ: Interpretation
2. ANS: D	DIF: Easy	OBJ: Comprehension
3. ANS: A	DIF: Easy	OBJ: Comprehension

4. ANS: B	DIF: Easy	OBJ: Interpretation
5. ANS: B	DIF: Easy	OBJ: Reading Skill
6. ANS: C	DIF: Easy	OBJ: Comprehension
7. ANS: D	DIF: Easy	OBJ: Interpretation
8. ANS: A	DIF: Easy	OBJ: Reading Skill
9. ANS: B	DIF: Easy	OBJ: Literary Analysis
10. ANS: D	DIF: Easy	OBJ: Literary Analysis

Vocabulary and Grammar

11. ANS: A	DIF: Easy	OBJ: Vocabulary
12. ANS: C	DIF: Easy	OBJ: Vocabulary
13. ANS: B	DIF: Easy	OBJ: Vocabulary
14. ANS: D	DIF: Easy	OBJ: Grammar

Essay

15. Students' essays should explain that at the beginning of the story Maibon fears growing old. When he gets the magic stone, he thinks all is well, but the stone causes more problems. Plants don't grow. The cow doesn't give milk. The baby's teeth don't come in. Maibon is able to get rid of the magic stone when he realizes that life is boring without growth and change. At the beginning of the story, he is afraid to grow old. At the end of the story, he is happy and proud to be old. Students should relate the universal theme to the idea that growth and change are a natural or important part of being alive.

    Difficulty: *Easy*

    Objective: *Essay*

16. Student essays should include three different purposes for reading different parts of "The Stone." One purpose might be to understand the basic plot. This would require a moderate to slow reading rate. Another purpose would be to enjoy the humorous dialogue. The reading rate would then be quick to mimic the easy flow of conversation. Yet a third purpose would be to understand Maibon's dilemma and how his feelings change throughout the story. In order to do this, the descriptive passages must be fully understood. The reader must see the world through the character's eyes. This requires a slow reading rate in order to take in all the details.

17. Students can use details to make a reasonable case for either position. Some may say Maibon would have avoided a lot of trouble if he had listened to his wife from the very beginning. Others may say he got to the right place on his own eventually and might not have learned his lesson if he had just gone along with his wife from the first.

Selection Test B, p. 196

Critical Reading

1. ANS: C	DIF: Challenging	OBJ: Interpretation
2. ANS: A	DIF: Average	OBJ: Comprehension
3. ANS: B	DIF: Challenging	OBJ: Interpretation
4. ANS: A	DIF: Average	OBJ: Interpretation
5. ANS: C	DIF: Average	OBJ: Comprehension

6. ANS: D	DIF: Average	OBJ: Interpretation
7. ANS: C	DIF: Average	OBJ: Interpretation
8. ANS: D	DIF: Average	OBJ: Comprehension
9. ANS: A	DIF: Challenging	OBJ: Interpretation
10. ANS: B	DIF: Average	OBJ: Literary Analysis
11. ANS: D	DIF: Challenging	OBJ: Comprehension
12. ANS: B	DIF: Average	OBJ: Comprehension
13. ANS: C	DIF: Average	OBJ: Literary Analysis
14. ANS: B	DIF: Average	OBJ: Literary Analysis
15. ANS: D	DIF: Average	OBJ: Literary Analysis

Vocabulary and Grammar

16. ANS: C	DIF: Average	OBJ: Vocabulary
17. ANS: D	DIF: Average	OBJ: Vocabulary
18. ANS: B	DIF: Challenging	OBJ: Grammar

Essay

19. Students' essays should identify the lesson that Maibon learns: Change is an important part of life. Students may recall that at the beginning of the story Maibon is afraid of growing old. The magic stone he gets causes Maibon to stop aging, but it also affects his family and everything that would normally be growing and producing on his farm. Finally, Maibon realizes the importance of change, and he gets rid of the magic stone. At the end of the story, he has lived many years and is proud of his white hair and beard. Students should explain that people in many cultures and throughout history have feared growing old; the idea that change and growth are a necessary part of being alive is a universal theme.

Difficulty: *Average*

Objective: *Essay*

20. Students' essays should clearly state whether they would or would not accept the gift of never growing older now or at any other age. They should support their position with three plausible reasons.

Difficulty: *Challenging*

Objective: *Essay*

21. Students can make a reasonable case for either position. Some may say Maibon would have avoided a lot of trouble if he had listened to his wife from the very beginning. Others may say he got to the right place on his own eventually and might not have ever been happy if he had just gone along with his wife at first.

"Lob's Girl" by Joan Aiken
"Jeremiah's Song" by Walter Dean Myers

Vocabulary Warm-up Exercises, p. 200

A. 1. wrestling
2. accompanied
3. proper

4. expert
5. condition
6. prevented
7. aware
8. intelligent

B. Sample Answers

1. F; A local store would be close so you wouldn't have to travel far.
2. T; Breeding cows will produce calves.
3. F; If you fetch something for a friend, you plan to carry it to him or her.
4. T; Injured people have been hurt in some way.
5. F; People close windows to prevent drafts from coming in.
6. F; Chirping is the sound that birds and some insects make.
7. F; You need two or more people to have a discussion.
8. T; If something has been assured, it has been promised.

Reading Warm-up A, p. 201

Sample Answers

1. struggling; I was *wrestling* with the idea of my parents splitting up.
2. (state); Today, I am in good *condition*.
3. learning how to seek out human smells; I was cold because I wasn't wearing the *proper* clothing.
4. (They learn quickly.) I think my history teacher is very *intelligent*.
5. The dogs have been trained to focus on a human scent. The coach gave *expert* advice on how to catch a football.
6. that some people may be trapped; To be *aware* of something is to know it exists.
7. (go along with); I *accompanied* my mother to the store.
8. (the deaths of thousands of people); I wish I had *prevented* my little sister from watching the scary movie.

Reading Warm-up B, p. 202

Sample Answers

1. (the farm would be filled with piglets); A farmer who is *breeding* sheep will soon have new lambs.
2. neighbor; I love my *local* supermarket.
3. (in a farm accident); John was *injured* playing football.
4. (talk); I love to have a *discussion* about food with my friends.
5. I'll bring you; When you *fetch* something for a friend, you go get it so that you can bring it to him or her.
6. (Trust me.) I *assured* my sister that I wasn't going to tell on her.
7. twittering noises; *Chirping* is what most birds do when they make noise.
8. (cold air/chill of the wind); I do not like to feel *drafts* because they make me shiver.

Writing About the Big Question, p. 203

A. 1. support
2. participation
3. influence(d)
4. community

B. Sample Answers

1. When I was having trouble in math class, my older sister helped me understand what the teacher had covered in class. When my dog died, my friends helped me organize a memorial service.

2. When my dog Honey died, I felt very sad and **isolated,** but as soon as my friend Rosemarie found out, she got some of our other friends **involved** in planning a memorial service. Each of them told about a nice memory of Honey or a story about a pet of their own, and I felt a wonderful **connection** to everyone, and to Honey.

C. Sample Answer

One time, our neighbors helped us clean up when a small fire damaged our kitchen. Their **support** helped us get past our **isolation** and shock. And then, over the next few weeks, each **family** in the neighborhood took turns making us dinner until we could use the kitchen again. Since we were new to the town, their kindness made us feel that we were part of a caring **community.**

"Lob's Girl" by Joan Aiken
"Jeremiah's Song" by Walter Dean Myers

Literary Analysis: Plot Techniques, p. 204

1. A. Lob's death; Lob's attempt to find Sandy
   B. Sandy was a good big sister.
2. A. Grandpa's death
   B. Macon has a special bond with Grandpa; Macon respects Grandpa.

Vocabulary Builder, p. 205

A. Sample Answers

1. Eager to stop the runner, Aaron threw the ball decisively to first base.
2. The club members made three resolutions about their plans for the year.
3. The story's sad ending made Li feel melancholy.
4. After the vet's clear diagnosis, we understood what was wrong with Spot.

B. 1. A; 2. D; 3. C

Open-Book Test, p. 207

Short Answer

1. The flashback shows that there is something royal—or special—about Sandy. Since her birth, Sandy has looked like the queen whose picture hangs in her grandmother's kitchen.

   Difficulty: *Average* **Objective:** *Literary Analysis*

2. She writes that the village is approached by a "narrow, steep, twisting hill-road" and describes a sign warning that the road is "DANGEROUS TO CYCLISTS."

   Difficulty: *Average* **Objective:** *Literary Analysis*

3. Lob was determined to join the family. He walked miles and miles to get to the family and kept coming back until at last his owner gave him to the Pengellys.

   Difficulty: *Average* **Objective:** *Vocabulary*

4. The narrator remembers that Ellie didn't want to hear Grandpa's stories anymore and didn't come to church much. Also, she used to rub her arms and face with cocoa butter, but now she uses a different product. It seems that Ellie has become more sophisticated.

   Difficulty: *Easy* **Objective:** *Literary Analysis*

5. Students may say that Ellie and Macon will date or marry. Many details support this prediction—for example, the narrator's speculation that Ellie is beginning to like Macon and his statement that Macon and Ellie's friendship seems "natural." Alternatively, students may predict that the narrator will learn to play the guitar, for at the end of the story, he says that he might learn the tune Macon has been playing.

   Difficulty: *Average* **Objective:** *Literary Analysis*

6. The doctor's identification of Grandpa's medical condition is not revealed. The doctor says only that Grandpa is seriously ill and will not live much longer.

   Difficulty: *Challenging* **Objective:** *Vocabulary*

7. The narrator appears to feel safe with Macon. He says that he would not have been able to stay in the room if Macon had not been there.

   Difficulty: *Easy* **Objective:** *Interpretation*

8. The flashbacks tell about important characters: Sandy in "Lob's Girl" and Ellie in "Jeremiah's Song." The flashback about Sandy's birth reveals that Sandy is like a queen. The flashback about Ellie reveals that she has become more sophisticated.

   Difficulty: *Challenging* **Objective:** *Literary Skill*

9. Both Macon and Lob are devoted. Lob keeps returning to Sandy. Macon keeps Grandpa Jeremiah company throughout his illness, up to the time of his death.

   Difficulty: *Average* **Objective:** *Interpretation*

10. "Lob's Girl": Lob will become Sandy's dog.

    "Jeremiah's Song": Macon will use his guitar to write a song for Grandpa Jeremiah.

    Students should say that foreshadowing adds suspense or engages the reader's interest.

    Difficulty: *Average* **Objective:** *Literary Analysis*

Essay

11. Students who write about "Lob's Girl" should point to the flashback of Sandy's birth and to one of several instances of foreshadowing (that Lob will become Sandy's dog, that the dangerous hill will figure in the story's plot). Students who write about "Jeremiah's Song" should point to the flashback describing Ellie's use of cocoa butter and to one of several instances of

foreshadowing (for example, that Ellie and Macon will form a deeper relationship, that the narrator will one day play the guitar). They should then comment on what the plot techniques add to the stories.

Difficulty: *Easy* **Objective:** *Essay*

12. In their essays, students should touch on the following points: For Grandpa Jeremiah, the stories are "the songs of my people"; they give people strength and form "a bridge." The narrator has a sense that the stories are important, but he is also frightened by them. He appears to be searching for their meaning. The stories' meanings for Macon are not clear, but they allow Macon to form a relationship with Grandpa Jeremiah. For Ellie, the stories stand for a way of life that is old-fashioned. For the doctor, the stories are "as good as any medicine."

Difficulty: *Average* **Objective:** *Essay*

13. Students should point out that the relationships are different, in that one is between an animal and a person, whereas the other is between two people. They should recognize that the relationships are similar, in that both are characterized by devotion. Students should also point to the role that death and grave illness or injury play in the stories.

Difficulty: *Challenging* **Objective:** *Essay*

14. Students writing about "Lob's Girl" might note that Cornwall has palm trees and beaches, so it is probably a more desirable place for a dog to live. On the other hand, they might point out that Lob appears to be drawn more to Sandy than to the community. For the dog, an individual is more important than any community. Students writing about "Jeremiah's Song" should point to ways in which Ellie has changed: She no longer listens to Grandpa Jeremiah's stories because they are not "true," she uses a different lotion, and she questions the doctor's diagnosis. Some students may say that the changes are positive: Ellie is becoming better educated. Others may say that the changes are negative: She is turning away from tradition. Some students may see Ellie's changes as having both positive and negative aspects.

Difficulty: *Average* **Objective:** *Essay*

Oral Response

15. Oral responses should be clear, well organized, and well supported by appropriate examples from the stories.

Difficulty: *Average* **Objective:** *Oral Interpretation*

Selection Test A, p. 210

Critical Reading

1. ANS: B   DIF: Easy   OBJ: Literary Analysis
2. ANS: A   DIF: Easy   OBJ: Comprehension
3. ANS: C   DIF: Easy   OBJ: Comprehension
4. ANS: A   DIF: Easy   OBJ: Interpretation
5. ANS: D   DIF: Easy   OBJ: Interpretation
6. ANS: C   DIF: Easy   OBJ: Comprehension
7. ANS: A   DIF: Easy   OBJ: Comprehension
8. ANS: B   DIF: Easy   OBJ: Interpretation

9. ANS: D   DIF: Easy   OBJ: Literary Analysis
10. ANS: C   DIF: Easy   OBJ: Literary Analysis
11. ANS: A   DIF: Easy   OBJ: Interpretation
12. ANS: D   DIF: Easy   OBJ: Comprehension

Vocabulary

13. ANS: D   DIF: Easy   OBJ: Vocabulary
14. ANS: B   DIF: Easy   OBJ: Vocabulary

Essay

15. Students should define foreshadowing as the use of clues to hint at what might happen later on, and flashback as a description of an event that took place earlier. Students should then give an example of each from the stories; for example, the DANGER sign posted on the road outside the Pengellys' house in "Lob's Girl" (foreshadowing) and the description of Macon as a younger boy in "Jeremiah's Song" (flashback). Students should also express and explain a preference for either foreshadowing or flashback. Most are likely to prefer foreshadowing because it creates suspense.

Difficulty: *Easy*

Objective: *Essay*

16. Students should explain in some way that the special bond between Lob and Sandy makes Sandy "Lob's girl." Sandy "owns" Lob's love. Students should also explain that "Jeremiah's Song" refers to the song Macon writes for Grandpa Jeremiah while listening to Grandpa's stories. It is called "Jeremiah's Song" because it was written in honor of him.

Difficulty: *Easy*

Objective: *Essay*

17. Students should note ways in which Ellie has changed: She no longer listens to Grandpa Jeremiah's stories because they are not "true;" she doesn't go to church with them; she questions the doctor's diagnosis. Some students may say that the changes are positive: Ellie is trying to change the direction of her life. Others may say that the changes are negative: She is turning away from tradition, and the changes hurt her cousin and grandfather. Some students may see Ellie's changes as having both positive and negative aspects.

Selection Test B, p. 213

Critical Reading

1. ANS: D   DIF: Average   OBJ: Literary Analysis
2. ANS: C   DIF: Average   OBJ: Comprehension
3. ANS: B   DIF: Average   OBJ: Interpretation
4. ANS: A   DIF: Challenging   OBJ: Literary Analysis
5. ANS: C   DIF: Average   OBJ: Interpretation
6. ANS: D   DIF: Challenging   OBJ: Interpretation
7. ANS: A   DIF: Average   OBJ: Literary Analysis
8. ANS: C   DIF: Average   OBJ: Literary Analysis

9. ANS: A	DIF: Average	OBJ: Interpretation
10. ANS: D	DIF: Average	OBJ: Literary Analysis
11. ANS: B	DIF: Challenging	OBJ: Interpretation
12. ANS: C	DIF: Challenging	OBJ: Interpretation
13. ANS: A	DIF: Average	OBJ: Comprehension
14. ANS: D	DIF: Average	OBJ: Literary Analysis

Vocabulary

15. ANS: A	DIF: Challenging	OBJ: Vocabulary
16. ANS: C	DIF: Average	OBJ: Vocabulary

Essay

17. Students should point out that "Lob's Girl" refers to Sandy, who is "chosen" by Lob and with whom Lob forms a special bond. Although Lob doesn't literally own Sandy, he watches over her and cares for her above all others. Students should also point out that "Jeremiah's Song" refers to the song Macon writes for Grandpa Jeremiah while listening to Grandpa's stories. Grandpa doesn't own the song Macon writes; rather, the song is in honor of him. (Some students may observe that, in a sense, Grandpa does "own" the song, much as he "owned" the stories that inspired it.) Finally, students should identify the title they found more surprising or moving and explain why.
   Difficulty: *Average*
   Objective: *Essay*

18. Students should define foreshadowing as the use of clues to hint at what might happen later in a story, and flashback as a description of an event that took place earlier than the story. Students should then choose one of these techniques, give examples of it from each story, and draw conclusions about which author relies upon it more. Students are likely to conclude that Aiken uses foreshadowing more frequently because her purpose is to create suspense, or that Myers uses flashback more frequently because he wants to show how and why characters change over time.
   Difficulty: *Challenging*
   Objective: *Essay*

19. Students writing about "Lob's Girl" might note that Cornwall has palm trees and beaches, so it is probably a more desirable place for a dog to live. On the other hand, they might point out that Lob appears to be drawn more to Sandy than to the community. For the dog, an individual is more important than any community. Students writing about "Jeremiah's Song" should point to ways in which Ellie has changed: She no longer listens to Grandpa Jeremiah's stories because they are not "true," she uses a different lotion, and she questions the doctor's diagnosis. Some students may say that the changes are positive: Ellie is becoming better educated. Others may say that the changes are negative: She is turning away from tradition. Some students may see Ellie's changes as having both positive and negative aspects.

Writing Workshop

Research Report: Integrating Grammar Skills, p. 217

A. 1. yes; 2. no; 3. yes; 4. no; 5. no
B. 1. "'Twas brillig, and the slithy toves" is a line in the short poem "Jabberwocky."
   2. The White House Web site has an article titled "Abraham Lincoln."
   3. "Snakes Alive" is an article in Sports Illustrated for Kids.
   4. Abraham Lincoln: The Prairie Years and the War Years is a book by Carl Sandburg.

Vocabulary Workshop—1, p. 218

On Tuesday, I got up on the wrong side of the bed. I was in the worst mood ever and I grunted at my mother when she came into my room. She looked hurt. Then she said, "Jude, I want you to go the extra mile today. Your little cousin Stanley is coming over." I hate Stanley! But I would have to go over the top to entertain him. I owed my mother that after the grouchy way I greeted her. I looked in the mirror and told myself that I would put my best foot forward. Just then, I heard Stanley's obnoxious voice downstairs. This was going to be hard!

Vocabulary Workshop—2, p. 219

1. There is no to write because the picture can tell the story just as well.
2. Mary rarely sees movies.
3. Kelly is predicting that bad things will happen.
4. Sally always told things clearly. She never avoided talking about important things.
5. Margot did not prepare at all.
6. They are not likely to come true.
7. Charlie ran slower; he was tired.
8. Jason acted as though he never saw the fight.

Benchmark Test 12, p. 221

MULTIPLE CHOICE
1. ANS: A
2. ANS: D
3. ANS: B
4. ANS: C
5. ANS: C
6. ANS: B
7. ANS: B
8. ANS: D

9. ANS: D
10. ANS: C
11. ANS: B
12. ANS: A
13. ANS: D
14. ANS: C
15. ANS: C
16. ANS: A
17. ANS: A
18. ANS: C
19. ANS: C
20. ANS: B
21. ANS: D
22. ANS: A
23. ANS: B
24. ANS: C
25. ANS: D
26. ANS: A
27. ANS: A
28. ANS: C
29. ANS: B
30. ANS: A
31. ANS: C

ESSAY

32. Students' invitations should use correct friendly letter form and an enthusiastic, welcoming tone appropriate to invitations. They should describe the event and give clear particulars about the date, time, and place, inventing details if necessary. If students invent a recipient instead of using another story character, they should make clear the character's relationship to this other person.

33. Students should identify the universal theme they wish to teach or illustrate. They should then list or describe the events of their stories, making clear the main characters and settings, the conflict around which the events revolve, and the resolution of the conflict.

34. Students should list library and reliable on-line sources and perhaps other sources, such as a museum or organization. They should include specific information on works to consult and make clear for what sort of information they will be consulted. Students should use italics and quotation marks properly in identifying sources.